Library of
Davidson College

VOID

# PAWNS IN A TRIANGLE OF HATE

# PAWNS IN A TRIANGLE OF HATE

The Peruvian Japanese and the United States

*C. HARVEY GARDINER*

UNIVERSITY OF WASHINGTON PRESS
*Seattle and London*

Copyright © 1981 by the University of Washington Press
Printed in the United States of America

All rights reserved. No portion of this publication may be reproduced or transmitted in any form or by any means, electronic or mechanical, including photocopy, recording, or any information storage or retrieval system, without permission in writing from the publisher.

**Library of Congress Cataloging in Publication Data**

Gardiner, C. Harvey (Clinton Harvey)
   Pawns in a triangle of hate.

   Bibliography: p.
   Includes index.
   1. World War, 1939–1945—Deportations from Peru.
2. World War, 1939–1945—Prisoners and prisons,
American.   3. Japanese—Peru—History—20th century.
4. Japanese—United States—History—20th century.
5. World War, 1939–1945—Peru.  I. Title.
D769.8.A6G37        940.53′1        81-51278
ISBN 0-295-95855-3        AACR2

# Contents

Preface  vii

1. The Japanese in Prewar Peru  3
2. Shaping a Deportation-Internment Program  12
3. Coming and Going, by the Hundreds  25
4. More Internees, More Repatriates  52
5. Grinding to a Halt  86
6. Beyond War's End  112
7. Challenging Human Endurance  132
8. Drawn Out Finales  160

Epilogue  173

Abbreviations  177

Notes  179

Directory  205

Bibliographical Essay 209

Index 214

## Maps

Hometowns of Deported Peruvian Japanese 26

Movements of the Peruvian Japanese, 1942–46 154

# Preface

Peru hated and deported them. The United States feared, hated, and interned them. Why?

Opportunity had beckoned in 1923 when Noriyoshi Endo, age twenty, entered Peru. Twenty years later he and his wife Tae, also still a Japanese citizen, had three children. Noriyoshi's bazaar in Lima was yielding him $240 weekly income, but two days after the Japanese attacked Pearl Harbor the United States government blacklisted his business. On June 15, 1942, Peruvian authorities seized him, and although no charge was made, much less substantiated, the entire family embarked on an American ship under American military guard for an unknown destination.

North of Lima, at Hacienda Esquivel, the birth of Arturo Shinei Yakabi in 1922 marked the second generation of that Japanese family in Peru. All of Shinei's family—parents, brothers, and sisters—lived there. Possessing little formal education, the youngster migrated to Callao where he worked in a bakery. There Peruvian authorities arrested him and, in June 1943, deported him aboard another American vessel, without a shred of evidence suggesting illegal activity.

Nine months later a much older Peruvian Japanese received similar treatment. Born in 1883, Genji Nimura had migrated to Peru in 1917 and five years later married Peruvian-born Juana Montoya. Shortly thereafter he became a naturalized Peruvian citizen. Seized early in 1944, by which time his wife had died, farmer Nimura, without benefit of charge, much less proof thereof, was hustled aboard yet another American ship.[1]

In every instance—that of resident alien Endo, naturalized citizen Nimura, and native-born Peruvian Yakabi (each with decades of law-abiding residence in Peru)—the United States not only encouraged and facilitated the arrests and deportations but also established the internment program which for years corralled them, along with the hundreds who preceded, accompanied, and followed them. Basic responsibility for the deportation-internment program rested with two chief executives, President Manuel Prado in Peru and President Franklin D. Roosevelt in the United States.

"When the security of the state requires it," reads article 70 of the Peruvian Constitution, "the Executive can suspend totally or partially . . . the guarantees set down in articles 56, 61, 62, 67 and 68. . . ." In the name of national security, Peruvian homes could be invaded and individuals detained without written authorizations, persons could neither congregate nor freely move about, and, finally, they could be removed from the country without legal recourse.[2]

In the United States, the Alien Enemy Act of 1798 permitted the summary apprehension and internment of nationals of states at war with the United States.[3] But in order to apply this 143-year-old law to Peruvian Japanese, authorities would have to get their hands on those enemy aliens and bring them within the range of American legal authority. That called for United States–Peruvian cooperation at the executive level.

Between April 1942 and April 1945 approximately eighteen hundred Peruvian Japanese were interned in the United States as despairing women and children joined their husbands and fathers. They represented 80 percent of all the Latin American Japanese interned in the United States, the remainder having been seized in and transported from twelve other countries.[4]

Totally unrelated to the much-publicized relocation program that put 110,000 Japanese Americans in ten centers administered by the War Relocation Authority, these Peruvian internees were quietly held—almost hidden—in special facilities operated by the United States Immigration and Naturalization Service.

This study of the deportation-internment program sets forth the cultural and diplomatic background and then details the deportations, internment, and ultimate release of the hapless pawns in a triangle of hate that involved the United States, Peru, and Japan during and after World War II. A dual coverage is sought throughout, one treating both the impersonal policies and actions of powerful governments and the personal experiences of powerless people.

The research, which has included wide travel in the United States, Japan, and Peru, has employed Department of State diplomatic files, intradepartmental correspondence and memoranda, interdepartmental correspondence involving the Departments of State, Justice, War, and Navy, FBI reports, Immigration and Naturalization Service records, passenger lists, internment camp records, court proceedings, files of attorneys and philanthropic organizations, and the personal recollections of former internees and officials.

For inspiration afforded, thanks go to two men: Edward N. Barnhart of Berkeley, California, for his early study of certain aspects of this theme and his continuing interest in it, and the late Kenji Nakane of Chicago, a gentle friend of many whose personal contacts with veterans of the deportation-internment program fired the writer's interest.

Assistance from individuals who helped to administer the program in Peru and the United States has come from R. Henry Norweb, John K. Emmerson, Raymond W. Ickes, James D. Bell, Tom Cooley, R. C. Tate, William H. Merritt, and Margaret Nan Williams.

Among the one-time deportee-internees whose conversations and correspondence have enriched the study are the late George Hisao Fujii, Kishiro and Teresa Hayashi, Yoshinari Honda, Kakuaki and Otari Kaneko and their daughter Mary Momoko Sato, Eugenia Yoshiko Kato, Paul Shuhei Katsuro, Masao Kishi, Kiyoko Naganuma Matsuoka, Shoichi Mishima, Ginzo Murono and his sons Eisuke and Seiki, Ricardo T. Nakagawa, Taro and Fusae Ohashi, Yasuhiko Ohashi, Yoshisada Shiga, John Kunio Takeshita, Victor K. Tateishi, Mitsutaro Tawara and his sons Toshiharu (Tosh) and Victor, Saburo Ushida, and Arthur Shinei Yakabi. For access to his autograph book, special thanks go to Tosh Tawara.

To Attorney Wayne M. Collins, Jr., of Berkeley, California, special thanks are extended for access to the papers of his father, Attorney Wayne M. Collins, whose services to scores of the deportee-internees were invaluable.

For photocopies of relevant materials appreciation is directed to H. Warren Mills and the United States Catholic Conference. For similar assistance concerning the ACLU Archives, thanks are extended to Nancy Bressler, associate curator of manuscripts, Seeley G. Mudd Manuscript Library, Princeton University. For access to a splendid file of the *Zavala County Sentinel* (Crystal City, Texas), thanks are conveyed to Dale Barker.

In pursuit of the texts of relevant laws, decrees, and regulations—Peruvian and American—as well as files of annual reports of the attorney general and the Immigration and Naturalization Service, the general and law libraries of the following institutions welcomed and assisted the writer:

University of Michigan, University of Illinois, University of Colorado, Stanford University, University of Kansas, and Southern Illinois University at Carbondale.

Although generous assistance has come from many, responsibility rests only on one, the writer.

C.H.G.

# PAWNS IN A TRIANGLE OF HATE

# 1

# The Japanese in Prewar Peru

The prospect of mutual advantage inspired Japanese emigration to Peru. For many years able-bodied Japanese, expendable workers from the pool of excess farm hands, had been available. As early as 1868 the first Japanese emigrants had gone abroad, to Hawaii, and soon others would go to mainland America, to the United States, Canada, Mexico, and southward. In late decades of the nineteenth century, as native and foreign agricultural interests in Peru expanded their sugar and cotton acreage, a need for able, dependable workers had arisen. For Peru it would not be the first experience with Oriental labor. That had come about decades earlier with the Chinese and had gradually led to animosity, a pattern which the Americas had recorded throughout the hemisphere. For the Japanese, however, the Peruvian venture, their first Latin American experience, would soon be joined by significant migrations to Mexico and Brazil.

The first phase of the Japanese migration to Peru began in the spring of 1899 when the *Sakura Maru* arrived at Callao with 790 Japanese. From the Japanese standpoint that movement stemmed from a combination of circumstances: unsettling economic prospects in the wake of the Sino-Japanese War, the desire of certain shipping companies and emigration agents to make a profit, the persistent surplus of skilled farmers, and an assurance that Peru would welcome such workers. That first migrant group, recruited in numerous Japanese prefectures by the Morioka Emigration Company, had gone to Peru aboard a vessel of the Japan Mail Line (Nippon Yūsen Kaisha). Four years later an additional 1,080 Japanese entered Peru, and in 1906 the third contingent numbered 774. Japanese willingness to migrate, matching Peruvian willingness to admit them,

3

fostered competition as the Meiji, Tōyō, and Overseas Development Companies joined Morioka in contracting immigrants.

Because the contract system held forth the prospect of more profit for the shipper, emigration agent, and plantation operator than for the worker, it soon invited criticism and change. By 1923 the emigration companies that had transported 17,764 Japanese to Peru were an anachronism. Agreements that required repayment of passage costs and fixed workers' wages for definite periods were no longer in vogue. The abolition of worker contracts in that year encouraged many to migrate independently. Also, by the 1920s, some of the earlier immigrants were established enough themselves that they could "call" relatives and friends and essentially sponsor the incoming immigrants. Such was the experience of twenty-four-year-old Hisao Fujii, who was "called" by his uncle Sadajiro Yumoto to assist him at chicken farming.

During the 1930s, at home and in Peru, the Japanese felt severe pressures. Although economic depression in Japan encouraged migration, a similar condition in Peru, along with mounting hostile legislation, made Japanese there consider returning across the Pacific. In a decade marked by no appreciable net gain in the number of Japanese immigrants in Peru, certain emotion-laden influences were also present—Japanese military involvement in the Far East and soaring prejudice on the part of native Peruvians. But the preceding decades had rooted most of the immigrants in Peru.

The Japanese who had migrated to Canada, the United States, Mexico, Brazil, and elsewhere were experiencing lives that mingled repetition with novelty. Prejudices dogged them. They fished the waters of British Columbia, operated truck gardens in California, deserted a colonization scheme in a Mexican jungle in search of opportunity, and labored so diligently on coffee plantations that Brazilian authorities wanted many more of them. A common denominator of the Japanese emigrants was their willingness to work.[1]

At first the early immigrants labored on sugar and cotton plantations along the coastal strip of Peru. But almost at once worker discontent surfaced. Health problems, especially in malarial zones, dictated some changes of setting. Often, too, the cane-cutting and other heavy work overtaxed the small physiques of many men. Miserable employer-employee relations, brought on by greedy operators who reduced wages and otherwise altered contract terms, combined with other complaints to encourage wholesale departures from plantations. The shortening of the contract period in 1906, from four years to six months, granted the Japanese even more mobility.

Although many one-time contract laborers gradually became operators of leased acreage and continued in agriculture, many others, by 1910, had traded the limited prospects offered by rural Peru for urban opportunities. The upward economic mobility that some pursued on rented land others sought in towns and cities, where any occupation increased the opportunity to master Spanish, learn Peruvian ways, and advance oneself. Some became household servants. Others, with meager resources, followed the lead of Ecuadorians and other aliens and opened barber shops. Eventually immigrants launched operations that required sizable outlays of capital—grocery stores, restaurants, and general merchandise outlets. Often, by the 1920s, newly arrived Japanese settled immediately in Lima, Callao, and other municipalities, skipping identification with any kind of farming. By 1940 approximately 80 percent of the Peruvian Japanese were living in the Lima-Callao metropolitan area. That year, when the Japanese numbered 17,598 and represented 28.08 percent of the foreign population of Peru, certain statistics reflected the economic side of their lives (see table 1).

The diligence that had commended the Japanese to Peruvian plantation operators seemed boundless once an immigrant launched his own commercial venture. His supplies and products came primarily from

TABLE 1
Economic Aspects of the Peruvian Japanese, 1940

| Category of Occupations | Male | Female |
|---|---|---|
| Owner-operators | 3,765 | 303 |
| Employees | 1,434 | 80 |
| Partnerships | 350 | 219 |
| Workers-farmers | 3,273 | 90 |
| Independent Workers | 973 | 44 |
| Unspecified | 677 | 399 |
| Total active | 10,472 | 1,135 |

Japan, and when a work force expanded, it embraced other Japanese. This approach to their economic endeavors, despite the competition it bred among the Japanese themselves, fostered a communal spirit vividly illustrated by their numerous business organizations. In 1938, thirteen Japanese commercial associations in Lima—the organizations of merchants, cafe owners, barbers, bazaar owners, charcoal dealers, chauffeurs, importers, jewelers, hotel owners, restaurateurs, peddlers, bakery owners, and building contractors—boasted 967 members. This strong commercial inclination enabled many Peruvian Japanese to achieve remarkable upward mobility.

By 1940, when Canada counted more than twenty thousand Japanese and the United States more than five times that number, many immigrants had moved from manual labor and rural settings to the cities and commercial enterprises. That rural-urban transition also characterized Brazil, where the Japanese population was burgeoning (as many as 23,299 entering the country in 1933), and Mexico, where discouragements had removed 64 percent of those who had been there a decade earlier.[2]

At all times, however, the Japanese were much more than economic beings. The cultural chasm between them and native Peruvians, along with their vulnerability as an ill-understood minority, prompted a huddling together, as it were, which showed itself in many ways. Love of homeland and a shared conviction that Japanese culture was superior, in addition to the initially held belief that Peru was just an interlude in their lives, encouraged the formation of organizations that emphasized their Japanese nature. Ordinarily an immigrant joined his prefectural society, proud of his roots in Fukuoka, Yamagata, Hiroshima, Okinawa, or elsewhere. In addition, Peru-based neighborhood and community-wide societies mushroomed. In turn these led to the creation, in 1917, of the Central Japanese Association of Peru (Perū Chūo Nihonjinkai). On occasion the Japanese also established athletic organizations and other specialized groups.

Unlike the Peruvian Chinese colony, which was 95 percent male, the Japanese migration soon included family units. Unmarried men usually made quick trips to the home country for brides as soon as they had established themselves. Later many bachelors married Nisei daughters of earlier immigrants. Typical Japanese—parents and children—readily accommodated themselves to the Roman Catholic Church, one of the more obvious proofs of their Peruvianization. Certain aspects of Peruvian Japanese society are reflected in table 2.

A sense of community and cultural pride joined a keen interest in the education of the children to encourage the founding of Japanese-language schools. In 1908 the first of fifty elementary schools opened. Supplementing this retention of Japanese culture, a succession of Japanese-language newspapers appeared. Lengthy sojourns in Japan for some children, usually teenage boys, also fortified the Japanese side of life. Stubborn retention of many facets of Japanese culture—language, music, flower arranging, games, and dietary preferences, among others—along with increasing immersion in the Spanish-Catholic life of Peru found many Peruvian Japanese straddling two worlds.

These aspects of the Japanese way of life in Peru were evident elsewhere in the Americas. In Canada, women-starved early immigrants welcomed "picture brides." Japanese fishermen established a hospital and founded associations. The Japanese inaugurated their first school in Vancouver in 1906, and three years later the Canada Japanese Association was functioning. The interests reflected in Peruvian and Canadian experience were found in the United States, Mexico, and Brazil as well.[3]

For decades before World War II, anti-Japanese sentiment had flourished in Peru. Not only did official colonization schemes continue to focus on Europeans, but the Japanese immigrants were heirs to the half-century-old Peruvian dislike of the Chinese. In rural areas early clashes—physical and otherwise—occurred between Japanese immigrants and native Peruvians. Soon many of the latter insisted that Japanese farmers had taken

TABLE 2
Social Aspects of the Peruvian Japanese, 1940

| Marital Status | Male | Female |
| --- | --- | --- |
| Married | 6,127 | 4,472 |
| Unmarried | 4,801 | 1,144 |
| Common-law unions | 369 | 59 |
| Divorced | 21 | 6 |
| Widowers, widows | 423 | 172 |
| Total | 11,741 | 5,853 |

over control of the fertile Chancay Valley and other select agricultural zones. In urban areas the cry of unfair competition and monopoly quickly engulfed Japanese barbers and others. The pride of race and culture that prompted Japanese to marry Japanese and set them apart socially was met by self-contradictory Peruvian reactions that exhibited a common prejudice: the Japanese, they said, defied Peruvianization because they would not mix, and they constituted an inferior race with which Peruvians should not mix. The issue of citizenship posed another paradox: although resenting immigrant retention of Japanese citizenship, officials often made the naturalization proceedings difficult for Peruvian Japanese. At the same time, on all fronts, the Peruvian press—especially that of Lima—reflected and fanned the growing hostility.

Early in the post–World War I period Peruvian authorities had begun to discuss antiforeign measures. How much their anti-Japanese bent reflected the trend in the United States—the U.S. exclusion law of 1924, for example—defies precise assessment. Soon, moreover, the economic distress of the 1930s compounded that anti-Japanese drift. The official government program to "Peruvianize" economic activity aimed principally at eliminating Japanese interests and enterprises. In 1934 Peru denounced the four-year-old treaty of friendship, commerce, and navigation. Legislation quickly required that 80 percent of any work force be native Peruvian and set quotas for imported cotton goods. In June 1936 the government established immigration quotas and regulations that especially hit the Japanese, the most numerous immigrant group in the country. In July the authorities suspended the granting of naturalization papers, and shortly thereafter late birth registrations were annulled.

Peruvians considered the *jus sanguinis* principle whereby an individual might enjoy dual citizenship a basic obstacle to Peruvian Japanese loyalty to Peru. They also cited, as proof of the continuing and essentially Japanese nature of the immigrant colony, the strong commercial ties Japanese merchants had with Japan and the custom of sending youngsters there to complete their education. Peruvians even viewed the Japanese aggression in China as a sign of what lay in store for their own country.

As the chasm widened between native Peruvians and Peruvian Japanese, journalistic outbursts inflamed an already irrational and emotional public. The economic position of the Japanese in the Peruvian economy was grossly exaggerated, as was the number of Japanese in the country. Rumor and half-truth spawned blatant lies that heightened the Peruvian resentment which the exclusive Japanese schools and societies had fostered.

The climax came in May 1940 when rioting Peruvians invaded and plundered hundreds of Japanese homes and businesses in Lima and Callao. Restaurant worker Yosei Arakaki lost his passport during the riot and barber Kenyu Miyashiro lost his shop (both losses were later made known to American authorities). Some frightened men hurried wives and children to Japan. Peru hurriedly enacted a decree that suspended temporarily the entry of immigrants; and while the government was counting its population, including the 17,598 Japanese hated by many of the other six million Peruvians, the Foreign Office revoked the citizenship of native-born Peruvians, such as the Nisei, whose parents had come from countries recognizing the *jus sanguinis* principle. Later the decree requiring that publications employing non-Latin alphabets carry parallel translations struck directly at the *Lima Daily* (*Lima Nippō*), the one surviving Japanese-language newspaper.

In Canada the anti-Japanese rioting of 1907 had sped the activities of the Asiatic Exclusion League, the formulation of annual quotas for Japanese immigrants, and the erection of various barriers that kept Orientals from certain professions. Concentrations of Japanese, as in British Columbia, parts of California, coastal areas of Peru, the Cauca Valley of Colombia, the ports flanking the Panama Canal, and the São Paulo region of Brazil, fueled outbursts of anti-Japanese sentiment. As the economic depression of the 1930s deepened, immigration quotas and economic restrictions increasingly plagued the Japanese at a time when the threat of international war was mounting.[4]

As the war in Europe intensified and its counterpart in the Pacific approached, cooperation increasingly characterized United States–Peruvian relations. Almost within the shadow of the European conflict, the Pan American Conference in Lima in December 1938 had stressed hemispheric unity in the face of totalitarian aggression. Periodic reporting by the American embassy concerning totalitarian activities in Peru accorded the Japanese detailed coverage. Specific U.S.–Peruvian meetings and arrangements in the aftermath of the Lima Conference were designed to implement that desired unity. In view of the critical turn of military events in Europe and the collapse of France, United States naval and military representatives conferred in mid-June 1940 with key Peruvian cabinet officers.

At a final meeting, "all three Ministers, evidently reflecting the President's views, again expressed the primary concern of Peru with respect to Japan." In July two agreements provided for American naval missions to improve the efficiency of the Peruvian navy and its aviation program. In the spring of 1941 a similar arrangement sent an American military adviser to the Remount Service of the Peruvian army. Tedious but eventually productive discussions focused on the American desire to buy certain critical and strategic minerals. Similarly protracted talks concerned a reciprocal trade agreement which would take into account the economic disruption Peru was suffering because of the war.[5]

Not long after the American Congress authorized the Federal Bureau of Investigation to engage in nonmilitary intelligence gathering throughout the Western Hemisphere, J. Edgar Hoover posted agents in Peru. At times, however, American officials fell willing victims of questing Peruvian politicians, as when Hoover repeatedly expressed confidence in a questionable Aprista appraisal of the Axis in Peru. Victor Raúl Haya de la Torre's out-of-favor party insisted that all the Japanese there had served in the Japanese army, that many were ex-officers, and that the Japanese community contained few women. The implication—a false one—was that a male could not migrate from Japan until he had served in the army. The Aprista assessment ignored the fact that Japanese reserve officers included few, if any, men who as impoverished sons of farmers had left Japan in early manhood. By ignoring the 40 percent of the Japanese community who were women and children and overemphasizing the male element, the Peruvians fed the already exaggerated fears of Americans, in Lima and Washington. Other unsupported assertions about the Japanese were concerned with their "military type" organization, their monopoly of small business, their threatened control of the Amazon basin, and their fifth column potential as allies of Peruvian Indians.[6] Unquestioning American acceptance of prejudiced and erroneous prewar Peruvian assessments of the Japanese presaged Peruvian-American wartime cooperation.

Not long before the outbreak of hostilities between Japan and the United States an American diplomatic assessment of the situation in Peru included the following: speculation that family ties rendered Foreign Minister Alfredo Solf y Muro pro-Axis, claims that the Japanese supported German propaganda there and were paying subsidies to some Peruvian newspapers, and rumor that Minister Ryūki Sakamoto intended to weld the Peruvian Japanese into a "nationalistic unit."[7] The prewar conclusions of American intelligence regarding the Japanese in Peru rested on an exceedingly fragile factual basis, and the lack of linguistically competent personnel sustained rumors that heightened the emotionalism that went hand in hand with ignorance, prejudice, fear, and hate.

# 2

# Shaping a Deportation-Internment Program

During wartime the internment of enemy aliens by belligerents has become commonplace, a practice accepted throughout the world. Within the United States, in 1942, such an operation involved the Japanese Americans, most of whom were neither aliens nor enemies. Its installation required many months. Abroad, any internment program to which the United States might become a party would be much more tedious and time consuming, since consideration had to be accorded the different perspectives—diplomatic, political, economic, military, social, psychological, and otherwise—entertained by the other state or states. International law, however subject to wartime abuse, might get passing consideration, but logistics, especially the availability of shipping, would require constant and compelling consideration.

In Peru, as well as throughout Latin America, the legal position of aliens made them readily susceptible to expulsion. Even the domiciled alien, whose position was stronger than that of the transient, possessed no absolute guarantee of a right to remain. The right of a state to expel an alien in defense of its interests required no express statement of law. Because "there is no available legislative or judicial definition of this phrase [i.e., national security] in Latin America," and because "International law authorizes the expulsion of an alien on the broad and not easily definable ground of 'public order or security,'" the vulnerability of the alien in wartime was complete. Generally, throughout Latin America, "the Chief Executive alone has the authority to order an expulsion; and this, it is said, can be done administratively, and summarily," and "the alien . . . has no right to judicial interposition in his behalf unless that right is expressly, or by necessary implication, given him in some law."[1] This control by the executive branch of a government permitted actions which, supplemented by loose arrangements with another government for internment, could spawn a deportation-internment program outside the range of legislative debate and public awareness.

Ambassador R. Henry Norweb's eagerness to contribute diplomatically to the American war effort by buttressing Washington's relations with a government whose economy could contribute significantly to that war effort fueled his desire to rid Peru of Japanese. "We may be able," he declared, "to assist the Peruvian Government by making available information and suggestions based upon our handling of Japanese residents in the United States." In the United States the four months following the outbreak of war had produced numerous developments. Anti-Japanese pressures by the American public, press, and politicians had prompted congressional delegations to recommend the internment of the Japanese, citizens and aliens alike. Many local, state, and federal law enforcement officials, paranoid on the subjects of sabotage and espionage, nurtured hysteria by issuing inflammatory and inaccurate reports, yielding civilian authority to the military, and considering the evacuation of citizens and aliens legal if deemed necessary militarily. Simultaneously, in furtherance of their desire to evacuate and intern everyone of Japanese ancestry, certain West Coast army commanders were operating outside normal channels, and many police officers were resorting to questionable search warrants. Military and civilian authorities had terrorized the Japanese, rendering them helpless and demoralized. Finally, ten weeks after the outbreak of hostilities, the American president, under the guise of "military necessity," had issued Executive Order 9066, the authority whereby military commanders could exclude any or all persons from proscribed areas. In mid-March the War Relocation Authority was created, and men, women, and children of Japanese ancestry were hurriedly crowded into assembly centers to await transfer to bleak windswept desert areas that the government avoided calling concentration camps. The first Japanese Americans to reach a relocation center did so in mid-1942. Almost immediately, while tens of thousands of other Japanese Americans were being transported to centers, in California, Utah, Idaho, Wyoming, Colorado, and Arkansas, the United States conducted "a survey of detention and internment camps to determine names of Japanese in confinement who wish to be repatriated." For Canadian Japanese the events of 1942 bore remarkable resemblance to those in the United States.

The step-by-step experience of the American government could not be applied to Peru and the Peruvian Japanese, but, in the aggregate, that experience conveyed one basic message: a government could abuse, even deny, the fundamental rights of individuals in the name of national security. Norweb believed that the American embassy could propagandize the Japanese threat, and he hoped to persuade Peru to deport between two hundred and three hundred "undesirable Japanese" in a matter of weeks.[2]

While Norweb was sketching his hopes regarding the Peruvian Japanese, the handling of the Panamanian Japanese already offered a record of accomplishment. There, before the outbreak of war, American and Panamanian officials had agreed, informally and orally, on the wartime internment of the Japanese. After the attack on Pearl Harbor, Panamanian and American agents immediately rounded them up. Panama quickly declared war against the Axis states, froze Axis funds, and not only permitted the transfer of the enemy aliens to the United States but also allowed the Panamanian Japanese to be exchanged for citizens of the Western Hemisphere held by Japan. This Panamanian cooperation was much like the World War I experience.[3] In 1942, however, it furnished a pattern that American planners in Washington and American representatives throughout Latin America, and especially those in Peru, desired to emulate.

### The American "Blacklist" and Peru

Two days after the attack on Pearl Harbor the American government expanded the blacklisting it had initiated in July 1941 regarding Germans and Italians to include Japanese. Essentially this economic warfare measure, formally termed the Proclaimed List of Certain Blocked Nationals, aimed at economic strangulation through government-sponsored boycott. For the Peruvian Japanese, however, the Proclaimed List could have only limited clout: the smallness of their businesses made them relatively insignificant, and few of their imports and none of their financing had come from the United States. Nevertheless inclusion on the American list was psychologically upsetting. It injected an element of uncertainty that precipitated premature assignments and sales of property. The American listing of the Japanese and their business interests probably also encouraged Peruvian authorities to adopt more cavalier attitudes in dealing with those individuals. That blacklist of December 9, for example, included the Lima light bulb factory of Jiro Hasegawa, the Lima sporting goods establishment of Yasuhiko Ohashi and Ginzo Murono, and the name of Huaral-based Nikumatsu Okada, operator of six cotton-producing haciendas. In June the successful farm administrator was deported to the United States. In January 1943 sporting goods proprietors Murono and Ohashi were shipped to the United States, and in mid-1944 the owner of the light bulb factory received similar treatment.[4]

The Department of State, acting in conjunction with three other cabinet departments—Treasury, Justice, and Commerce—as well as the Administrator of Export Control and the Coordinator of Commercial and Cultural Relations Between the American Republics, published the Proclaimed Lists. Personnel and criteria additionally confounded the end product. Throughout the wartime period the preponderant role of the Japanese on the American lists for Peru was clearly evident (see table 3).

In the absence of records and in the presence of so many other relevant facts, the precise economic effects of the "blacklist" on individuals, families, and the entire Japanese community cannot be measured. But individuals did occasionally point an accusing finger publicly at the American operation. Hikoichi Hamamura, a merchant in Huancayo, de-

**TABLE 3**

The Japanese and Selected Proclaimed Lists for Peru

| Date | Japanese | Axis Total |
|---|---|---|
| December 9, 1941 | 159 | 159 |
| August 10, 1942 | 668 | 1,005 |
| November 12, 1942 | 741 | 1,078 |
| April 23, 1943 | 771 | 1,161 |
| October 7, 1943 | 781 | 1,176 |
| March 23, 1944 | 781 | 1,170 |
| September 13, 1944 | 772 | 1,153 |
| February 28, 1945 | 777 | 1,117 |
| December 20, 1945 | 773 | 938 |
| June 6, 1946 | 0 | 0 |

SOURCE: U.S., DS, *The Proclaimed List of Certain Blocked Nationals* (all lists and supplements) (Washington, GPO, 1941–46).

clared that after he was put on the "blacklist" (December 9, 1941) his business was ruined.

Exactly how an entry, individual or business, originated—by whom initiated and for what reasons—remains unclear. The utility of the listings, however, can be questioned, because (1) the addresses of some persons were never ascertained; for example, that of Jorge Yasaki, on the Proclaimed List as early as March 1942, was never established during the entire wartime period; (2) some names, stated in inverted order, were never listed correctly in any subsequent listing; (3) fanciful transcriptions of Japanese names persisted throughout the entire span of their inclusion on the lists; (4) some compiler (or compilers), rooted in Spanish and ignorant of Japanese, injected confusion; for example, Honda entered as Jonda, Ohashi as Ojasi; (5) occasionally a person assumed multiple identities (Pedro Tomio Nabeta was listed as both Pedro Nabeta and Tomio Nabeta, and Juan Ichisuke Fujimoto was listed under three versions of his name); (6) the tendency to employ Spanish rather than Japanese first names resulted in the listing of adopted names and the omission of legal names. Later, however, those compiling the evacuation lists of persons being sent to the United States and those building the data files of the U.S. Immigration and Naturalization Service (INS), looking askance at Spanish names as aliases and therefore something to be avoided, went to the other extreme and listed only the Japanese names. This means that often it is difficult to correlate official listings, even when, for example, José Tanaka and Hiroshi Tanaka are in truth José Hiroshi Tanaka.[5]

Year after year, ignorance of language, cultural prejudice, economic envy, and wartime emotion rather than firm criteria that advanced the prosecution of the war combined to make easy the inclusion of Peruvian Japanese businessmen on the Proclaimed Lists, their removal therefrom impossible.

### The Rio Conference and the Emergency Advisory Committee

While struggling with specifics, the United States also wanted a more general and forceful identification of all Latin America with the widened war. Beyond the desire to achieve unanimous support of a resolution binding all the American republics to sever diplomatic relations with the Axis states, the American delegation to the Rio de Janeiro meeting of foreign ministers led the fight to incorporate a detailed resolution (XVII) regarding subversive activities in the Final Act of that January 1942 conference. To prevent subversive activities, recommendations were advanced in four areas: (1) the control of dangerous aliens, (2) the prevention of the abuse of citizenship, (3) the regulation of international travel, and (4) the prevention of acts of political aggression, such as espionage, sabotage, and subversive propaganda. To study and coordinate these recommendations, the conference provided for the prompt creation of the Emergency Advisory Committee for Political Defense.[6]

That committee, a seven-man body composed of representatives from Argentina, Brazil, Chile, Mexico, the United States, Uruguay, and Venezuela, established itself in Montevideo and in the course of its first fifteen months of operation (April 1942–July 1943) submitted to the governments of the Western Hemisphere twenty-one programs of action based on the recommendations. Some proposals were so detailed that no government ever fully implemented them. Such was the case with those related to the registration and reporting of all Axis aliens. Less cumbersome proposals received more sympathetic attention from the authorities. The entire program represented a continuing pressure for unified outlook and action within the hemisphere, something that the United States desired and could not hope to attain through occasional conferences alone. The willingness of individual governments to adopt and implement the proposals of the Emergency Advisory Committee fluctuated widely, as administrations changed, as their perception of the war shifted, and as military events unfolded.

By the time Peru was named to the committee, in October 1944, as a replacement for Argentina, most of its innovative labor had been accomplished. Lack of direct identification with the committee during the first thirty months of its life possibly induced Peruvian reluctance to implement its proposals. However, the views of the United States, Peru, and the committee coincided quite early on the subject of internment.

The committee's Resolution XX, entitled "Detention and Expulsion of Dangerous Axis Nationals," concluded that "there are two procedures for safeguarding the security of the Hemisphere: a) Internment of dangerous Axis agents and nationals for the duration of the emergency; b) repatriation of the same." After detailing reasons why internment was preferred to repatriation, the resolution added, "by reason of lack of facilities or similar reasons arising out of local conditions, some of the Republics may not find themselves in a position to adopt a program of detention within their territories to the extent desired for the security of the Continent. Accordingly, paragraph 3 recommends local detention within each Republic, and in addition urges a complementary program of expulsion of aliens to other American Republics, for the detention of such aliens for the duration of the current conflict." More than a year before Resolution XX was approved in committee (May 21, 1943) and transmitted to the governments (June 4, 1943), the United States and Peru had established a full-blown deportation-internment program.[7] In such instances, in addition to circulating a potentially normative program for all interested governments, the committee's proposals accorded an air of legitimacy to actions already taken. In a real sense the economic pressures of successive issues of the Proclaimed List and the political pressures of successive resolutions of the Emergency Advisory Committee were complementary aspects of the American wartime program.

## Developments in Peru

The military events of December 7 also spurred activity in Peru. Japanese newspapers were closed, and gatherings of more than three persons were forbidden. Unverified reports had the Peruvians "controlling and watching all movements of Japanese," with special attention focused on the northern ports of Talara and Zorritos and the chief port of the country, Callao. The U.S. War Department received word from Lima that "now is a very favorable time to resume consideration for the placing of American military and naval units in Latin American countries for reconnaissance, security, and support of these governments pledging solidarity with the United States."[8] Present was the germ of the reciprocating outlook—Peruvian dislike of her Japanese, and American desire to defeat the Japanese—that later enabled Peruvian-American cooperation to include a program of deportation and internment.

Except for new port regulations and a boom across the entrance to the inner harbor at Callao, the six weeks following the outbreak of war between Japan and the United States produced little that associated Peru with the war in the Pacific. In that interval, however, the United States was agitating for and then looking forward to the conference of foreign ministers at which Washington hoped to win unanimous support for a resolution binding all the American governments to break with the Axis. Argentine and Chilean reluctance blocked unanimity of action at Rio de

Janeiro, but Peru, as of January 24, did fulfill that American desire. That same day in Lima, Japanese Chargé Masaki Yodokawa, in his farewell message, told the Peruvian Japanese that "with regard to the Japanese residents of Peru, neither the Peruvian Government nor the Peruvian people hold any animosity towards the Japanese and . . . there need be no change in the lives or occupations of the Japanese." Troubled by the rioting of 1940 and the tardy Peruvian reimbursement of its victims, the Japanese community knew that Yodokawa was unwarrantedly optimistic. Faring better in the minds of the Peruvian Japanese was his reminder that "no Japanese should forget his pride as a subject of the Empire." He further reminded them to be prudent in word and deed, to try to continue their work, to obey Peruvian laws and officials. "Even if . . . unjust oppression should be suffered," Yodokawa said, "maintain discretion and good sense."[9] In January 1942 no one could foresee the dimension of oppression the war would bring or the need for good sense it would require of those oppressed.

Peru promptly determined the number of Axis officials who, with their families, needed to be repatriated. At the same time the Peruvian Foreign Office wondered whether the United States would "permit repatriation of Axis nonofficial women and children and men not of military age or known to have engaged in subversive activities should such persons be deported by Peruvian Government for travel by way of the United States." Peru, obviously considering the wartime period an excellent opportunity to rid itself of many Japanese, was somewhat in advance of American thinking, because Assistant Secretary of State Breckinridge Long penciled on the document, "ignore this . . . in replying."[10]

Peruvian acceptance of the American proposal that all Axis officials be repatriated via the United States afforded Lima officials an entrée regarding the repatriation of nonofficials as well. Added support for the Peruvians came when the Japanese government insisted that ten businessmen, representatives of Japan-based trading companies, be repatriated along with the officials. A week later Peru indicated a desire to expel seventy nonofficial Axis nationals, a number that quickly grew to 236. Almost simultaneously Peru reiterated her request for a statement of the American position regarding repatriation. Early in March, by which time the limited capacity of the ships scheduled by the United States for repatriation purposes was known, Peru regretted that only dangerous nonofficial Axis nationals would be accommodated. Peru had expected that facilities would be made available to all who wished to depart. Still hopeful, the Peruvian Foreign Office again sought American views concerning the eventual repatriation of all Axis nationals who might desire to leave Peru.[11]

To say, however, that Peru was enthusiastic and the United States reluctant regarding the repatriation of all of the Axis nationals in Peru would oversimplify a complex issue. Peruvian enthusiasm varied with different nationalities. Because there were few nonofficial Peruvians in Japanese hands and there were thousands of disliked Japanese in Peru, Lima pressed hardest concerning the Japanese. The Germans, on the other hand, posed problems. For one thing many of them had worked themselves into the fabric of Peruvian society—upper strata at that—in a manner totally unknown to the Japanese. Furthermore, the number of Peruvians, among them prominent individuals, in Germany tempered the Peruvian approach to that repatriation with a caution that contrasted with the near abandon characterizing their approach to the Japanese.[12]

The United States was reluctant to endorse full-scale repatriation of the Japanese, or any other Axis nationality, for a number of reasons. The magnitude of the problem staggered Washington officials who faced the prospect that any program instituted for one Latin American state might have to be extended to a dozen or more. Furthermore, because such repatriation would be on a one-for-one basis, American officials could assume that a relatively limited number of citizens of the Western Hemisphere in Japanese hands (a view which would later change) would require a limited number of Latin American Japanese for exchange purposes. Beyond such policy problems of the Department of State loomed a logistical one, the availability of shipping for such an activity. The Departments of War and Navy, busy expanding American military operations, could be expected to deny shipping for any massive repatriation program. Added to all else, at a time when the internment of 110,000 Japanese Americans had been decided on but not yet accomplished, the question of the vaguely indefinite internment of countless Axis nationals from Latin America in anticipation of their hoped-for repatriation hinted at administrative headaches no one wanted to indulge.

A flurry of negotiations and agreements increasingly identified Peru with the American war effort. One arrangement, part of the American defense of the Pacific approach to the Panama Canal, placed a small United States military force at Talara, near the oil fields of northern

Peru. That combination of circumstances soon sped the deportation of certain Japanese. In Washington, less than a week after the arrival of that American contingent at Talara, officials signed the lend-lease agreement which promised Peru about $29,000,000 worth of armaments and munitions, the largest such consignment in all Spanish America. Negotiations also concerned Peruvian rubber, cinchona bark, and other strategic needs of the United States, Export-Import Bank credits for Peru, and a reciprocal trade agreement geared to the wartime requirements of both countries.[13] Along with all else, the dimensions of the repatriation issue widened.

Posed first by the shipment of enemy aliens from Panama, the question of the unity of internee families quickly arose in U.S.–Peruvian relations. The Department of State and the Peruvian Foreign Office agreement that family unity should be preserved prompts one to wonder how much the decision stemmed from elementary humanitarianism and how much it reflected the expedient control of even larger numbers of aliens.[14]

While some negotiations and decisions dealing with the indefinite future easily materialized, others concerning the initial removal of Axis nationals from Peru often proved tedious. Following a conversation during which the Peruvian official pledged cooperation in the removal of individuals on both the British and American lists of undesirables, the American embassy reported, "I am hopeful . . . [Minister of Government and Police] Garrido Lecca's ready response to our representations . . . may be found to consist of something more than amiable volubility. . . . as a means of promoting action and preventing subsidence into the inertia which is all too frequently a characteristic of Peruvian official action, or rather inaction, an officer of the Embassy . . . will keep in close touch."[15] Later, administrative lethargy would not be the only charge leveled at Peruvian authorities.

In Washington, in the same season, officials encountered a representative anti-Japanese outburst. Jorge Larrañaga, a former member of Peru's Financial and Economic Advisory Committee, insisted that the United States had underestimated the Japanese in Peru. Larrañaga's picture included the Japanese servant "with an alert ear," shop owners who "could set the city of Lima on fire overnight," restaurateurs who could "inject drugs . . . according to Tokio's prefixed plans," and so on. He urged the confinement of all the Japanese in concentration camps.[16] This emotional and irrational assessment of the Peruvian Japanese by an educated official of Peru, who proved to be a persistent propagandist, coincided with the assessment of the Japanese Americans indulged by many American officials. Almost simultaneously conversation between Under Secretary of State Sumner Welles and Attorney General Francis Biddle regarding Latin American citizens among the internees that had arrived from Panama and Costa Rica concluded that (1) the situation posed no legal difficulties and (2) the Department of Justice was the only agency that should handle the question of the internees from Latin America.[17] Accordingly, before the first enemy alien left Peru for the United States the way was clear for the deportation and internment of Peruvian citizens, whether naturalized or native-born Peruvians. It was also evident that the War Relocation Authority, established on March 18 to administer interned Japanese Americans, would have nothing to do with the internees from Latin America. For the Department of Justice, whose Immigration and Naturalization Service was accustomed to holding only limited numbers of aliens for short periods, the future held the prospect of indefinite detention of large numbers of persons.

While Washington focused attention on Attorney General Biddle regarding the detention of Latin American internees, the American embassy in Lima looked increasingly to Third Secretary John K. Emmerson for the selection of the prospective deportee-internees. Probably the only person with a command of Japanese at any American diplomatic mission in all Latin America, Emmerson had gone to Lima in February because of the relatively heavy concentration of Japanese in Peru. A month later, within the Auxiliary Section of the embassy, he was methodically assessing the Peruvian Japanese community—studying old files of a Lima-based Japanese newspaper, translating materials that the embassy conveyed to Peruvian officials, lengthening future supplements of the Proclaimed List by the addition of more Japanese, and seeking informants who knew the Japanese community, a move that soon involved Chinese cooperation. For twenty months in 1942–43 Emmerson played a pivotal role in the deportation of Peruvian Japanese. Thirty-five years later he would declare, "During my period of service in the embassy, we found no reliable evidence of planned or contemplated acts of sabotage, subversion, or espionage."[18]

In the closing days of March 1942, the United States orally satisfied Peruvian insistence that Axis officials going to Europe via the United States would not be surrendered until it was certain that the Axis powers had freed the corresponding Peruvian officials. On a broader front that included the Japanese, Norweb reported to the State Department that he had informed the Peruvian Foreign Office, "the United States Government is prepared to transport from Peru to the United States for immediate repatriation and exchange not only the Axis officials... but also nonofficial Axis nationals. My Government will interpose no objection to the repatriation of any category of Axis personnel, including men of military age, with certain exceptions such as airplane pilots and submarine commanders, who may be interned locally."[19] Subsequent arrangements between the United States and Peru concerning the deportation, internment, and repatriation of the Japanese were also not in writing. Wartime uncertainties, as well as haste and differing priorities, objectives, and perspectives help to explain why such arrangements were intentionally nebulous. Later, different interpretations of the oral arrangements would plague U.S.–Peruvian relations regarding the internees.

The perfection of the lists of deportees was all that remained to be accomplished, but day after day those lists, revised and confused, remained incomplete. From the standpoint of Washington, the Peruvian experience was not unique: problems and delays attended the deportation programs in Bolivia and Ecuador, which were integrated for ship-scheduling purposes with that of Peru.[20] For their understanding of the total problem, the Department of State sent the embassy in Lima in early April 1942 its estimate of the number and handling of the enemy aliens to be removed from the west coast of South America (see table 4). Plans called for the following: 237 officials and 237 nonofficials aboard the *Acadia,* 700 nonofficials aboard the *Etolin,* and additional shipping for

**TABLE 4**

Estimate of Axis Nationals To Be Shipped to the United States from the West Coast of South America

| Country | Officials | Nonofficials | Total |
|---|---|---|---|
| Bolivia | 63 | 83 | 146 |
| Peru | 104 | 949 | 1,053 |
| Ecuador | 37 | 78 | 115 |
| Colombia | 33 | 400 | 433 |
| Total | 237 | 1,510 | 1,747 |

the remaining nonofficials. The *Etolin* already lay at anchor at Callao, ready to take aboard what its skipper considered prisoners of war.[21]

In the United States the events of December 7, 1941, had immediately crystallized a massive, nationwide hatred and fear of the Japanese, but the noninvolvement of Peru militarily promoted no equivalent sentiment there. Instead, anti-Japanese feelings in Peru built up gradually. While American politicians, especially those from Pacific Coast states, routinely exploited the hatred of the Japanese, equivalent political animus scarcely surfaced in Peru. But the early arrest of many Japanese Americans by the FBI and other law enforcement agencies was paralleled months later in Peru as a result of considerable official American agitation and cooperation. In both countries the arrests often violated the legal norms regarding warrants, charges, hearings, and so forth. In the United States, families worried as waves of hate engulfed them—as jobs were lost, businesses boycotted, withdrawals from schools forced, and epithets rained upon them. In Peru Japanese assets were frozen and successive issues of the Proclaimed List of Certain Blocked Nationals by the United States repeatedly brought economic distress to the Japanese community. The fears of Peruvian Japanese multiplied as they witnessed the increasing alignment of Peru with American wartime aims, as the Lima press mounted attacks on the Japanese, and as Peruvian police fashioned the lists of prospective deportees that encouraged the solicitation and acceptance of bribes from men of means in return for the opportunity to hide and escape deportation temporarily.

For Japanese the months of December, January, February, and March had been characterized by uncertainty, fear, and helplessness accompanied by the disturbing awareness that they were victims of discriminatory and unjust actions by the governments of the United States and Peru. Ahead, during the spring of 1942, in both Peru and the United States, more uncertainty and tension would besiege the Japanese. Soon the American government would corral its Japanese in the horse barns of Santa Anita and other "assembly" centers en route to the isolation of desolate "relocation" centers. In the same period, selected Peruvian Japanese, scheduled for internment they knew not where, would fret in the jails of Lima and other Peruvian cities, hounded by mounting fears.

# 3

# Coming and Going, by the Hundreds

As preparations to facilitate the repatriation of Japanese diplomatic and consular officials advanced, an accompanying move aimed at the early departure of many nonofficial Japanese. In Lima hundreds of Japanese had hurried to the Spanish embassy—Spain being charged with the protection of Japanese interests—to indicate their desire to be repatriated to Japan. Before the first Japanese was put aboard ship, some 460 "volunteers" had registered with the Spanish mission. At the same time the American embassy concerned itself with the prospective expulsion of certain "dangerous" individuals. Simultaneously Peruvian authorities interested themselves in ridding their country of a few Italians and the numerous German seamen whose ships had been scuttled in Peruvian waters, along with as many Japanese as space permitted.

## The First Ship

The *Etolin*, an old oil-burning steam vessel built in 1913 and long in passenger service in the Pacific as property of the Alaska Packers Association, wore a new coat of gray with the flag of the United States and the word DIPLOMATE on both sides. When she sailed from Callao early on April 5, 1942, the *Etolin* had 325 male passengers aboard—173 Germans, 141 Japanese, and eleven Italians. Numerous problems had attended their embarkation. The baggage search, conducted by the prefect of Callao, detectives from Lima, and customs officers, had proceeded without a hitch until Foreign Office representatives ordered a halt to the search of the passengers' clothing. At first, Peruvian authorities had confiscated any money in excess of specified amounts, but this practice also quickly ended.

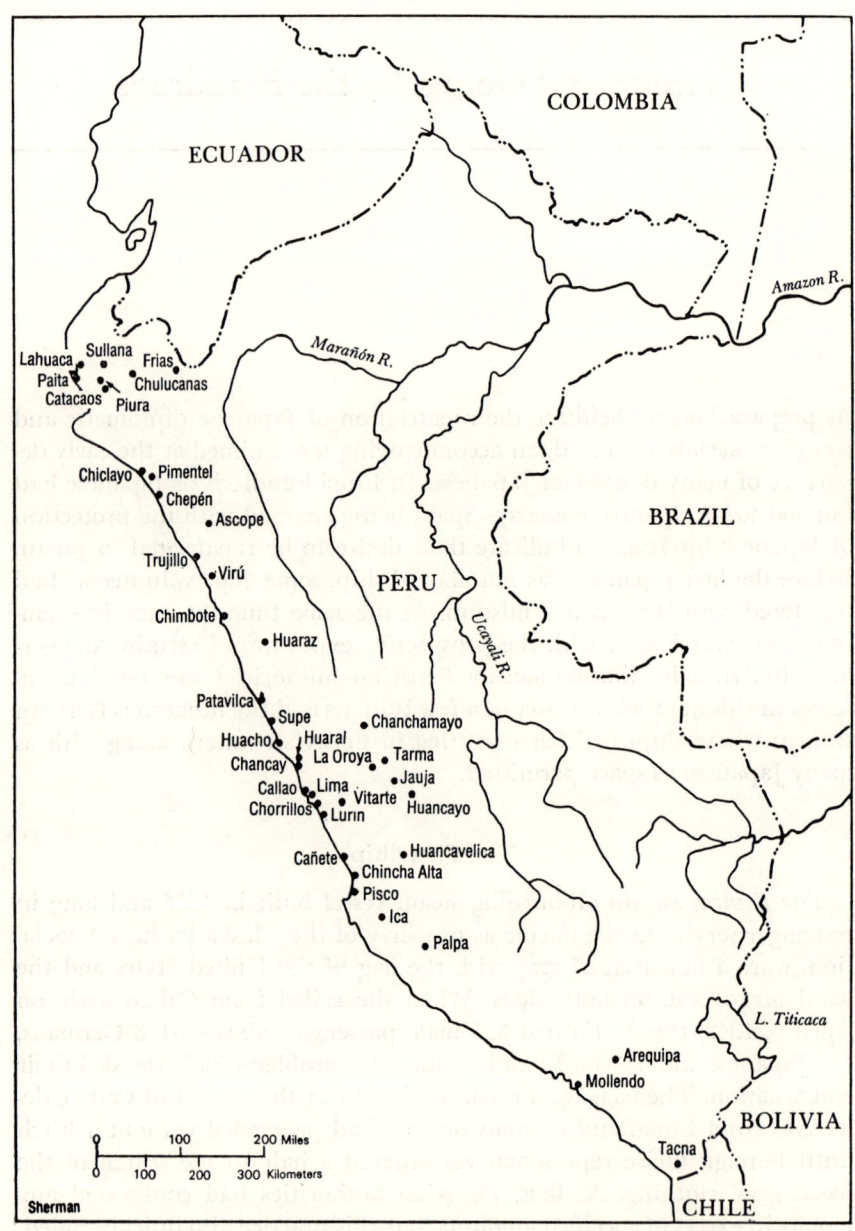

Map 1. Hometowns of Deported Peruvian Japanese

Medical examinations of the deportees, on the other hand, could not be stopped. None had occurred.

In this nine-hour nighttime operation the Japanese, orderly and even good-natured, were the last to go aboard. Their names, often incomplete and incorrect, were frequently misspelled. Family and given names were often transposed. The American embassy list of Japanese deportees became a shambles when thirty-two men scheduled to appear failed to do so and twelve unlisted ones did appear. Of the latter two seemed extremely young. Questioning them, Peruvian authorities learned that the runaway boys hoped to join the Japanese army. They were turned away. The inspection of the Japanese produced incidents which, however humorous to onlookers, reflected the fears and uncertainty plaguing the deportees. Some carried cooking utensils, many had food. Even some of the Japanese laughed when one of their number had to discard three dozen hard-boiled eggs.

Basic to much of the confusion was the haphazard preparation for the embarkation by the Peruvian Foreign Office. For weeks before the arrival of the *Etolin* the Foreign Office had been preparing "final and definitive lists," which invariably proved neither final nor definitive. When, two hours before the passengers boarded the ship, the American embassy finally received the Peruvian list of prospective deportees, the list was incomplete.[1]

Analysis of the 141 Japanese deported on the *Etolin* reveals much. No charge, Peruvian or American, had been leveled at any of the men and no hearing of any kind had been conducted. The ages of the men, more than 90 percent of whom were from the Lima-Callao metropolitan area, ranged from nineteen to sixty-four, averaging thirty-six years of age. Their residence in Peru averaged more than fourteen and one-half years. None had a police record in that country. The group included merchants, barbers, teachers, carpenters, farmers, blacksmiths, students, journalists, commission agents, restaurant owners, tailors, and seamen. Approximately half of the men were waiters, salesmen, clerks, and other lowly employees. More than half of the Japanese were unmarried, and the family of virtually every married man was already in Japan. Less than 5 percent of the group were on the Proclaimed Lists, and five of the seven there were representatives of Japanese companies—Tōyō Menka, Mitsui, Asano Bussan, Showa Tsūsho, and Iwai Shoten. (Then, as now, the Japanese government accorded special consideration to the overseas representatives of trading companies. All of those company representatives were destined to return to Japan on the first repatriation vessel, along with the officials.) The other two on the American blacklist were a dry goods merchant from Arequipa and a Lima toy seller, the former with weekly earnings of sixteen dollars, the latter with forty dollars weekly income. Less than 12 percent of the men were being expelled; the others had recorded their willingness to leave Peru with the Spanish authorities. Only one of these men—he died in the United States in June—failed to return to Japan. A few would sail on the M.S. *Gripsholm* in mid-1942, and 126 of them were aboard the same ship the following year.[2]

In addition to the sloppy, incomplete lists, spur-of-the-moment additions and subtractions, quixotic and erratic inspections, and the lack of coordination between the Peruvian and American authorities, this first deportation operation exhibited no recognizable criteria for deportation. Almost all the men lacked social, economic, and community significance. Were the Peruvians ridding their country of any and every Japanese possible? Were the Americans selectively attempting to further a war effort? This limited operation answered neither question. Also unanswered was the question why there were so many volunteer deportees. Were they simply seeking to rejoin their families in Japan or were they superpatriots eager to don Japanese military uniforms?

Despite long residence in Peru these men were essentially Japanese. Just one, a Nisei, possessed Peruvian citizenship; all the others, born in Japan, had retained their Japanese citizenship. Years earlier, before the China Incident had merged into World War II, many Japanese in Peru had contributed money to purchase aircraft for the Japanese army and navy. That patriotic fervor was felt not only by the young runaways who failed to get aboard the *Etolin* but also, quite possibly, by certain young men in their twenties and thirties who volunteered for deportation, seeing the transfer to the United States as the first leg of their return to Japan and service in the war effort. The seventy-seven unmarried men had meager social ties with Peru, and those who were earning $3.20 or $4.80 per week as employees possessed scant economic stake in Peru.

Consider eight of these volunteers, all Okinawans named Higa who had migrated to Peru between 1919 and 1929. They were farmers, merchants, barbers, and clerks. Lack of material success plagued most of them. Although one earned as much as ninety-six dollars weekly, five had weekly incomes of less than five dollars. Of the seven Higas who were married, all had evacuated their families to Japan before the Japanese-American hostilities. Now the men sought to rejoin their wives and children. If these families had fled Peru after the rioting of 1940, as many others had, did not the follow-up departures of the men indicate they had given up on Peru?[3] One wonders, too, since Okinawans were by far the most numerous Japanese among these volunteer-deportees, whether the strong Okinawan prefectural society had encouraged departure. Unfortunately, at this late date, not every question has an answer.

This first shipload of deportees was exceptional in that so many were volunteers, so few "blacklisted" or "dangerous," but it was only a weak harbinger of other matters, among them the social cost of deportation. What happened, for example, to the one-time dependents of restaurant employee Arakaki, coffee shop operator Nakasone, and Hideo Oshio, all of whom were divorced? Social turmoil also resulted when merchant Shimamura abandoned his common-law native Peruvian wife, Victoria. No records deal with such issues, much less permit calculation of the social calamity of deportation.[4]

On its northward course the *Etolin* picked up additional enemy aliens: thirty-eight Germans and ten Japanese in Ecuador and 149 Germans and three Italians in Colombia. On April 20 the anchor dropped at San Francisco, where every one of the 525 men, in a brief encounter with personnel of the U.S. Immigration and Naturalization Service, learned that he was completely at the mercy of American authorities, since he was entering the United States illegally, without benefit of visa or passport. Commenting on the "bizarreness of the program," Jerre Mangione, a wartime official of the Immigration and Naturalization Service, added, "an Immigration Service camp commander told me, 'Only in wartime could we get away with such fancy skullduggery.'" To guarantee this state of affairs American consuls in Peru and elsewhere had followed instructions and issued no visas.[5] Next the disgorged human cargo of the *Etolin*, in the custody of the Immigration and Naturalization Service, boarded an eighteen-car special train for a "blacked out" run to Texas.

## Kenedy Internment Camp

The pressing need of the U.S. Immigration and Naturalization Service for internment centers happily coincided in one south Texas town with a community effort to make use of an abandoned federal facility. Terming an enemy alien camp a "great benefit in many ways," business leaders of Kenedy, an agricultural community of about twenty-nine hundred, spearheaded the transfer to the INS of the defunct Civilian Conservation Corps (CCC) camp, a twenty-two-acre installation on the edge of town. The buildings included nine 20 by 120 foot barracks and some lesser structures. Immediately the remodeling and construction required to accommodate an anticipated eight hundred to two thousand aliens got under way. Workers hurriedly erected more than two hundred prefabricated huts, each to house five or six persons. Barbed wire enclosed the detention area, and guard towers and powerful searchlights commanded strategic positions. Anticipating the imminent arrival of the first internees, the carpenters, electricians, plumbers, and other workers frantically built a dining hall, kitchen, hospital, headquarters building, quarters for officers and nurses, warehouses, and latrines.

In pursuit of efficient camp administration the officer in charge supervised a number of departments, among them Surveillance, Supply, and Liaison. All employees were repeatedly informed that the camp operation must comply with the terms of the Geneva Convention of 1929, a lengthy document regarding the treatment of prisoners of war. A Censor Division, which required personnel competent in Japanese, German, and Italian, scrutinized the outgoing and incoming mail of the internees. The Surveillance force required dozens of civilian guards who had to be trained in many matters. Nor were the guards alone in this; the Immigration and Naturalization Service, in only its second year of operation as part of the Department of Justice, was in a period of transition, adjustment, and expanded duties and personnel. Every area of camp administration, initially undermanned and in need of training, would experience problems regarding food, housing, clothing, mail, discipline, work assignments, and so forth. The Kenedy camp had received only about eighty-five internees, from various sources, before the arrival of the *Etolin* contingent.[6]

On April 23 most of the townspeople turned out to witness the unloading of the heavily guarded internees from South America. Only authorized personnel could use cameras, but newsmen were permitted to report what they saw. Alighting from the eighteen cars, each group of twenty men was flanked by two civilian guards and two INS border patrolmen. At the rear of each contingent a mounted officer fingered a rope. Several of the 525 men were so infirm that they required transportation by automobile, but the others trudged across the grassy plot between the blacked-out train and the barbed wire enclosure. A local reporter considered most of the Germans "young and smart looking." The Japanese, few of whom were well dressed, he termed "small, unshaven, insignificant." The distinction made in Pacific Coast states between Japanese Americans and German Americans that especially denigrated the former was also at work in south Texas. The Japanese, housed in old CCC structures while Germans occupied small new huts, quickly raised the cry of racial discrimination.[7]

Soon the spokesman for the Japanese relayed to a Department of State inspector the question of his colleagues: How long would they be held? When could they go home? When could they receive money from Peru or send it there? What would happen to their families? At the same time Officer-in-charge Aubrey S. Hudson, who remarked that he "experienced the least trouble with the Japanese and most with the Germans," was approaching the hot Texas summer with an order that no ice water would be provided the internees.[8]

The expansion of the Kenedy camp, which more than doubled its area to forty-seven acres, began less than sixty days after the facility opened. Seven acres were assigned to recreational purposes. At midyear the overall pattern featured an expanding number of internees, almost all of whom were from Latin America, despite the occasional removal of men as repatriation voyages to Europe—four such groups of Germans totaled 564— and the Far East materialized.[9]

Meanwhile, two cases plagued the camp administrators and begged for consideration in Washington and Lima. During his first two weeks in Texas, Taiichi Onishi, a thirty-seven-year-old Lima merchant who had volunteered to leave Peru in the hope of being reunited with his family in Japan, had attempted suicide four times. His need for hospitalization produced a pitiful exhibition of bureaucrats dodging responsibility as the INS, holding the Department of State primarily responsible for his presence in the United States, tried to relieve itself of the troubled internee. In turn the State Department, lacking the needed facilities, suggested that the War Department, experienced in handling insane soldiers, surely had the needed capability. It developed that the War Department had lately tried to pass some "mentally queer people" to the INS. This buck passing ended only when Texas admitted the ailing Japanese to one of its state hospitals. In the same season Yukihiko Kobashigawa, the first total casualty of the internment program, died of pulmonary tuberculosis.[10] One wonders whether his illness should have been detected in Peru. Would the supervisors of future operations subject deportees to physical examinations?

Although questions remained unanswered for some men, the hopes of others, particularly the twenty-three who left Kenedy in mid-June to board the Swedish motorship *Gripsholm* for repatriation, were fulfilled. The few nonofficials fortunate enough to sail on that voyage included, at the insistence of the Japanese government, the representatives of the trading companies. To assure their sailing on June 18, these men were rushed to New York by plane. Their baggage failed to keep up with them and had to be forwarded fifteen months later on the second exchange.[11] They had stayed at Kenedy less than two months, not long enough to filter into the voluminous files the INS soon began to compile on each detainee. Their early repatriation, on the other hand, encouraged the remainder of the *Etolin* contingent to apply promptly for repatriation.

Early in August a Department of State representative accompanied Spanish Consul José María Garay on an inspection of the facilities. They learned that 283 of the 294 Latin American Japanese then at Kenedy were from Peru; that 160 Japanese were housed in the old wooden CCC barracks, the remaining Japanese occupying prefabricated huts; that trousers, shirts, shoes, socks, sheets, pillows, pillowcases, and blankets had been issued; that smoking tobacco, soap, toothpowder, and razor blades were issued free of charge; that the central laundry handled the larger items, while the internees were responsible for washing the smaller ones; that a Japanese-operated canteen sold soft drinks, toilet articles, and tobacco products, and its profits, if any, were pledged by the camp authorities for use "for the benefit of all detainees." Some internees complained that they received insufficient food allowances, but the Spanish official learned that their principal concern was repatriation. Two weeks later Ivan Williams arrived from another INS detention facility, took charge, and introduced tighter administration at Kenedy Internment Camp.[12]

Keeping track of the internees prompted two daily line-up counts, at 9 A.M. and 4:30 P.M. The language problem inspired the compilation of an album containing a picture of each man. In the company streets, which were segregated by nationality, the internees elected captains who assisted when the siren sounded and the line-ups occurred. The staff conducted three, sometimes four bed checks nightly. Mounted patrols supplemented the nighttime guards, who were so posted that they changed positions every hour. Anyone who touched the barbed wire fence activated an electric alarm system. The thwarting of the single escape effort—nationality unknown—during the first eighteen months attested both the completeness of the security system and the docility of the internees.

Almost as if to greet and challenge the new officer in charge, a devastating hurricane struck the camp. Fortunately a thirty-minute advance warning enabled the authorities, in the middle of the night, to move the men from the fragile prefabricated huts into more substantial structures. For ten hours high winds ripped at the camp. The staff and the internees weathered the hurricane, but an inventory, on August 30, listed many demolished buildings, downed electric lines, broken gas mains, and numerous damaged and weakened structures. During ensuing weeks the internees, led by an uncooperative old German ship captain who knew the terms of the Geneva Convention, stubbornly refused to assist in clearing the debris or repairing the buildings.[13]

This episode is characteristic of a state of affairs that repeated itself in different camps in which the Japanese and Germans from Latin America were thrown together. In marked contrast to the docile, disspirited, confused, and ill-organized Japanese, the hefty German seamen were well organized and belligerent. Younger and more recently from their native land, the Germans exhibited a fanatical loyalty to Hitler that far surpassed the identification of the average Peruvian Japanese with Emperor Hirohito. Furthermore, thanks to the retention of their shipboard leadership, the Germans, possessed of superior awareness of the Geneva Convention and better command of the English language, represented a unified and potent force in formulating and articulating requests, complaints, and demands. At Kenedy the Japanese fell in line, quietly supporting postures initiated by the Germans. Only much later, when Japanese-language texts of the Geneva Convention were available to them and the Spanish embassy reinforced their positions, did the Japanese openly agitate for their rights under international law.

Denied internee assistance, the camp authorities retaliated by dissolving all internee organizations. As the administrators took over all internal functions, they prepared the assignments that placed the individual internees in the position of either cooperating or suffering the consequences. Firm administration and hard work quickly restored the camp physically.

The large recreational area contributed significantly to the release of tensions and to the reestablishment of more harmonious conditions generally. Adjacent to the main detention area and available to the men throughout the daylight hours, it included a soccer field (which led to the formation of a soccer league), softball and baseball diamonds, tennis and handball courts, horseshoe pitching areas, vertical bars, and trapeze rings. As with all else, racial and national groups formed cliques and teams of their own. Those who engaged in the gardening project, most of whom were Japanese, received no pay for their labor but did win exemption from all other duties.

Indoors the sedentary ones had chess, checkers, and other games. A "hobby shop" equipped with work benches and woodworking machines occupied scores of craft-minded individuals. One large building served the school program, housing the classes in navigation, engineering, bookkeeping, art, mathematics, and languages that operated continuously except for the unbearably hot days of July and August. Every week two movies were shown, in an open air theater during the summer, otherwise in the 30 by 120 foot recreation hall. The latter, equipped with a stage and internee-produced scenery, encouraged the production of plays, several of which internees wrote. The Japanese created a special outdoor theater for the presentation of their distinctive plays. Some of these activities obviously reinforced the nationalistic nature of the internees.

Despite every effort by camp authorities to promote harmony, there was still tension, discontent, and friction among men eager to be elsewhere. The would-be suicide was not the only pathological case overwhelmed by problems. During the interval between mid-1942 and mid-1943, when no further repatriations removed any Japanese internees from the camp, those problems persisted.[14]

### The Second Ship

Eight days after the *Etolin* cleared Callao with its Kenedy-bound internees, another vessel, the smaller ten-year-old *Acadia*, formerly in passenger service out of Boston, departed the Peruvian port. The Japanese contingent from Peru, only forty-six in all, included diplomatic and consular officials and their families, plus a few nonofficials and their wives and children.

The Japanese mission in Peru, the officials and their families, amounted to twenty-five persons. Leading them in the absence of Minister Ryūki Sakamoto, who was conferring with colleagues in Washington when hostilities erupted, was Chargé Masaki Yodokawa. His group included the second secretary-interpreter, economic and military attachés, consular officers, servants, wives, and seven young children. For weeks before they sailed they had been housed by the Peruvian government outside Lima, at nearby Chosica.

Although the *Acadia* was primarily scheduled to pick up Japanese officials from Bolivia, Peru, Ecuador, and Colombia, space permitted a few nonofficial passengers to board the vessel at Callao. Totaling twenty-one, they included six male adults, five of whom were accompanied by their wives and children. The reason for their preferential treatment is unknown, except for one family, the Kurimotos, who were related to Kane Sakamoto, the stranded wife of the absent minister. Two of the men, Lima merchants Kenzi Amemiya and Motozo Nonomiya, had appeared in supplements of the Proclaimed List. Also departing, after seventeen years in Peru, was thirty-five-year-old Susumu Sakurai, author of a recent volume containing informative biographical sketches of prominent Latin American Japanese. There is no indication that any of these nonofficials were being expelled. Like most of those who had sailed the previous week on the *Etolin*, except that these were family units, they had volunteered to leave Peru. Needless to say, the special consideration accorded the officials extended to all members of this small group, and their embarkation occurred without confusion or incident. There was, however, friction aboard the *Acadia* between the captain, the armed guard personnel, and the union crew. Twelve days later, in New Orleans, considerable confusion attended the debarkation of the passengers. The experience of the *Acadia* would dictate better planning of future voyages.

By the time the *Acadia* had transited the canal, 654 enemy aliens—491 Germans, ninety-four Japanese, and sixty-nine Italians—were aboard. In New Orleans the officials and nonofficials were separated. The former journeyed north, to be housed with other Japanese officials in the custody of the Department of State, while the nonofficials entrained for Texas. Because the camp at Kenedy was an all-male facility, the families from the *Acadia* became the first Peruvian Japanese assigned to the Seagoville Internment Camp. Their stay in Texas was also brief, for they joined the throng that sailed for the Far East aboard the *Gripsholm*.[15]

## Seagoville Internment Camp

Of the three installations in Texas in which the INS eventually interned Peruvian Japanese and other Latin American deportees, the one at the edge of the village of Seagoville, about twenty miles southeast of Dallas, was the most remarkable. It resembled neither the enlarged CCC camp at Kenedy nor the soon to be expanded migrant labor facility at Crystal City. Reporting an official inspection of Seagoville, two Department of State employees declared, "It more closely resembles a college or school rather than a reformatory or a detention station."[16]

In 1940, on a tract of several hundred acres, the Department of Justice had erected a model federal reformatory for female offenders. The buildings, which included dormitories, an auditorium-school, hospital, and an industries center, faced on two quadrangles. The architectural style of the one- and two-story red brick structures with their cream limestone trim was contemporary Southern Colonial. Each of the six steam-heated dormitories contained from forty to sixty-eight rooms furnished with combination chests of drawers, desks, chairs, and beds. Every dormitory also had common living rooms and laundries, bathing and toilet facilities, dining room, and a kitchen equipped with refrigerators, gas stoves, and electric dishwashers. The maple tables in the dining rooms seated four persons, but they could be combined for large groups or families. These living quarters would shelter many internees under better conditions than they had known in Peru.

The Industries Building, in addition to housing the internees' canteen and the sewing and weaving areas, provided space for various projects and activities such as folk dancing and exhibitions. Outdoor activities included gardening, baseball, and badminton, among others. Many middle-age internees spent considerable time walking about the grounds, a very popular activity among the Japanese.

The auditorium-school building, with twelve classrooms, a full-time educational staff, and a library of about three thousand English-language volumes and magazines, also had film projectors, pianos, and an organ to serve numerous religious and entertainment purposes. The sixty-bed hospital shared its building with a three-chair dental clinic, an eye, nose, and throat clinic, and an operating room—all staffed by the U.S. Public Health Service.

The transfer of this establishment from the Bureau of Prisons to the INS early in 1942 had prompted the additional construction of some temporary buildings. These included a cluster of fifty sixteen-foot-square plywood huts, a central kitchen and dining hall, laundries, baths, and toilets. Initially the Japanese, and all the internees, occupied the red brick dormitories, but the new huts proved best suited to the needs of families, and the removal of the Japanese to them increased their sense of community. A high chain-link fence surrounded the grounds, which had only one entrance. The internees understood that the white line down the middle of the road around the cluster of buildings set the limits beyond which they were not allowed.

In May Seagoville held 319 enemy aliens, the majority of them from Latin America. Of that number 118 were Japanese. Their spokesman under the Council-Spokesman system, instituted by the authorities to generate internee cooperation, was one of the men who had sailed on the *Acadia*. Preparation of the food by internees guaranteed its palatability, and the daily portions of rice for the Japanese reflected administrative concession to dietary preference.

A variety of complaints, which were not limited to Seagoville, arose among the internees of all nationalities. They resented that they could mail only three letters and one postcard weekly. This restriction was an effort to lessen the burden on the censors, but the administration relented when it was pointed out that opportunities for repatriation called for considerable writing to make arrangements and settle personal affairs. Although internees resented the censoring of their personal letters, it continued.

The authorities denied the requests of some internees—primarily Europeans—that they be allowed to go to Dallas to buy clothes with their own funds, but they did make various mail-order catalogues available to the internees. All nationalities quickly took to scanning the catalogues and placing orders for merchandise. For most this rush to do business with Sears, Roebuck and Montgomery Ward, far from being a sign of affluence, reflected the meagerness of their wardrobes.

Not unexpected, since they were being held against their will, were various complaints of internees concerning their treatment. When some older persons complained that their work was too strenuous, the officer-in-charge replied that only when a medical examination confirmed that charge would they be relieved of their duties. Some Germans and Italians —again more demanding and belligerently aggressive than the Japanese— insisted that they had been informed in Latin America that they would receive the same treatment as diplomats, namely lodging in hotels. They also charged that they were being held in a penal institution, citing their immediate supervision by Warden Amy N. Stannard of the Bureau of Prisons and the presence among them of fifteen women who had been prison inmates at Seagoville. Diplomats, they insisted, were not required to operate kitchens and conduct their own janitorial and maid service. This pattern of complaints produced no discernible change for any internee.

Finances figured prominently among the Seagoville complaints. Japanese internees, forced to yield approximately ten thousand dollars to American authorities in the Panama Canal Zone, complained that only a few of them had received receipts and those receipts had been written on plain white paper by an American army captain. This matter exceeded the responsibilities of the camp administration and was referred to the Spanish authorities as the custodians of Japanese interests.

Still another monetary issue focused complaints on the operation of the canteen. When internees charged that canteen prices were too high, the administration pointed out that the markup was only 10 percent on counter goods and no more than 20 percent on mail-order sales, some of which had to absorb freight charges and possible loss on perishable goods. The hope voiced by the administration that the internees could soon establish their own canteen organization and relieve the operation of the need for government employees did much to silence this kind of complaint.

Three months later, when Spanish Consul Garay visited the camp, some changes were noticeable. Successive repatriations to Europe had removed some internees, and others had arrived. The fifteen female prisoners had departed, and internees alone occupied Seagoville. In general the internees were in good health, none having died during the interval that had witnessed two births. Reduced prices at the canteen and a wider variety of merchandise had increased the popularity of that establishment, as had the summer heat. The sale of ice cream and cold drinks had skyrocketed. Among the 386 internees, the 202 Japanese registered no complaints but evidenced continuing interest in repatriation prospects. When asked whether Axis nationals at Seagoville could be repatriated against their wishes, the Department of State responded that although they had been received for repatriation, "information as to their individual wishes might prove useful."[17]

## On Other Fronts

Meanwhile propagandist Larrañaga continued to verbalize his anti-Japanese stance as he offered American officials specific recommendations: the transfer to Peruvian ownership of all the cotton-growing properties the Japanese held, and the establishment of a zone along the coast of Peru in which no Japanese could remain. The latter idea, reflecting awareness of the removal of the Japanese Americans from the Pacific coast of the United States and related activity by Mexico, also drew the attention of Minister of Finance David Dasso while visiting Washington. Besides requesting details on the removal of the Japanese Americans, Dasso unsuccessfully sought the loan of one or more Japanese-speaking Americans to serve official Peruvian purposes.[18]

While the first two shiploads of Japanese were still en route to the United States, Washington entertained suspicions and fears that virtually guaranteed additional deportations. The embassy in Lima was instructed to investigate one American's insistence that a certain Japanese-held plantation near coastal Bellavista was a likely site for aircraft operations. Washington also quickly requested a list of the Japanese secret agents in Peru, exhibiting a fear reinforced by a Japanese reaction. Japan, having learned via Spain of the shipments of Japanese nationals from a half dozen Latin American countries in recent days, had protested. This led Washington to conclude that the Japanese objection to that removal program indicated "that the Japanese Government desires them to remain in Peru for some purpose of its own."[19]

In assessing the problem, Ambassador Norweb concluded that the undesirable Japanese and Germans, including their families, numbered about 450, a figure which he soon increased on learning that the Spanish mission had the names of more than a thousand Japanese who were clamoring for repatriation.[20] Most of all, however, it was Emmerson's conclusions and recommendations, endorsed and forwarded, that directly influenced future policy.

Emmerson had concluded that the Japanese, vastly underestimated, posed a serious problem. He considered their Peruvian colony, led by a relatively small number of powerful individuals, to be dangerous, well organized, and intensely patriotic. To counteract this influence, he recommended that "Japanese leaders believed to be dangerous should be expelled from Peru." Since no more than ten important or potentially dangerous persons—undesirables—had embarked on the *Etolin* and the *Acadia*, the Auxiliary Section had readied a list of some 250 Japanese for expulsion. "These include," Emmerson declared, "officers of Japanese associations, businessmen who have been active in the Japanese colony, journalists, directors of educational and propaganda organizations, and teachers in Japanese schools." Prompt and favorable reaction within the Department of State established these recommendations as the cornerstone of the ensuing deportation program.[21]

Pivotal in this statement of criteria for expulsion are the words "believed to be dangerous." Many persons on Emmerson's list of prospective expellees, named by Peruvian authorities, could well be the objects of economic envy, cultural detestation, irrational and emotional outbursts, and whimsical dislike. To Peruvians the Japanese constituted social and economic—not military—dangers, and the designation of "dangerous" men by Peru largely ignored the American concern about the conduct of a war. Since Emmerson's expulsion criteria required no proof that a person was dangerous, the American authorities were willing to ally themselves with Peruvians in a program that honored blind prejudice and emotion and ignored legal rights and formalities. It was happening that way with the Japanese Americans in the United States, so why not in Peru.

Norweb quickly assessed 978 Japanese who had filed applications with the Spanish embassy. The 235 families included 748 women and children. More than 90 percent resided in the Lima-Callao area. Merchants, employees, barbers, and farmers constituted almost 80 percent of the group, which counted not a single teacher or journalist. This was not the kind of list then being compiled by the combined efforts of Peruvian authorities, the British and Chinese diplomatic missions, and the American military, naval, commercial, and legal attachés—a list which, for example, included three journalists and 108 teachers. Noting that the American and Spanish lists coincided only in reference to three men, Norweb observed, "There is no indication that, outside of these three, there is a single individual among the 978 who is either important in the Japanese colony or a dangerous alien." The "little people" would be ignored "until all persons recommended for expulsion by the Embassy and the Peruvian Government have been accommodated."²² At this time one level of this U.S.–Peruvian pursuit shifted when President Manuel Prado set out on a state visit to the United States.

For both governments President Prado's visit to the United States proved rewarding. The pomp—staying at the White House, addressing the Senate, being the cynosure of numerous gala functions and the recipient of several honorary degrees—pleased the vain little aristocrat. In addition to basking in the aura of recent American-Peruvian agreements, he and his colleagues won additional concessions, one regarding long-staple cotton in the new reciprocal trade agreement. Still others concerned credits. All eased the economic and fiscal pinches that war had brought to Peru. Visits to service academies, to tank and aircraft factories, and to shipyards impressed Prado and his party with the American determination to win the war, as did the outcome of the distant Battle of the Coral Sea. A friend of the United States before he came, Prado's two-week stay buttressed his willingness to cooperate with Washington.²³

While the Prado-Roosevelt relations were proceeding smoothly in Washington, a significant difference surfaced between Peruvian and American authorities in Lima regarding the deportation program. When Lima's chief of detectives asked the American embassy to supply information against each person to warrant his repatriation, he was informed that the United States was not prepared to investigate each individual. The Americans, ignoring both law and legal formality, simply wanted to weaken the Japanese community by seizing and expelling its leaders. In the United States at that time a similar abuse of human rights found Attorney General Biddle moving to cancel the citizenship of hundreds of naturalized American citizens. Two weeks later American authorities would insist that citizenship should not stand in the way of their efforts to deport individuals from Peru.²⁴

Expressions of concern became the order of the day. The problems posed by large numbers of Latin American Japanese arriving in the United States troubled the Department of State. The latest concerns relayed to American officials by propagandist Larrañaga included his fears that the Japanese might seize the fort in Callao and turn its guns on American ships, that they might destroy the naval base and dry dock, and that they might destroy the oil depot of the American-controlled International Petroleum Company.²⁵ In Lima, in view of Minister Garrido Lecca's continuing inactivity, Peruvian promises to restrict the movements of Japanese, to remove them from certain coastal districts, to deny them fishing licenses and the right to own guns, and to require the renewal of all other licenses held by them—these were not enough. It also disturbed American officials to learn that "persons recommended for expulsion have later been notified by the Peruvian authorities that their departure will not be necessary." Emmerson reiterated his concerns as "First, the expulsion of the leaders of the Japanese colony; Second, the control of their movements and activities; and Third, measures to counteract Axis propaganda." In pursuit of them Emmerson, in company with George Tsung-yuan Woo of the Chinese legation, had spent a day enlisting the cooperation of the Chinese colony in investigating Japanese activities to the north of Lima in the Chancay Valley. Although the embassy considered this and future Chinese cooperation productive, the liaison was of questionable value, since the Chinese admitted that they had had "no relations with the Japanese since the beginning of the Sino-Japanese conflict.[26]

## The Third Ship

While concerns mounted and President Prado remained abroad, American authorities assigned another ship, the *Shawnee*, to deportation purposes. Owned by the Atlantic Gulf and West Indies Steamship Company, the fifteen-year-old passenger vessel, out of New York and larger than the *Acadia* but smaller than the *Etolin*, could accommodate about a thousand passengers. The rising tempo of the war made difficult the assignment of shipping for deportation duty, so Washington urged the embassy in Lima to "impress upon the authorities the fact that this will be the last opportunity they will have to get rid of dangerous Axis aliens." One estimate suggested that except for 150 deportees from Bolivia, Japanese and Germans from Peru could complete the passenger list. In view of recent experience it was comforting to learn that the *Shawnee* had a superior crew. The embassy was also instructed to compile complete alphabetical lists of all the passengers by nationality, unifying families and specifying relationships, age, and sex. It was easy for Washington to ask for such advance preparations but difficult for the embassy to comply, given its problems in winning Peruvian cooperation. On June 16, however, all was in order and the *Shawnee* raised gangplanks and anchor and sailed from Callao with 342 Japanese, 106 Germans, and 10 Italians from Peru.[27]

Preparations for the loading of the *Shawnee* had emphasized maintaining family unity, and numerous families were being deported. The *Shawnee* transported the following family units: forty-four married couples accompanied by their 118 children, four men in the company of their eight children, one woman accompanied by her three children, and twelve childless married couples.[28]

Although only seventy-six passengers claimed to be single, not all of the remaining men were unmarried. At least eleven men had wives in Japan and four were leaving families behind in Peru. The motives of the latter left unanswered questions: Was barber Luis Yoshitake Mochizaki of Chimbote abandoning his native Peruvian wife and their six children or had she refused to go with him? Did bakery owner Tomiji Nishio consider it necessary to leave his wife and three children in Lima to safeguard assets valued at $7,200?

Detailed information regarding twenty-five married couples reveals that the average husband was seven years and eight months older than his wife. Accounting for this was a sequence common to many men: initial migration as a well-nigh penniless unmarried male, years of hard work and saving, and a quick trip to Japan for a bride. The women, frequently young mothers of large families, were particularly dependent on their older husbands. Their vulnerability—economic and otherwise—without them was extreme. Accordingly the removal of families, the male heads as involuntary deportees and the wives and children as voluntary deportees, mingled humane treatment with the urge to maximize the number sent out of Peru.

With two exceptions all of the men had retained Japanese citizenship. The two Peruvian citizens, one a twenty-two-year-old Nisei, the other a Chimbote merchant who claimed to be a naturalized citizen, were living proof that Peruvian citizenship was no obstacle to deportation. Since many of the men had resided in Peru for ten, twenty, thirty, and more years—Nikumatsu Okada of Huaral had lived there forty-three years—one might wonder about such stubborn retention of Japanese citizenship. Basically it derived from two things: a strong feeling of superiority (after all they were representatives of the Yamato race), and a realization that Japan could defend them, diplomatically and otherwise, if need arose. Prior and subsequent groups of deportees also exhibited this refusal to accept and identify themselves fully with their adopted country, a fact that justifiably fueled Peruvian hatred.

Their homeland origins, coming as they had from more than half of the prefectures of Japan, were more diverse than their places of residence in Peru. Two-thirds of the deportees had lived in Lima, while others were from coastal communities such as Callao, Chancay, Huacho, Chimbote, Trujillo, Chiclayo, and Cañete and interior places such as La Oroya, Huancayo, and Junín. For the occupations of 163 heads of families, see table 5.

Within the Japanese colony merchants commonly played leading roles —as employers of other Japanese, as supporters of the Japanese-language schools, and as senior members of the community whose influence extended to local societies and to the Japanese consular and diplomatic officials in Peru. Merchant income varied greatly. Specializing in dry goods in Lima, Tatsujiro Kurotobi was earning $9.60 weekly, while Choki Ishu, featuring shoes in his store, earned $25 per week. Another Lima merchant, Kotaro Sakata, averaged $240 each week from his general merchandise establishment, and Chitsu Kadena's bazaar and importing business yielded him $800 monthly. When he was arrested and deported, Kadena left behind assets valued at $88,000. Thirty-nine-year-old Noriyoshi Endo, who had entered Peru at age twenty, was turning his back on assets estimated at $137,600.

The expelled teachers, almost half of whom were from Lima, were considered "dangerous" by American and Peruvian authorities for several reasons: Japanese tradition placed them in a coveted and respected role within the community, their mental alertness and idle hours might be

**TABLE 5**
**Occupations of Deportees**

| Occupation | Number | Occupation | Number |
|---|---|---|---|
| Merchant | 39 | Journalist | 4 |
| Employee | 39 | Restaurant owner | 3 |
| Teacher | 30 | Mechanic | 3 |
| Barber | 9 | Tailor | 2 |
| Representative of Japanese firm | 9 | Miscellaneous | 15 |
| Farmer | 8 | No occupation | 2 |

SOURCES: See note 28.

dedicated to intelligence gathering, and their comparative youth and relatively short stays in Peru—many had been there less than ten years—meant that they were products of the increasingly nationalistic, militaristic Japan of the 1930s. Their weekly salaries ranged between $6.40 and $12.80. The four ousted journalists, all from Lima, had earned salaries up to sixteen dollars weekly before their newspapers, *Perū Jihō* and *Lima Nippō*, had ceased publication.

The incomes of many men ranged between four and fifteen dollars weekly, and wide gaps separated those of employers and employees. However, room and board at employers' expense supplemented the meager earnings of numerous farm laborers, apprentice barbers, retail clerks, and others. Alongside these "little people" were men who, by dint of energy and ability, had achieved phenomenal success. Nikumatsu Okada's rise from ordinary laborer to manager of six cotton-producing haciendas in the Chancay Valley, where he was acknowledged as the leading farmer, demonstrated how much a Japanese immigrant could achieve. After thirty years his achievement had prompted a decoration by the Japanese emperor; thirteen years later that decoration categorized him as "dangerous." In urban Peru, where most of the Japanese lived, the $480 weekly income of Fukuichi Ikeda had the sweet smell of success as the products of his Lima bus and car-body factory sped over countless streets and roads. The Peruvian labor of this forty-four-year-old, which had spanned twenty-three years, ended when he boarded the *Shawnee*.

A few deportees, eighteen from Lima and eight from as many other communities, had been placed on the American blacklist, a measure that guaranteed their receiving special attention. They had appeared on the Proclaimed List as follows: ten on December 9, 1941, seven in February, three in March, one in April, three in May, and one, strangely enough after he was behind barbed wire in the United States, in July 1942. Often the listing of a business establishment was followed by the specific inclusion of the individual. However it happened, one's appearance on the Proclaimed List became a danger signal. Consequently, harried owners shifted titles of businesses to Nisei children, to native Peruvian employees or friends, to almost anyone, in moments of desperation, in an effort to safeguard assets. Another result of the blacklisting, one related directly to the deportation program, was the recognition by employees of designated operations of their personal vulnerability. In Peru the blacklisting, which did little to advance the hoped-for American military victory, did produce incalculable anguish, social stress, and economic hardship within the Japanese community.

In Lima, while the *Shawnee* was steaming northward, an American assessment of that operation included the following: (1) the introduction, removal, reintroduction, and repeated removal of names on the deportation list had represented a tug of war between American and Peruvian officials that could not be pressed beyond certain limits by the Americans; (2) high officials had freely admitted that politicians, serving as "living guarantees," had saved certain Japanese from deportation when it was evident that the list exceeded the capacity of the ship; (3) the remarkable cooperation by President Prado was matched by an utter lack of cooperation by Minister Garrido Lecca; (4) within areas based on their strategic importance the American lists of individuals to be deported had focused on teachers, reserve officers, and leaders of organizations, and had considered, at all times, the Japanese from the main islands (*naichijin*) both more influential and more dangerous than those from Okinawa; and (5) a larger percentage of undesirables and "extremely dangerous" individuals had been deported than on previous occasions. The *Shawnee* operation clearly pointed up practices to be repeated as well as ones to be avoided, if possible, in the future.

At New Orleans, where the *Shawnee* arrived June 23, the INS began its processing of the ten Italians from Peru, the 175 Germans from Bolivia and Peru, and the much more numerous Peruvian Japanese. Each confrontation between official and deportee left the latter aware that he was in the United States illegally. Forty-eight hours later all were in Texas, the unattached males at Kenedy, the family groups at Seagoville, with the exception of a few married men who had to go to Kenedy until more family housing units could be completed. Separating the baggage of such broken families proved maddening. At both internment camps the newly arrived not only encountered other Peruvian Japanese but also word that others had recently departed, for Japan.

## The M.S. *Gripsholm*

Even before the completion of the casualty count at Pearl Harbor, American and Japanese officials, aided by Swiss and Spanish intermediaries, were negotiating the exchange of diplomatic and consular personnel and other nationals. The Japanese accepted an American proposal that the exchange take place at the east African port of Lourenço Marques (now Maputo), and the United States quickly expanded the number of people in whom it was interested by including Canadian and Latin American government personnel in Japanese hands. As the two governments amplified their proposals, quibbling and delay set in. Japan balked at rounding up designated enemy nationals in recently overrun areas, and the American military services, smarting under early defeats, opposed the Japanese idea of exchanging nonofficials "without limit as to their number and without question of their usefulness for the prosecution of the war."

The American desire to unify the Western Hemisphere regarding the war, which had promoted the Rio de Janeiro Conference and the mounting rupture of relations with Japan, now increased the number of officials and nonofficials to be exchanged. At the same time, the Japanese surge into wide areas of the southwest Pacific was increasing the number of people likely to be involved in any exchange. With each passing week the problem grew, and it might have become insurmountable had not both Washington and Tokyo agreed on the basic desirability of the exchange, much of which the historic concern of governments about their official personnel prompted.

By early spring, when Washington was still arranging to transport Japanese officials from Latin America to the United States in anticipation of their repatriation, the Department of State hinted that as many as five hundred nonofficial Latin American Japanese would accompany those officials to Japan.

A multifaceted sequence thus prompted the movement of many nonofficial Japanese from Latin America to the United States. The insistence of both Japan and the United States on exchanging their officials and, at the same time, the widening of the war, both militarily by the Japanese and diplomatically by the United States to include many Latin American states, were factors supplemented by other concerns: loyal Japanese wanted to return to Japan, the United States wished to retrieve many civilians, some Latin American governments hoped to rid themselves of unwanted aliens whom they held suspect, Washington feared that Latin American governments would not control prospective saboteurs, and the United States was willing to organize and effect the exchange of nonofficials much as it was handling the exchange of officials. One thing had led to another and, as capstone to all else, the size of the ships to be used suggested the inclusion of nonofficials in the exchange program. Only later would the question arise: would the ever-expanding number of interned nonofficials—unlike the relatively small and fixed number of officials—actually be repatriated? Delay, or failure to agree on subsequent exchanges, could result in long periods of internment in the United States, something that no one in Washington then seriously considered.

By mid-May 1942 the Japanese officials from Latin America were in the United States, as were hundreds of nonofficials, some coming from Panama and Costa Rica aboard the *Florida*, others from Peru and Ecuador aboard the *Acadia* and *Etolin*. Irritated that those four countries had forced her nationals out, Tokyo specified that those Japanese should receive preferential consideration on repatriation lists.

When the Swedish motorship *Gripsholm*, chartered by the U.S. government, sailed from New York on June 18, after the final diplomatic flurries regarding passenger lists and safe conducts, there were 1,065 Japanese and 18 Thai nationals aboard. That total of 1,083 would be raised to 1,500 by the addition, at Rio de Janeiro, of Japanese from eastern South America. From Louisiana and Texas, Latin American Japanese had been rushed to New York.[29]

More than 10 percent of all the Japanese put aboard the *Gripsholm* were nonofficials from Latin America. Among them were every nonofficial Japanese that had accompanied the diplomatic personnel from Peru aboard the *Acadia*. Indeed, those twenty-one had grown to twenty-two, because a birth had occurred while in American custody. But of the 141 Japanese aboard the *Etolin* only thirteen won places on the *Gripsholm*. Most of them, incidentally, represented Japanese businesses—Tōyō Menka, Mitsui and Company, Showa Tsūsho, Sanko and Company, Asano Bussan, and Iwai Shoten, illustrating anew the special consideration Japanese authorities accorded such individuals.[30] To the thirty-five Peruvian Japanese, Panama and Costa Rica added at least ninety-three men, women, and children to the repatriation list for the *Gripsholm*.

These Japanese from Panama and Costa Rica were unlike those from Peru who would also travel on the exchange ship. While the Peruvian group, weeks after Pearl Harbor, had voluntarily placed themselves in American hands, the Isthmian Japanese had been quickly apprehended by the police on December 7 and immediately turned over to American military authorities. Unlike the friends of diplomats and the representatives of powerful business interests from Peru, the individuals from Costa Rica and Panama were primarily "little people."

The security of the Panama Canal had dictated the speed and thoroughness of the roundup of these Isthmian Japanese. In Costa Rica, at Puntarenas on the Gulf of Nicoya, numerous fishermen, some of whom resided in Ensenada, Mexico, were seized. Promptly transferred to the Panama Canal Zone and later to the United States, these men from Mexico and Costa Rica frequently confused American record keepers. Except for several farm families, this group was entirely male. The larger Japanese colony in Panama was also predominantly masculine when compared with the Japanese in Peru, Brazil, and elsewhere in Latin America. Most of the men worked either as barbers or as employees of Japanese-operated stores in the cities of Panama and Colon, in occupations and locations that hinted at intelligence gathering. The Panamanian roundup also included about twenty complete families.

The Costa Rican and Panamanian Japanese had skills that many American officials hoped to retain—the seamanship of the fishermen and the information potential of the wide-eyed and attentive barbers and salesmen. These men stepped off the *Florida* at New Orleans before the first all-male facility of the INS, at Kenedy, Texas, was ready to receive internees. Accordingly the American military, having held them for over one hundred days in the Panama Canal Zone, continued to do so, at Camp Livingston, near Alexandria, Louisiana. A few went to Fort Sill, Oklahoma. It proved much easier to fall into and remain in the clutches of the military than it was to get away from them.[31]

As the U.S. Army retained the men and the Department of Justice yielded their Seagoville-based wives and children to the *Gripsholm*, the tragedy of their detention and separation climaxed. Minor children burdened most of the confused and exceedingly dependent women. Aiko Suzue of Costa Rica got ready to sail to Japan with three youngsters, and Ichitaro Sugiyama's wife Toyo also prepared to leave Seagoville with her three. Mitsue Tateyama, wife of a Panamanian barber, shepherded two daughters toward Japan, while the wife of Shigeo Ohara had to fend for five children. Very few families remained together in this troubled period. Of those, Masato Nagakane, his wife Francisca, and their four children boarded the *Gripsholm*. Another fortunate family was that of Masao Ikeziri. His wife, Kiyoko, pregnant at the time of their apprehension and shipment to the United States, had given birth at Seagoville to Shoichi. Mother, father, and the two-week-old American citizen boarded the repatriation vessel.[32]

The separation that sent so many wives and children away while husbands remained in American custody seemed rather trifling alongside the wrenching and wrecking that some families experienced. Kiroku Nobuhira, already divorced and wanting his son to go to Japan with him eventually, planned to leave his daughter with his ex-wife in Panama. Kazuo Kawano's native Panamanian wife was reluctant to leave Seagoville for an unknown Japan with three children. Another native Panamanian wife, Cecilia de Gracia Uno, equally a stranger to Japan and mother of seven, also hesitated to cross the Pacific.[33]

However, by mid-1942 the United States, aware of the entrapment of additional thousands of Americans by Japanese military successes, could only hope to regain those nonofficial Americans by giving up an equal number of nonofficial Japanese. Battlefield casualties did not then constitute the sole body count. Very carefully one counted and matched the number of persons promised in any exchange with the enemy. When the United States put the women and children from Costa Rica and Panama, the men from Peru, and the occasional family from any of those countries aboard the *Gripsholm*, those Latin American Japanese, not one of whom had been charged, tried, or convicted of espionage, sabotage, or subversive activity, were pawns in a human traffic Washington hoped to continue.

The sailing of the *Gripsholm* aroused a kindred optimism in unlike peoples. At the internment camps at Kenedy and Seagoville both the administrators and the internees welcomed the departure of the repatriates. To administrators the exchange constituted a safety valve, an assurance that facilities would not become overcrowded. To the *Etolin* group it meant they might be next, and so the men eagerly filled out the forms requesting repatriation. The *Shawnee* group, who reached Texas seven days after the departure of the *Gripsholm*, also anticipated a short stay in the United States. In Washington, as soon as the exchange ship got under way, American officials were preparing tentative passenger lists for a second exchange.

No interested party, in June 1942, would have believed that fifteen months would elapse before the second exchange with Japan could occur, nor that it would be the last one. Old obstacles persisted—the slow transmission of communications, the delays and language problems inherent in working through two protecting powers and four languages, and the problem of obtaining assurance of safe conduct once the long and complicated passenger lists had won approval. New problems included stiffer American resistance to the repatriation of fishermen, seamen, journalists, priests, and army and navy reserve personnel, the refusal of Japan to consider the repatriation of about five thousand Japanese nationals not named by it but who had volunteered for exchange, and the refusal of both the Department of Justice and the War Relocation Authority to force the repatriation of any individual against his will. There was one subtle but overriding difference between the first exchange and subsequent ones: the validity of the effort to recover officials was taken for granted, but the repatriation of miscellaneous private citizens was increasingly questioned. Also, after the United States had launched its offensive on Guadalcanal, military plans in both the United States and Japan resulted in shipping shortages for other purposes.[34]

# 4

# More Internees, More Repatriates

Recent events had encouraged false optimism. A growing number of Latin American governments had severed diplomatic relations with the Axis. By means of lend-lease and reciprocal trade agreements, the extension of credits, special contracts for strategic and critical materials, and more, the United States had strengthened its ties within the hemisphere. Intergovernmental cooperation was on the increase—especially, in the case of Peru, after President Prado's visit to the United States. Three vessels had transported Japanese, Germans, and Italians northward from western South America. The INS was taking its responsibilities in stride, pleased that repatriation was paralleling internment. But any prospect of the early fulfillment of American and Peruvian hopes regarding the Peruvian Japanese quickly dimmed, set upon by multiple frustrations.

### Frustrations of 1942

Concerning their Japanese, most Peruvian officials continued to promise the Americans much more than they delivered. Dr. Hernán Bellido of the Foreign Office anticipated no serious trouble from the Japanese but conceded that any potential danger could be eliminated by placing them in well-guarded concentration camps. Minister of Government Garrido Lecca's assurances that Peru would control her Japanese in detention camps evaporated as quickly as his previous pledges. His successor, Ricardo de la Puente, spoke of stricter measures, including the expulsion of several hundred Japanese leaders, but time and shipping would test his assurances. Meanwhile the promised removal of Japanese from two haciendas near Lima languished, presumably blocked by bribed officials.[1]

President Prado, "still glowing with the cordiality and enthusiasm of his visit to the States," proved consistently amenable to American desires. Hoping to rid Peru of the Japanese permanently, he embraced the idea of their continuing deportation and repatriation and sought arrangements for their internment in the United States that would assure they would never return to Peru. He and Pedro Beltrán, destined to become the Peruvian ambassador in Washington in mid-1944, agreed that the removal of thirty-thousand Japanese they claimed were in the country would be the most welcome aid Washington could render Peru. Raising no objection to an internment program at U.S. expense, Prado maintained that any legal issue related to the shipment of the Japanese from a nonbelligerent to a belligerent state might be avoided if that movement was for the purpose of repatriation.[2] However, even the deportation of the Japanese, the first phase of this program, remained frustrated by the shipping shortage.

Aided by George Woo of the Chinese legation, John K. Emmerson continued his assessment of the Peruvian Japanese. Immediately after the sailing of the *Shawnee* a short trip took them south to Arequipa, Nasca, Pisco, San Vicente de Cañete, and Chincha Alta. Two weeks later they undertook an eleven-day survey of twenty-five towns and eleven haciendas to the north of Lima. The American installation at Talara encouraged visits there as well as to Sullana, Piura, Paita, and Catacaos in the far north. Colony after colony, both urban and rural, between Chiclayo and the capital drew the investigators, who, in every instance, solicited the cooperation of the local Chinese. But bitter hatred and lack of close contacts between Japanese and Chinese minimized the information the latter could supply. Nonetheless, competing Chinese merchants did seize the opportunity to encourage the addition of Japanese competitors to the Proclaimed List. Emmerson also learned that (1) although many Japanese had moved into the sierra from coastal cities, others not only remained in areas from which Peruvian authorities had presumably cleared them but also moved about freely, (2) numerous Japanese schools continued to operate, and (3) influence and money invalidated regulations everywhere. Two months later a survey of thirty-nine haciendas near Lima and Callao revealed not only unemployed and disgruntled Japanese with diminishing resources and uncertain futures but also the increasing victimization of those people by Peruvians guilty of robbery and murder. Recalling his Peruvian excursions with Woo, Emmerson later wrote, "we learned nothing reliable or convincing about subversion."[3]

In midsummer the ambassador, whose springtime recommendation had been the expulsion of dangerous Japanese leaders, concluded that "the most satisfactory solution would be the removal to . . . the United States of all persons in Peru of Japanese race." Norweb could base his conclusion on many factors: (1) the desire of the Peruvian authorities to rid the country of the Japanese, (2) the labors of his own staff—Emmerson's surveys, his commercial attaché's operation of the Proclaimed List, his legal (FBI) attaché's investigations, his military and naval attaché's reports—all of which had produced copious and growing files on the Japanese individually and collectively, and (3) the realization that Peruvian officials from the lowest police to cabinet officers showed indifference, laxity, and corruption in their administration of regulations and in their cooperation with American authorities. As for the Japanese themselves, it was evident that many, apprehensive of worsening conditions, would willingly leave Peru, that the removal of one group of leaders would only give rise to new ones, and that the *Shawnee* operation had clearly indicated the desirability of deporting entire families.

Conscious that the wartime realities that denied him any shipping rendered this large-scale undertaking a pipe dream, Norweb advanced certain "immediate considerations": the expulsion of Japanese "whether or not they are naturalized citizens," expulsion of known leaders on the first available ship, removal of all Japanese from designated strategic areas and also from a zone within a specified distance from the coast (propagandist Larrañaga had suggested 200 kilometers from the coast for one hundred years), "the establishment of relocation centers in the interior for small groups of Japanese," the closing of every Japanese school, the assignment of special, well-paid (presumably incorruptible) police in Japanese districts, a ban on Japanese-owned short-wave sets, and the use of radio broadcasts to counteract any pro-Japanese propaganda.[4]

In sum, a frustrated ambassador was calling for ceaseless diplomatic efforts to achieve an unrealistic measure of cooperation. To expect that Peruvian officials would turn their backs on influential Japanese, stamp out the venality of local police officers, close schools whose standards they admired and recognized as better than Peruvian state schools, and establish and administer effective and secure relocation centers was to expect Peruvians to change their natures.

Accompanying this and other statements of the situation in Peru went a plea for shipping which the Department of State noted and sympathized with but could not satisfy. One conclusion of the department, that it "might have to go to the President to have the Army and Navy ordered to make a ship available," proved unproductive.[5]

In Washington the Department of State continued to focus attention on the Peruvian Japanese. Ambassador Joseph Grew, returned from Japan on the *Gripsholm*, had speedily informed the department and the president of the shipboard conversation in which Peruvian Minister to Japan Ricardo Rivera Schreiber had urged the United States to "leave nothing undone to impress upon the Peruvian Government the seriousness of the Japanese future threat." Although hesitant to encourage Peru to break international law by sending Japanese from a nonbelligerent to a belligerent state, Washington nonetheless wanted the Japanese out of Peru and believed that Peru would accept specific American proposals for their removal and internment. While approving Norweb's mid-August proposals, the department did view the deportation of Nisei and naturalized Japanese as a knotty problem and suggested that the latter be "denaturalized." Always the principal concerns remained the removal of the Japanese leaders and the shipping required to achieve that.[6]

When the lack of shipping persisted, the Department of State considered interning the Japanese in Peru at American expense, along lines of a new but untested Cuban internment scheme. In the same season Nelson Rockefeller's oral report on the Japanese situation in Peru led President Roosevelt to respond with a vague promise to help the Peruvians manage their Japanese in local concentration camps. When the Department of Justice supported the State Department's request for funds to establish an internment camp in Cuba for dangerous enemy aliens, the likelihood of extending the plan to Peru momentarily increased.[7]

As the shipping shortage shifted its plans from the sequence of deportation, internment, and repatriation to simple internment in the country of residence, the Department of State summarized the situation throughout much of Latin America. In general the Central American and Caribbean states, having declared war against Japan, had willingly sent enemy aliens to the United States without placing any limitation on American disposition of them. Venezuela, on the other hand, had refused to transfer Axis aliens to American custody, and Mexico, Colombia, and Ecuador had exacted explicit guarantees from Washington before turning over any aliens. Because of its location on the south Atlantic, the blind side in reference to Japan, and a deep-rooted tradition of racial tolerance among other reasons, Brazil never transferred any Axis aliens to the United States. Nonbelligerent Peru had repeatedly expelled Axis nationals, entrusting them to American authorities without any firm American promise regarding their final disposition. Not only because wives and children of deported men had increasingly become a focus of anti-American propaganda, but also because of mutual acceptance of Peru's anti-Japanese outlook, the Department of State believed that any future program should involve entire families. Furthermore, the larger the number of Japanese in American hands the larger the number of Americans the United States could expect to recover from the Japanese. In August Secretary of State Cordell Hull had calculated that there were thirty-three hundred American citizens in China alone who desired to return to the United States. "In exchange for them," he told President Roosevelt, "we will have to send out Japanese in the same quantity." To do so he urged the continuance of "our exchange agreement with the Japanese" and "our efforts to remove *all* the Japanese from these American Republic countries for internment in the United States."[8]

Since one section of the Department of Justice, the Immigration and Naturalization Service, was charged with the care and keeping of the internees from Latin America, it naturally followed that other components of that department would concern themselves with those enemy aliens. When Attorney General Biddle, citing the flow of enemy aliens into and out of the United States, concluded that it was quite likely that many internees from Latin America might be on American hands for the duration of hostilities, he suggested, "If they are not to be repatriated . . . , the Department of State should arrange for them to be returned to Central or South America or the same procedure should be adopted with respect to them as now applies to other Axis aliens apprehended in this country on Presidential warrants, and that each case should be decided on its merits to determine, after proper hearing, whether the individual alien should be released, paroled, or interned for the duration."[9]

Whether this was a serious proposal to lump the Latin American Japanese together with the Japanese Americans or simply a whimsical desire to intone peacetime legal norms mattered little, the issue threatened basic American policy and relations with more than a dozen Latin American states. In an early follow-up the Department of Justice added that while encouraging Latin American governments to transfer dangerous enemy aliens to the United States, the Department of State must effect their repatriation. The State Department scarcely needed to be reminded that repatriation from the United States was more difficult than deportations from Latin America. At the same time, the department was studying demands that the Axis nationals deported from Mexico to the United States either be repatriated or returned to Mexico. When another twist of the same issue arose, namely the matter of the return to Panama of native Panamanian wives of Japanese internees, it developed that there was not even a firm and written agreement with Panama regarding the internment program. Without reference to specifics, the State Department admitted to the Justice Department that the laws of Latin American states made impossible the internment of enemy aliens from Latin America for the duration of the war.[10] Accompanying that conclusion within the Department of State must have been prayers for transportation—ships to take enemy aliens to Japan as well as vessels to bring more of same from Latin America.

In the autumn, although the internee factor remained numerically constant—no deportations increasing the number and no repatriations reducing it—the two departments drifted farther apart. "The investigative agencies," asserted a Department of State memorandum, "desire that these people be either repatriated or interned in the United States. They do not want any of these Japanese to return to the other American Republics where they may go free." Almost simultaneously the attorney general, learning of a conference of Navy and State personnel, deplored Assistant Secretary of State Long's announcement of a policy of repatriating Japanese, both American and Latin American Japanese presumably, against their will. "Any involuntary repatriation appears to raise serious questions of law as well as of policy," said the attorney general.[11] Years later American lawyers would go into court to battle the Department of Justice over the issue of involuntary repatriation. Meanwhile, as 1942 receded, the differing outlooks of the Departments of State and Justice regarding various aspects of the program of interning Latin American Japanese promised almost as much confrontation as cooperation.

For the Japanese already interned in the United States, the second half of 1942 represented a shakedown period. As they awaited the next repatriation for which many promptly applied, the Japanese, stimulated by the example of German internees, gave the conditions of their internment increasing attention. After a delay of months, copies of the Japanese text of the Convention Relative to the Treatment of Prisoners of War (Geneva, 1929) became available to internees. There, among the ninety-seven articles, they found answers to many questions about fences (art. 9), food (art. 11), clothing and canteens (art. 12), hygiene (arts. 13–14), work (arts. 27, 29), pay (art. 34), mail (art. 36), censorship (art. 40), petitions (art. 42), and other subjects of interest to them. When the Seagoville camp became crowded and no other family facility existed, many separated families of the *Shawnee* group rained protest upon the Spanish embassy.[12]

Routinely the protecting power also received the forwarded official Japanese lists of those internees to be accorded preferential consideration in the next repatriation. Some communications flowed in the opposite direction, as when the Department of State informed Spanish authorities that Japanese nationals entering the United States would be allowed to carry the equivalent of three hundred dollars for exchange. For internees who wanted funds from Peru the transfer involved the Banco Popular del Perú and the Chase National Bank.[13]

Various reports and complaints, the former from INS administrators and visitors from the Spanish embassy and the Department of State, the latter from the internees, emanated from the internment camps. Throughout the year the U.S. Army retained at Camp Livingston, Louisiana, the 184 male Japanese received in April from Panama and Costa Rica. At Livingston the enemy alien internees complained that they were limited to one fourteen-word message per month, that mail from the Spanish embassy failed to reach them, that they needed winter clothing, and that the relatives of ailing men should be informed.[14]

At Kenedy the sole midsummer complaint, that food allowances were insufficient, paled to insignificance after the hurricane heavily damaged the facility. At the end of 1942, Kenedy's roster of 685 civilian internees included at least 320 Latin American Japanese.[15]

At Seagoville, for a while, matters of first importance were the expansion of facilities to enable men from Kenedy to rejoin their families and the investigation of charges that American authorities in the Panama Canal Zone had seized approximately ten thousand dollars from Japanese internees while in transit. A lesser complaint, one more readily remedied, concerned the "mark up" on goods sold in the camp canteen. At the end of 1942, conditions in the barber and beauty shops, agitated primarily by German internees, posed continuing problems. By then the 302 Latin American Japanese at Seagoville, all but fourteen of whom were from Peru, included fifty-four heads of families whose October appeal had surely hastened their transfer there from Kenedy.[16]

As 1943 dawned the Panamanian and Costa Rican Japanese men remained in Louisiana, and the other Latin American Japanese were at either Seagoville or Kenedy, Texas. In all those settings the summer heat of 1942 and other climatic factors had multiplied the hardships of internment. Camp life had introduced circumstances and conditions that adversely affected many, possibly most, internees. Lack of privacy, for quiet and introverted individuals, constituted a continuing calamity. Forced proximity for months—always the same faces and the same voices—bred trivial but bitter antipathies. Often a general listlessness undermined staid and sober people, rendering them frivolous. The pattern of living behind barbed wire reduced otherwise dignified individuals to scandal mongering. Camp operations contributed to the weakening of family ties. Even where family unity was theoretically intact, it broke down, as did parental discipline, in mess halls and other public areas. Gradually, as all this intensified and worsened in 1943, 1944, 1945, the camps bred rivalries that even produced confrontations between social gangs. Meanwhile, hypochondria set in. Imaginary illnesses sent internees running to the doctors, really seeking escape from monotony. At the same time, the docile side of their Japanese nature prompted them to come to terms with their jailers.

About 120 miles southwest of San Antonio, at Crystal City, Texas, the Department of Justice established what became the largest facility of the INS for the detention of enemy aliens. It derived from a decision of October 1942 to house, pending repatriation, the growing number of interned Japanese families from Latin America.

At the edge of Crystal City, an agricultural community of about sixty-five hundred that termed itself the spinach capital of America, stood a migratory farm labor camp which consisted of forty-one small three-room cottages, 118 one-room structures, and some service buildings. That camp served as the nucleus for the INS installation. As at Kenedy, months earlier, the new use required considerable construction. This was all the more necessary as INS officials faced the needs of men, women, and children of various ages, races, and nationalities as well as the continuing uncertainty regarding the early repatriation of any internees, and especially the Japanese. The Departments of Justice and State cooperated to support the priorities of the INS as it gradually constructed 219 temporary housing units of duplex, triplex, and quadruplex design, fifteen additional three-room cottages, and 103 plywood huts of the type that had failed to withstand the August hurricane at Kenedy. The completed camp would accommodate 962 families, chiefly Japanese but some Germans.

Each housing unit included an oil stove with oven for cooking and heating, a kitchen sink with cold running water, and essential cooking utensils and dishes. Some basic furniture and furnishings the internees produced themselves, using materials supplied by the camp administration. Within the duplex, triplex, and quadruplex units toilet and lavatory facilities were shared. The internees laundered personal apparel at stationary tubs in a central hand laundry. Other items, including sheets, pillowcases, and work clothes, went to the central power-operated laundry. The provision of superior family facilities at Crystal City promptly routed all such groups there rather than to Seagoville. The ten-foot fence, the floodlights, and the guard towers guaranteed the isolation and security of the camp.

The acreage permitted, in addition to the establishment of communities based on nationality and race, a wide range of land-use activities. In a climate that averaged 250 frost-free days annually, the internees had more opportunities to volunteer for a paid-work program than their counterparts elsewhere. For their work they received ten cents an hour. Agricultural-minded internees planted and tended sizable and varied vegetable crops. The production of eggs, poultry, honey, and meat, and the slaughtering and curing of meats, sausage making, laundry and bakery work, shoe repair, the manufacture and repair of clothing, preservation of foods, and the manufacture of mattresses and furniture occupied hundreds. Some helped the administration with its paperwork, others delivered ice or worked in the canteen, still others became instructors, and so forth. The work program occupied so many individuals so much of the time that it became a major contributor to the harmonious operation of the camp.

The INS administration at Crystal City reflected not only the particular circumstances of that camp but also some of the accumulated experience of other camp operations. While the administrative services officer took care of fiscal matters, maintenance, construction, supplies, and internal security (including policing, fire protection, and censorship), an internees relations officer handled all internee services, including recreation and education. He maintained the dossiers on each internee, supervised the assignment of living quarters, and, on occasion, served as arbitrator. He handled the minor complaints which, if ignored and allowed to accumulate, could become major, even disruptive, problems. As at other camps, each national and racial group had its representative in the Council-Spokesman system.

As time passed and the internment program expanded, an increasing interest in the welfare of the internees developed. In addition to routine inspections by the protecting powers—Spain for the Japanese—the International Red Cross, the War Prisoners Aid of the YMCA, the YWCA, the American Friends Service Committee, and the National Catholic Welfare Conference, not to mention numerous local clergymen, concerned themselves with internee well-being.

The camp gradually came to resemble a small town in many respects. The ratios of men to women, parents to children, old to young—all took on the appearance of a normal community. The establishment and operation of stores, schools, a hospital, churches, beauty and barber shops, movies, and numerous recreational facilities also furthered the sense of community, albeit one which the local newspapers termed a "concentration camp."[17]

Early in 1943 the first internees, a small number of Germans, took up residence at Crystal City. Greater secrecy, reflected in the sparse press coverage locally, attended the launching of the Crystal City installation than had been the case at Kenedy. When, in mid-February, another group of internees arrived, the local newspaper could only report, "The number is never officially given and we did not learn if they were Germans or Japs." Between mid-1943 and mid-1944 its population would expand rapidly, and about the time hostilities ended in Europe the Crystal City Internment Camp would house more than thirty-three hundred internees.[18]

### The Stresses in Peru

Ten times during the second half of 1942 revisions and supplements of The Proclaimed List of Certain Blocked Nationals appeared, and the *Shawnee* was only three days out of Callao when the supplement of June 19 added approximately one hundred Japanese individuals and businesses to that "blacklist."[19] As America's economic warfare against her Far Eastern enemy further invaded Japanese life in numerous towns and cities of Peru, many who had escaped deportation in June felt a gnawing fear that did not diminish as successive lists appeared. The psychological effects of the Proclaimed List, either as *fait accompli* or as future threat, cannot be calculated. The realization that the next list, only weeks away, could victimize others denied any enemy alien more than momentary relief.

With the passage of time internees who had sailed on the *Etolin*, *Acadia*, and *Shawnee* wrote letters telling of shipboard and camp experiences as well as inquiring about friends, relatives, conditions in Peru, the transmission of funds, and other matters. Reports that camp life had produced neither torture nor persecution, that the prospects for repatriation were good, that living, however uncertain, was relatively easy—all this hurried not only wives and children of internees but others to consider Peruvian deportation and American internment as the lesser of evils. Continued residence in Peru, on the other hand, meant facing a growing number of uncertainties and hazards.

As usual, the letter of Peruvian law and its enforcement proved to be two different things. Japanese bank accounts, frozen by the decree of December 8, had to be registered by the Superintendencia de Bancos. Obligations entered into before that date escaped the regulations, and depositors could withdraw up to five hundred soles (eighty dollars) monthly.[20] Often persons with multiple accounts, influential friends, and some money to be used adroitly to win favors did not feel the harsh impact intended by the anti-Axis measures. Enforcing regulations required men of competence and integrity, qualities that were often lacking, especially among individuals who ostensibly were not paid for their services.[21] Under such circumstances it was not uncommon for anti-Japanese natives to consider the despoiling of Japanese a patriotic act, one which also enabled greedy and unprincipled men to latch onto Japanese assets—as had happened in California. The cancellation of contracts, termination of leases, and expropriation of properties—all represented presumably legal Peruvian assaults whose cumulative effects demoralized more and more Japanese.

The prospect of deportation, which was viewed variously as threat and release, introduced yet another ambivalence into the Japanese community and divided it. To keep abreast of hostile developments, the Proclaimed Lists, the surveys of the Americans, and the laws, regulations, police investigations, and public sentiment of the Peruvians, the Japanese became a more closely knit community in their search for the latest information and solutions for personal dilemmas. But even as they figuratively huddled closer together—thus increasing Peruvian suspicions and hostility—estrangement set in. An air of "if they must take somebody, let it be you not me" invaded the Japanese community. For different reasons, a similar sentiment was evident in wartime United States: "We must stand together against the Nazis and the Japs, but I'm glad your draft number is lower than mine." Or, "My sons have family responsibilities yours don't have." No man and no country had a monopoly on selfishness prompted by the urge to survive. In Peru, as in many other countries, it was a time that tested moral fiber.

The discovery by Peruvian police that Japanese tailors in Lima were producing a military style uniform launched a flurry of concern and activity. The tailors explained that the jumperlike uniforms were a wartime economy measure for civilians, but others thought they might be military uniforms. Word from Lima suggested a search of the baggage of thirty-year-old Akira Masami Uesugi, who had represented the Japanese shipping line Kawasaki Kisen in Peru before his departure on the *Shawnee*. Two green cavalry uniforms were found, minus insignia. A few weeks later, when Peruvian authorities discovered nine Japanese with Japanese military uniforms, the United States sought custody of the men. Not unrelated to this issue, which received attention in high American official circles, was the concession by the War Department "that a few Japanese might be moved by Army planes from Peru to the Canal Zone."[22]

On December 15, a U.S. Army plane departed Lima with twenty unwilling passengers. Most of the fifteen Japanese were tailors and merchants. Representative of the tailors were Okinawa-born forty-year-old Kohei Gushiken and Yaichi Murata, a twenty-five-year resident of Peru, both of whom left families behind, as did most of these deportees. In the Panama Canal Zone the twenty enemy aliens quickly occupied quarters other deportees had used earlier. But even before these men had arrived there, the Defense Command had registered its opposition to any kind of internment of enemy aliens in that strategic area.[23]

Suddenly, about this time, shipping prospects for the removal of Japanese from Peru improved. Uncertain is the cumulative effect of the appeals for ships by Peruvian authorities, the American embassy, and the Department of State. Uncertain, too, is the impact of the Japanese uniforms, the tailors, and their removal and detention. What is certain is that in the closing weeks of 1942 the frustrations born of inaction which many officials had long endured were coming to an end.

### Men Only: The Fourth Ship

When the Department of State sought cooperation in the matter of bringing approximately one thousand Japanese from Peru, the Department of Justice considered more than the simple question of physical facilities. Biddle wondered anew "whether the Department of Justice should undertake to receive such people if it cannot accord them the same privileges with regard to hearings, etc. that it accords enemy aliens taken into custody in the United States." Meanwhile the State Department was hoping that instructions to the military, naval, and legal attachés in Lima by the War and Navy Departments and the FBI would endorse its program.[24]

While indicating that the INS could and would cooperate in the program, Biddle introduced some related matters. Informed that some internees might safely be subjected to less strict handling, he raised the question of parole within small inland communities, an idea he possibly had borrowed from the WRA's approach to Japanese Americans. The attorney general also wanted the opportunity to conduct reviews of the facts in Lima to help determine which persons should be deported and interned. Although physical facilities, budgetary matters, and personnel were curbing the enthusiasm of the INS regarding the internment program, the attorney general's outlook apparently stemmed from more laudable legal considerations, and when shipping became available, his concerns intensified. Since repatriation was not likely in the foreseeable future, the Justice Department insisted that it could justify the detention of the Latin American Japanese only if some satisfactory means were instituted to determine whether the enemy aliens were dangerous.[25]

Peruvian enthusiasm for another deportation, meanwhile, remained high as Secretary General of the Ministry of Foreign Affairs Dr. Javier Correa Elías urged the removal of all the Japanese. The International Brigade of the Ministry of Government was extending lists that already included 560 heads of families—lists that invited comparison with the 250-plus prospective deportees compiled by Emmerson. In Lima neither

Peruvian nor American officials viewed favorably the internment of the Japanese in Peru, an idea that recurred in circles in Washington.[26]

Once again, as the U.S. Army Transport *Frederick C. Johnson* approached Peru for deportees, the effort to reconcile Peruvian and American lists resembled something of a contest. Influence at the highest level occasionally deleted a name, as when the wife of the Peruvian president blocked the deportation of Tadao Taniguchi, a Lima merchant who in the course of twenty-nine years in the country had become a devout Roman Catholic, a naturalized citizen, and the husband of a native Peruvian.[27] One hundred sixty-eight Japanese lacked Taniguchi's good fortune.

On Sunday, January 6, 1943, Ginzo Murono and Yasuhiko Ohashi had gone fishing. On their return, as they approached Yasuhiko's home, they saw two men standing there, in plain clothes. Asking for Yasuhiko, who promptly identified himself, they took him off immediately to the district police station. Ginzo, hoping to aid his business associate and friend, followed and from a telephone in a nearby store tried to contact someone of influence. While telephoning, Ginzo was accosted by two men in plain clothes and asked to identify himself. Immediately he joined Yasuhiko and a considerable number of other Japanese in the large detention area of the police station. No charges were ever made; no hearings ever took place. Married and the father of two preschool children, thirty-four-year-old Murono had lived in Peru for sixteen years and was a partner in a sporting goods and stationery business which the Americans had put on the Proclaimed List two days after Pearl Harbor. The American record against him read, "Said to be in charge of Murono Company, one of the most powerful Japanese firms in Lima, meetings reported at Murono's house." Thirty-five years later the first charge amused him, the second he denied.[28]

In the early afternoon, that same day, Taro Ohashi was napping when the police came and hurried him off to a police station. At age twenty-five, in 1927, he had migrated from Kyoto Prefecture to Lima, where he had continued his interest in farming as well as establishing a ribbon business which the Americans had blacklisted, his supplies coming principally from Japan and Germany. Peruvian authorities recommended his expulsion because he was a former president of the Japanese society in Miraflores.[29]

For Kakuaki Kaneko the two days still stand out, the celebration of his thirty-sixth birthday on January 6, his seizure by the police on January 7. Aware of previous arrests and of his own vulnerability, Kakuaki and his wife Otari had instructed the maid to respond cautiously to any ringing of the doorbell or knocking on the door. Between 5 and 6 A.M. that morning the bell rang and the maid, warily opening the door, inquired, "Who is it?" Two Peruvian policemen pushed their way in, arrested Kakuaki, and hustled him off to a police station. Who was this prospective deportee? From a farm in Fukushima he had migrated, in 1928, to Peru, where he and a younger brother, who was destined to be deported on the same ship, operated a glass business. The business had put Kakuaki on excellent terms with many prominent Peruvians. He had worked on President Prado's residence, and the president's legal counsel had been godfather to Kakuaki's four-year-old daughter. Kakuaki was prominent in the Fukushima prefectural society, one of the largest such groups in Peru, and also in Japanese athletic organizations and activities. He had won races at 100 and 200 meters and was a champion pole vaulter. Lawyer Rivera Schreiber, through whom Kakuaki had aided friends, had enabled Kakuaki to escape deportation on earlier occasions, but in January 1943 no help was at hand for one whom the Peruvians sought to expel because he was "active in the Japanese colony."[30]

The same fate awaited Saburo Ushida far to the north in Chiclayo. At age twenty-one, in 1921, Saburo had left Yamanashi Prefecture for Peru. Working hard, he had established first one store, then a second, and yet another in Chiclayo, outlets for groceries and sundry merchandise. A fourth store he opened farther north in Piura. Accepted and trusted by his Peruvian customers, friends, and relatives, as well as by the native Peruvian wife who had borne his four young daughters, Saburo Ushida had prospered. In June 1942 the police had interviewed him, and soon thereafter he had prepared for the seemingly inevitable by closing two stores and counseling his wife and a trusted nephew concerning his remaining business affairs. Nonetheless the knock at the door at 6 A.M. on January 7 jolted him. Hurried off to police headquarters by a detective, Saburo was immediately jailed. The authorities who considerately honored his request and sent to his home for some personal effects were the same ones who put him, along with other Japanese, aboard a truck that left the city before the end of the day. No specific reason accompanied the American recommendation that he be expelled.[31]

Unlike any other embarkation, earlier or later, that of January 10, 1943, occurred at a northern port, Talara, for several reasons. For one thing, crowds, confusion, and the last minute nonappearance of men scheduled to go, as well as the rapid substitution of others, had irritated American officials on previous occasions. Pursuit of the security of the American air detachment at Talara and the protracted Emmerson-Woo survey of the region north of Lima had pinpointed many Japanese for deportation. So it was that instead of short runs from Lima police stations, those seized in the capital and elsewhere traveled north by trucks and buses, escorted by armed police. During an arduous two-and-a-half-day 600-mile trip from Lima, the Peruvian police made no special provision for food. A final check at Talara resulted in the release of seventeen men, owing to age or infirmity as well as because they "could not be cited as dangerous." A telephone call, plus money, also deleted Shoichi Mishima from the passenger list. The release of Huacho carpenter Sumitaka Nishimuta from this contingent was coupled with the illness of his wife.

This joint Peruvian-American effort put 173 men (168 Japanese and five Germans) aboard the *Frederick C. Johnson,* a vessel capable of accommodating 500. Presumed to be "dangerous," the 168 had been selected as follows: by Peru, fifty; by the United States, forty-four; by both Peru and the United States, forty-two; and unknown by whom and on no prior list, thirty-two. Among the twenty-six deported because they were "resident in strategic area," twenty-five were so designated because they were "near Talara," although some lived more than 100 miles distant from that base. This one deportation removed more than 10 percent of the total Japanese population in the entire Department of Piura.

Every passenger was male, despite the Peruvian and American desire to ship out entire families, because the trip to the United States was going to be interrupted by an indeterminate stay in the Canal Zone in facilities designed for men. Most of the deportees, who ranged in age from twenty to sixty-one, had lived in Peru for considerably longer than a decade—Eiichi Sakoda, a Piura barber, had counted Peru his home for forty-two years. Occupationally the group included merchants (seventy-one), barbers (twenty), commercial employees (sixteen), farmers (fourteen), teachers (six), mechanics (four), glass workers (four), carpenters (three), tailors (three), gardeners (two), and cooks (two), plus at least one each of the following: engineer, photographer, dentist, blacksmith, dairyman, commission agent, painter, chauffeur, garage owner, soap manufacturer, and flooring contractor. American officials had placed more than 40 percent of them on the "blacklist." Fourteen men, attuned to the worsening position of Japanese in Peru, had sent their families to Japan.

No arrest produced either charge or hearing, much less a trial. Most were considered community leaders, for one reason or another, sometimes seemingly for no reason at all. Two were Nisei, twenty-nine-year-old Manuel Enrique Ikari, a Piura merchant who had married a native Peruvian, and twenty-year-old unmarried Koshio Shimabukuro, a clerk in Lima. Two men had become Peruvian citizens: Carlos Shinkyu Taira, an Okinawa-born farmer naturalized in 1934, whose wife Mercedes was a native Peruvian, and Shigeyuki Tanaka, a Trujillo barber, whose twenty-six years in the country included fifteen as a citizen. The retention of Japanese citizenship by 164 of those men represented a monstrous irritant to Peruvian pride. That these Japanese had lived and prospered many years in the country but refused the final legal identification with Peru humiliated and enraged Peruvians. The Japanese, for the most part, knew that retention of Japanese citizenship, an act that indulged an arrogant sense of cultural superiority, nevertheless guaranteed them leverage that reduced the prospect of being victimized by Peruvian authorities. In devastating fashion, that peacetime asset of sorts, Japanese citizenship, had become a distinct wartime liability. Rare was the Peruvian voice raised publicly at this time on behalf of a Japanese, but one such from Arequipa did appeal to American authorities on behalf of Yoshihisa Muto. Citing Muto as a thirty-third degree Mason, a twenty-year resident married to a Peruvian woman, and as one opposed to Japanese policy, the nonproductive appeal went to President Roosevelt.

Although Lima, as usual, contributed the largest number of deportees (seventy-one), two dozen other communities also lost Japanese at this time, among them Chiclayo (twenty), Trujillo (eighteen), Piura (fourteen), Huacho (twelve), Sullana (five), Arequipa (four), Huaral (three), Callao (three), Pimentel (two), and Paita (two), plus at least one person from each of the following: Paiján, Catacaos, Ascope, Chiclín, Chulucanas, Vitarte, Frias, Chepén, Huaura, La Huaca, Chacra, and Virú. In addition to the relationship of this roundup to the security of the American installation at Talara and to the wide-ranging survey by Emmerson and Woo, there was a psychological factor, studied or otherwise, behind the seizure of men from so many different areas.

Another impact of the roundup and deportation, that upon wives and children, was distinctly social and economic. The marital status of the men was as follows: 123 married, thirty-seven unmarried, five widowers, and three unknown. The families of fourteen married men were in Japan, but the wives and children of 108 others were being left in Peru. Records concerning twenty-five of those families indicate that they averaged 2.6 children and the wives averaged seven years younger than their husbands. Obviously hundreds of dependents, like the deportees themselves, faced an uncertain and difficult future, one that would bring from both groups repeated requests that the families be reunited. Eventually many wives and children did join these heads of families in internment. Later, more than sixty of these families would be repatriated to Japan, as were an overwhelming number of the unmarried men, fourteen men rejoining their families, and four individuals who were deserting families in Peru as they opted for Japan. Unrecorded is the torment created when fifty-two-year-old Shigeru Kawakami, whose native Peruvian wife had mothered his family, declared to American authorities, "Although I have a Peruvian-born wife and six Peruvian-born children, I shall repatriate to Japan myself as soon as possible" and did so.[32]

When the *Frederick C. Johnson* reached Panama, the enemy aliens were trucked into the Canal Zone, where they joined the fifteen Japanese who had flown out of Peru in mid-December. For a couple of weeks, the time apparently needed to make shipping arrangements, the men lived under constant military guard in barracks in a wilderness setting in which they even had to construct toilet facilities. Saburo Ushida recalls that the food was meager—two meals a day—and not to the Japanese taste. There was black coffee, grapefruit, scrambled eggs, bread—never any rice. Next the Japanese were transported to the U.S. Army Transport *Puebla*, again in trucks that allowed them to see nothing. On the run to San Pedro the men, although permitted on deck once daily, were required to perform many duties, including laundering the apparel of their American armed guards, without any remuneration. When a man named Takahashi refused to work, he was incarcerated for insubordination. Before landing all were required to sign papers that signified that they had been well treated afloat.

At San Pedro, on February 6, the men encountered INS officials. As each man in line reached the man seated at the table, he was asked, "Do you have a passport?" Since all passports, whether Japanese or Peruvian, had been collected as soon as the *Johnson* had cleared Peruvian waters, each man, with varying degrees of suppressed bitterness, responded firmly, "No." Each heard an official declare, "You must recognize the fact that your entry into the United States is illegal." This status that rendered them pawns of American authorities would persist indefinitely.

From registration by the INS the men were bused to the well-shaded Tuna Canyon Detention Center, a converted CCC camp north of Los Angeles in the San Gabriel Mountains, a facility described by one Department of State representative as "one of the best internment or detention camps in the United States." There the hungry, weary, disspirited Japanese were pleasantly surprised. Greeted by a Japanese American Issei internee, chef Kawasaki, the men were served rice and fish in abundance. One of the many who gorged themselves that day, Kakuaki Kaneko, recalls, "We went back even three times." Their brief stay at Tuna Canyon momentarily brightened the lives of many bewildered men. Soon, however, the group, minus one individual whose tubercular condition hospitalized him, entrained for Kenedy, Texas, where, on February 12, they joined that growing community of internees.[33]

### The Next Deportation and Another Assessment

As those deportees were sailing away from Talara, the Departments of State and Justice were seeking an accommodation regarding Latin American internees. Biddle, insisting that many cases did not warrant internment, added, "Some of the cases seem to be mistakes." When the State Department suggested that any formal investigations in the United States might be interpreted as an attack on the integrity and sincerity of Peruvian officials (which the State Department's personnel freely indulged in intradepartmental communications), Biddle defended his department's right to review any case and hoped to eliminate many problems by sending Raymond W. Ickes of the Justice Department's Alien Enemy Control Unit (AECU) to Lima to assist in the selection process. Before Ickes's departure, weeks later, Biddle conceded that his department would not put cases concerning Latin American internees through the procedure of alien enemy hearing boards, but he doggedly maintained the right to review cases.[34]

In the post-Talara assessment of that operation the Peruvians and Americans agreed that all future deportations should be from Callao.

American officials continued to resent the limited cooperation and outright obstructionism of some Peruvians, even as they hoped for success when another opportunity materialized. Informed that a vessel would come soon for more male enemy aliens, Lima organized new lists of the unwanted, a matter complicated by the Peruvian preference, almost insistence of late, that the Japanese wives and children accompany the men to be ousted.[35]

Except for the switch from Talara to Callao and the participation of AECU's Ickes in the determination of the passenger list, this late February operation resembled the January one in that the ship was the *Frederick C. Johnson* and an indeterminate stay in the Canal Zone awaited the "dangerous" men.

For Ickes the working days in Lima were long ones. However much or little information there was for each person on the lists, only one question had to be answered: was the enemy alien actually or potentially dangerous? As Ickes allowed one and denied another expulsion and his careful screening delayed the scheduled sailing, gone was easy American acquiescence in whimsical Peruvian selections based solely on a desire to rid the country of its Japanese. When the *Frederick C. Johnson* cleared Callao harbor on February 24, the ship that could accommodate 500 carried only twenty-six Germans and 119 Japanese.[36]

More than 60 percent of these Japanese deportees resided in the Lima-Callao area. Most of the others came from the region south of Lima: from Cañete (sixteen), Arequipa (five), Pisco (five), Ica (two), Lurín (two), and other communities. Very few lived north of Lima: in Chancay (two), Huacho (two), Huaral (one), Supe (one). And rarely did any come from the interior, as did one each from Huancayo and Jauja. Most of the men were merchants (eighty-eight), but the group also included barbers (nine), farmers (six), teachers (five), and a few others. Since only thirty-one were blacklisted by the United States, the 119 appeared to be of less economic consequence than their predecessors in January. They ranged from twenty-one to sixty-two years of age, and their average residence in Peru was considerably in excess of a decade. José Shinichi Ohashi had lived there for thirty-five years. As for citizenship, 117 were Japanese, two—Isamu Kurotobi and Arturo Shinei Yakabi—were Peruvian Nisei. None had been naturalized.

On the social side they included eighty-four married, twenty-two unmarried, two widowers, and eleven unknown. Information regarding fifty-nine marriages indicated that the families averaged 3.4 children and the age difference between husband and wife averaged 7.9 years. Once again the plight of wives and children separated from their breadwinners promised to be a dismal one buoyed up only by the remote hope that some future ship would reunite the families.[37] Again the general account of a group invites mention of individuals.

Apprehended by police in Cañete, Mitsutaro Tawara spent February 22 in the local jail. The following day he was in the custody of Lima authorities and then he was put aboard ship, separated from his wife and five children as well as the land he had known for decades. In 1917, twenty-two-year-old Mitsutaro and his wife Kiwa had been among the 1,455 Japanese encouraged by Japanese emigration companies to seek their fortunes in Peru. After a year on a sugar plantation at Cañete, they had moved north to Huaral to farm cotton. Fourteen years and three children later the family returned to Cañete where they raised cotton and bananas on leased land and operated a grocery store. There two more children were born and there, too, the police seized Mitsutaro.[38]

At the same time, far to the south in Arequipa, the police were taking merchant Octavio Taijiro Tochio into custody. Yokohama-born and high-school educated, he had entered Peru in 1915 and after working five years for another Japanese had opened his own bazaar. He wooed and married a beautiful native Peruvian, Luisa Villanueva, who, besides matching his interest in tennis, bore his three children. Happy family, successful business (blacklisted in April 1942)—that and more disintegrated the day he was arrested and hurried off to Lima.[39]

In Lima, that George Washington's birthday, Kunio Takeshita was enjoying his afternoon siesta when the police arrived. His brothers—he had four—awakened him and the police, once they had identified Kunio, trucked him off to jail. In 1917, when Kunio was two years old, his parents had left him in Fukuoka Prefecture with relatives when they migrated to Peru. In 1929 he joined them and his four younger Nisei brothers. In the neighborhood of the Jesús María Japanese School, the family store specialized in picture frames. When his father died in 1940, Kunio had become the head of the family, acquiring also that special vulnerability which singled him out to the police.[40]

Another Japanese rudely awakened by police that fateful day was bakery worker Arturo Shinei Yakabi. The twenty-one-year-old Nisei, born at

Hacienda Esquivel, Chancay, was the oldest of the five children of a couple that had migrated from Okinawa. As the eldest child in an economically struggling rural family, Shinei's opportunity for schooling was limited. With only four years of formal education, he set out, at age fifteen, to work in nearby Callao. Working for other Japanese, first in a grocery, then in a bakery, he received scant wages, but the arrangement included room and board. While sleeping in his quarters behind the bakery, Shinei was awakened and seized by Peruvian police. He was no leader of the Japanese community, no official of a Japanese society, no businessman on or destined for the Proclaimed List. Nor was it a case of mistaken identity. He was a sacrificial victim. His employer apparently was escaping deportation by bribing the police and offering them a substitute, Shinei. Hustled into a police van, he soon was joined by others seized in the Callao roundup. In Lima they were all jailed in a common enclosure. During three weeks there three memorable things occurred: Shinei's mother visited him repeatedly, occasionally a Japanese was called out to confer with officials and never returned, and police officials informed Shinei that if he had money "they could work it out." At 3 A.M. February 24 the penniless young man was among those trucked to the pier. All of his possessions, a few articles of clothing, he carried in a flour sack.[41]

Another evacuation prompted another assessment, this time by both Justice and State Department personnel. The summation by Ickes represented both a review of the recent operation and a statement of AECU policy. No individuals would be sent to the United States except actually or potentially dangerous alien enemies about whom credible evidence existed. In an effort to establish parameters warranting internment, Ickes accepted the following: service as an officer of a Japanese society, residence in Callao and other (unidentified) strategic areas, attendance at Japanese meetings (which abused, if it did not contradict his insistence that mere membership in a Japanese society was nonincriminating), visits at embassies and legations of other enemy countries. Allegations, alone, that a Japanese was "influential" would not warrant internment, although such unsupported accusations by Peruvian citizens and police had already sent scores of men to the United States. Aware of Peruvian obstructionism—only fifteen of the 119 Japanese deported had been on the American list—Ickes suggested two "get tough" measures: (1) by transmitting embassy lists direct to President Prado the obstructionist tactics of indifferent and venal subordinate Peruvian officials could be avoided, and (2) the United States should insist on the expulsion of those on old American lists before considering those named on Peruvian lists.

Ickes offered three more recommendations. His idea of encouraging Peru to establish American-financed concentration camps in that country, which appealed to the Department of Justice because it would lessen the internment problem in the United States, lacked appeal to embassy personnel well acquainted with Peruvian ways. A second suggestion, welcomed by all, concerned the early removal of the families of aliens already deported. Lastly, Ickes hoped for better timing, "to avoid the frantic haste and consequent confusion which came so close to making the February 24 sailing of the SS Johnson a complete 'fracaso.'"

Norweb basically agreed with Ickes and anticipated the cooperation of the AECU in the future. Meanwhile he wanted no additional shipping unless women and children could be removed, something he hoped to achieve within three or four months. Questionable, in part, was the ambassador's conclusion, "The removal of Axis nationals from Peru has been of value in breaking up the German and Japanese organizations, in contributing to Hemisphere security, and in affecting Axis morale." As he set about cultivating Peruvian officials once more, Norweb, who would soon be solicitous of Peruvian enforcement of the law of March 22 which provided for the cancellation of the naturalization papers of subjects of Axis origins found guilty of subversive activities or spreading propaganda, and of the decree of April 10 that promised the expropriation of "all properties of Proclaimed List nationals not transferred to Peruvians . . . by May 31st," buttressed his own opposition to internment camps in Peru by citing embassy personnel who shared his opinion.[42]

To Ickes's conclusions and recommendations, Biddle added another. Since many Axis nationals had been and continued to be brought to the United States in anticipation of repatriation that might fail to materialize, would it not be well to arrange with the Latin American governments for their return to Latin America at the conclusion of hostilities? Totally contrary to Department of State policy and to promises made to numerous foreign governments, this suggestion was not the only evidence of interdepartmental disharmony in Washington. Of more immediate concern was Secretary of War Stimson's proposal, "Enemy aliens . . . in countries south of the line formed by the northern border of Brazil and the northern border of Peru will not be interned by the United States."[43] On the verge of terminating its custodial role by transferring the Latin American Japanese at Camp Livingston to the INS at Kenedy, Texas, the War Department apparently thought that other agencies could and should lessen their internee burdens.

### Friction in the Camps

Meanwhile neither Lima nor Washington monopolized the problems and frictions of the time, witness some of the issues originating with the internees. The Panamanian and Costa Rican Japanese, still in the hands of the U.S. Army, continued to protest both the seizure of funds while in the Canal Zone and the restrictive regulations at Camp Livingston. Not long before these men were finally transferred to INS custody, nine of them unsuccessfully petitioned to be returned to Panama, where at least three had left Panamanian wives and children.[44]

Another matter, ostensibly a private one involving one man's finances, soon assumed more significance. Nikumatsu Okada, deported in June 1942 and interned at Seagoville, sought permission to return to Peru to protect his property from a rapacious adopted daughter who, he charged, had insisted that he and his wife were dead as she withdrew $150,000 from his Peruvian bank account. The Department of State refused Okada's request but it did urge an investigation. The episode quickly revealed the laxity of Peruvian controls over the funds of Axis nationals, a truth that displeased both Okada and the United States but surprised neither.[45]

Month after month the internees waged an unrelenting struggle to reunite their families. The limited capacity of the Seagoville facility and the opening and enlargement of the one at Crystal City brought requests to be transferred there pending repatriation.[46]

Internment officials faced an endless variety of problems and circumstances, ranging from a wintertime shortage of underwear at Seagoville to the death of an internee in California. Ichiroku Yatomi's death raised questions. Yatomi, whose hospitalization had separated him from the *Puebla* group in February, had died a month later in Los Angeles General Hospital of advanced pulmonary tuberculosis. Routinely his twenty-three-year-old Nisei widow and their two children would be notified and disposition made of his funds and belongings. But even then a haunting question would persist: what was the state of Yatomi's health at the time he, one of the tailors who spent three months in a Lima jail before being airlifted to Panama, left Peru? Peruvian insistence that he departed in good health was countered by Norweb's doubt "that police physicians ever bothered to investigate the condition of their [prisoners'] health." Reporting that many in the same group had been ill, the INS suggested that the U.S. Public Health Service be charged with the inspection of deportees at the port of embarkation, an idea with which the AECU concurred. By the time a distraught Aiko Yatomi let it be known that she wanted to bring her two small children with her to claim her husband's ashes, this case would present additional complications.[47]

As the spring of 1943 advanced and no relative or friend had received word from any man deported in February, justifiable concern focused on the 119 who had been put ashore in Panama. In the Canal Zone, from which the 183 Japanese of the December and January contingents had recently departed, these new arrivals had encountered rugged conditions. Within a fenced area every corner of which was manned by soldiers with machine guns, the men, in groups of three to five, lived in square tents, most of which leaked badly in the developing rainy season. The heat, humidity, and insects plagued the men and to such as young Yakabi the rain came as a total surprise. Every morning at 6 A.M. a reveille bugle summoned them to line up for a routine count. The half hour allotted for breakfast afforded them additional grounds for disgruntlement as they consumed food Japanese did not consider palatable. By 7:45 A.M. those on the garbage detail were rounding it up to be trucked off to the dumping area. Then the ten-man work groups, each guarded by two MPs, formed.

Day after day the labor—required, not volunteered—consisted of clearing away more of the Panamanian jungle, extending the perimeter of the camp. For more than one hundred days, under increasingly unhealthful conditions as the rains beat down, the men were forced to work without remuneration. Denied communication with their families, unaccustomed to the hard labor, resenting the unsavory food and their inadequate shelter under intolerable weather conditions, the men understandably put forth no special effort. In return guards occasionally kicked, beat, or nicked with their bayonets some passive worker. One day a brush-cutting ex-bakery worker paused, asked for a drink of water, and received instead a blow from which he still carries a scar.

One Japanese, thirty-one-year-old Tetsuo Suwa, a merchant from Ica, became mentally upset—berserk in the words of many. One day he dashed barefoot for freedom, in his pajamas. At the fence machine-gun bullets from one of the towers crumpled him. Hospitalized and sobered, he survived the episode. For all of the apprehensive Japanese, however, the stay in Panama that lengthened into months was a torturing hell. One man, merchant Tochio of Arequipa, had a talent for expressing those feelings. Written as he and his closely knit and embittered companions were leaving Panama, his "Song of Farewell" included the following:

> To the Cross on Telegraph Isle
> We bid our last farewell ...
> We are the hostages
> Damn it, take us any place. ...
> What hard labor, the armed watch,
> We don't give a damn ...
> Sadly there is no way to ward off
> Anxiety over our dear families
> Abandoned in Peruvian land ...
> Bear it, bear it, the raindrops whisper. ... .[48]

Shortly before the June departure of the 119 from Panama, an inquiring Naval Intelligence officer was told, "it was impossible to provide earlier for their transportation to the United States."[49]

The first group of Peruvian Japanese to experience a long and tedious delay en route to the United States, the 119 were also unique in that travel to Texas did not follow swiftly their arrival. The S.S. *Monterey*, larger and offering better food than the *Johnson*, had transported the men from Panama to San Francisco, where they landed on June 15 and encountered the INS reminder that they were entering the country illegally. After that frustrating glimpse of American bureaucracy, the men boarded U.S. Army trucks and rode a short distance down the peninsula to Sharp Park, where the INS operated one of its many temporary centers intended for aliens pending hearings or the determination of final decisions. There the barracks were old and the nationalities many. Although the pall of uncertainty still enveloped the group, the men were better off in terms of climate, food, housing, and the opportunity to communicate with Peru. The do-nothingness that built up in the course of their eight weeks at Sharp Park was relieved briefly when trouble flared up with the Chinese, who were divided into pro-Kuomintang and pro-Communist groups. The fracas featured a Chinese flag which, once it was raised, was lowered and seized by Japanese, the Japanese Americans and Peruvian Japanese joining forces in the melee.

The train that the men boarded early in August headed north, to Missoula, Montana, where the INS operated a general detention facility. There the Peruvian group, reduced by one hospitalized in California, joined large numbers of Italians and some Germans at an abandoned army post which the International Red Cross had recently inspected and termed a "well-ordered community."[50]

## Women and Children

By June, things once again had fallen into place, a ship was promised and the files of the American embassy, the Peruvian Foreign Office, and the Spanish embassy yielded potential passenger lists of wives and children eager to join husbands and fathers as voluntary internees. Because the stepped-up tempo of the war precluded further cooperation by the War Department, the War Shipping Administration came to the aid of the Department of State and contracted with the Compañía Sud Americana de Vapores of Chile for the transportation of enemy nationals between Peru and the United States.[51]

Since an operation involving women and children promised to be different, some unusual questions and answers passed between Lima and Washington. What is the baggage allowance? It is 32 cubic feet per adult and proportionate amounts for each child. May mothers carry medicines for their children? Yes. May the women carry sewing machines and typewriters? No, to both. How much money can an adult woman carry? Up to three hundred dollars.[52] This information, and much more, the Spanish officials in Lima relayed to the interested women.

Except for three men, whose early repatriation the Japanese government had requested, the passengers were families of internees. The three men, all traveling alone, were forty-two-year-old Nobuo Yatoh of Lima, whose family was in Japan, thirty-two-year-old Masagi Yamamoto of Lima, and Jorge Kame Tameshiro, a twenty-six-year-old Nisei from Callao. One doubly fractured family consisted of motherless six-year-old Tokio Aita accompanied by his eight-year-old brother Hisao, the father of whom had been deported in January. The other passengers included twenty-eight women—one accompanying her married daughter, one with her daughter-in-law—and fifty-five children. Only one woman possessed Peruvian citizenship, but all of the Nisei children did. Five women were wives of men flown out of Peru in December 1942, nineteen were married to men of the January 1943 contingent, and two were wives of men of the February group—men who had themselves just recently arrived in the United States. The passengers included twenty-seven-year-old Hisako, wife of Ginzo Murono, who was interned at Kenedy, and their two children, four-year-old Toyoko and one-year-old Eisuke. Another mother, Fusae Ohashi, wife of Taro who also was at Kenedy, was accompanied by son Ken (age five), daughter Mirako (four), and son Mamoru (two).

The passenger list of eighty-six Japanese, all of whom were examined in Callao by a U.S. Public Health Service physician, was surprisingly, disappointingly small. Departing Callao on June 29, the *Aconcagua* landed them at New Orleans on July 15. The three men were shepherded to Kenedy, the remainder to Crystal City and family reunions. These reunited families overwhelmingly petitioned repatriation to Japan at the earliest opportunity. That proved to be a longer wait than the interval of separation just ended, and all settled down to the routines of camp life. Before leaving Texas fourteen of the twenty-six wives would give birth to a total of eighteen young American citizens. As Margaret Nan Williams, then a secretary at the Crystal City Internment Camp, put it, "There wasn't much else to do."[53]

The *Aconcagua* was still steaming toward the United States when a second vessel of the Chilean shipping line, the *Imperial*, called at Callao for more Japanese women and children. For a time the American embassy advocated sending several Peruvian police officers with the deportees, to enable them to observe American methods of handling the Japanese and, more subtly, to improve relations with the Peruvian Division of Investigation, but the idea, approved by the Department of State, was vetoed by the Peruvian Ministry of Government. Meanwhile the efforts of Peruvian, Spanish, and American officials were producing a passenger list of 105 Japanese and one German, all of whom were subjected to physical examinations at the Anglo-American Clinic. Because most of the families had come from towns north of Lima (Huacho, Chiclayo, Trujillo, Pimentel, Ascope, and elsewhere), they had been lodged temporarily in Lima in Japanese hotels that were reopened expressly for their convenience.[54]

Twenty-six of the thirty families were those of men deported from Talara in January, two anticipated reunion with men flown out in December 1942, and the remaining pair were families of February deportees. Accompanying twenty-nine mothers, three of whom were Peruvian Nisei, were seventy-three children who ranged in age from one to twenty-three. Management of the youngsters, none of whom fell overboard or suffered injury, combined shipboard regulations with firm parental discipline. Without the latter, Yasuko Higa's trip with a brood of seven, only one of whom was a teenager, could have been a nightmare.

For Chieko Nishino the whole affair was a sequence of heartbreaks. According to reports, she, after the deportation of her husband in January, had been living with a Peruvian officer. She no longer favored the voluntary internment she had once requested. When informed she must leave on the *Imperial*, she threatened to jump overboard with her two children. While gathering some personal belongings at her Lima residence, she did attempt suicide. How much of the social chaos injected into this family derived from American and Peruvian policy cannot be established. But close surveillance saw her and the children safely to America, where the estrangement ended. Eventually the reunited family would leave for Japan.

On July 27 the *Imperial* docked at New Orleans and the authorities ushered the Japanese onto a train bound for Crystal City. There, a few days later, their husbands and fathers, transferred from Kenedy, joined them. Like the families reunited by the voyage of the *Aconcagua*, these speedily petitioned repatriation. But before that occurred, ten of the wives who had come on the *Imperial* would give birth to eleven baby Texans.[55]

## Report from Lima

From midsummer to the end of the year no ship sailed with deportees, making 1943 resemble 1942, with some differences. The evasions, bribes, limited cooperation, frustration, and overall disappointment attending the evacuation of the Japanese aboard the *Shawnee* contrasted strongly with the trouble-free operations for the *Aconcagua* and *Imperial*. In mid-1942 word had come that the War Department could provide no more shipping; in mid-1943 word came that no more Chilean vessels would transport internees.[56]

In Lima Second Secretary Emmerson, the American most closely identified with the deportation of the Japanese, thought that his job was done, that the Japanese colony constituted no threat if, indeed, it ever had.

While looking forward to reassignment, Emmerson summarized the aims and accomplishments of the program in Peru under the following headings:

1. *Deportation of Leaders.* "Excluding diplomats, women and children, 606 Japanese have left Peru since April 4, 1942." On other occasions he had bemoaned the fact that so many of these deportees were inconsequential small fry and volunteers rather than expellees.

2. *Closure of Schools and Organizations.* These closures by the Peruvian government, with teachers and officers deported, had prompted some clandestine meetings, but the police had harassed the Japanese by arresting many for congregating.

3. *Prohibition of Travel.* Bribery and lax enforcement had weakened the effectiveness of the requirement that all Japanese possess government-issued safe-conduct passes (*salvo-conductos*) in order to travel from town to town.

4. *Withdrawal of Licenses.* Questionable enforcement had also attended the regulations that no Japanese could acquire licenses to hunt, fish, or possess firearms.

5. *Removal of Telephones.* Peruvian authorities had removed 150 of the 500 Japanese-held telephones which the American embassy had requested be disconnected.

6. *Prohibition of Short-wave Radios.* Recommended by the Americans, this step had not been acted on by the Peruvians.

7. *Censorship.* Despite Peruvian reluctance to institute official censorship, certain confidential arrangements had allowed American officials to examine a cross section of the Japanese mail.

8. *Cooperation with Police Authorities.* The statement, "The Embassy has enjoyed excellent relations with the Peruvian police authorities," suggests a diplomatic capacity to forget the inefficiency, lethargy, venality, and other complaints that had crowded communications between Lima and Washington.

9. *Removal of Japanese from Strategic Areas.* Peruvian orders and efforts to remove Japanese from certain areas, especially coastal towns, had never included any large-scale relocation program and had produced spotty results.

10. *Relocation of Japanese.* The serious problem resulting from the unemployment of many Japanese had provoked no official Peruvian action.[57]

Before his departure from Peru, Emmerson would also write a lengthy (over a hundred pages) report entitled "Japanese in Peru." A narrative-analytical account, the concept for which possibly derived partly from his recent study of Antonello Gerbi's writing about the Peruvian Japanese, it received considerable attention.[58]

"This looks like the kind of thing that will do the Department good when (after necessary editing) it is published," one official had said. For the sake of the Department, vigorous editing ensued. Next, in Lima, for the sake of the embassy, it was considered "advisable to rewrite pages 12 and 13 so that no member, or former member, of the staff of this Embassy could be open to the criticism of charging former officials of the Peruvian government with graft in connection with the Japanese emigration." Then, Peruvian sensitivity, among other things, prompted more changes in Washington. Next, after nine months of consideration and delay within the Peruvian Foreign Office, it was preferred by and for the sake of Peruvian officialdom that publication of the report be delayed. After the elections which were in the offing, Peru also reserved the right to suggest deletions and changes of phraseology.[59] By mid-1945 the aging report nestled in the files, for the sake of the kind of international harmony that avoids unpleasant truths.

## The Montana Camp

In the meantime, during the summer of 1943, the reunion of many families had lessened discontent at Kenedy and introduced stability and a certain felicity into life at Crystal City. Special problems, however, did persist—the case of Nikumatsu Okada's Peruvian funds, questions about the death and property of Ichiroku Yatomi, the hospitalization of sick children, and complaints about luggage damaged by eager American port officials. As usual, Spanish officials played their role as the protecting power.[60]

On the other hand, one large group of Japanese men, the 118 sent to Montana, faced problems of adjustment in this season. Fort Missoula, located approximately four miles southwest of Missoula on the bank of the Bitter Root River at an altitude of 3,000 feet, surrounded by irrigated tracts and ranching country, lay between two mountain ranges.

The INS facility, an abandoned army post, included many brick buildings. Those within the stockade housed the internees. The hospital, recreation building, and numerous warehouses stood outside the enclosure, as did the houses occupied by INS personnel and numerous barracks formerly used as a CCC camp. The detention area was enclosed by a high woven-wire fence along which the occasional towers were manned by armed border patrol officers. Staffing the hospital were two doctors and two nurses, employees of the U.S. Public Health Service.

Even though hundreds of Italian seamen, a few Germans, and an unknown number of Japanese Americans were already there, the coming of the Peruvian Japanese produced no crowding. Each man had beside his bed, which was either a standard army bed or a folding cot, a locker and a stool or a bench. Since the Montana winter brought temperatures of 15 to 20 degrees below zero, it was well that the heating systems were efficient.

The enclosure was divided into two sections, one for the Japanese, the other for the Italians and all others. Separate mess halls allowed the different nationalities and their native cooks—as one of them, Kunio Takeshita earned ten cents an hour—to cater to the desires of the two groups: lots of rice for the one, much spaghetti for the other. The laundry work fell mainly to the Japanese, the bread making to the Italians. One estimate was that thirty-six cents sufficed to feed one man for one day.

Tobacco products and miscellaneous items were available at reasonable prices in the two canteens. A welcome regulation permitted internees to write as many as two letters and four postal cards weekly, plus unlimited business correspondence.

The forty acres dedicated to recreation included fields for soccer and baseball, and volley ball and tennis courts. By far the most popular activity, soccer attracted so many participants that leagues were formed. Shinei Yakabi remembers playing on an Italian team. Frequently, in small groups, the internees made their way under guard to the nearby Bitter Root River for a dip in the swimming hole or a bit of fishing.

The organization and operation of this camp, like the other internment centers, relied heavily on the cooperation of the elected spokesmen of the different national groups. Complaints went to the INS officials by way of the spokesmen. Minor problems, not those related to camp regulations, were also handled by the spokesmen, who often assigned additional duties to those requiring disciplinary action.

The stay at Missoula, which acquainted them with summer, autumn, and winter in the Big Sky country, was easily the best chapter to date in the Peruvian Japanese experience—better than the temporizing at Sharp Park and not to be mentioned in the same breath with their Panamanian torment. Missoula conformed to the requirements set down in the Geneva Convention. Most men gained weight. Yet things were not as desired. One leader, the same Tochio who had earlier written the "Song of Farewell," now set down the bitterness of his forced exile from Peru and his loved ones in a communication which probably never reached the addressee, the Imperial Government of Japan.[61] In the meantime the second repatriation program had exchanged hundreds of Japanese for an equal number of Americans.

### The M.S. *Gripsholm*

Fifteen months had elapsed since the first exchange of nationals between the United States and Japan—months during which internees, Americans in the Far East and Japanese in the United States, had eagerly anticipated a second exchange and diplomats had doggedly tried to arrange it. Many delays previously met had recurred: the Japanese demands for designated individuals, objections raised by American agencies, language problems, transmission by way of the Swiss and Spanish representatives, and the refusals of some who were expected to repatriate. Throughout the negotiations Latin American Japanese moved in and out—the ten international merchants from Peru and Bolivia and twenty-five Japanese residents of Mexico designated by Japan, and the 226 Peruvian Japanese neither designated nor desired by Japan. Finally, however, on September 2, 1943, 1,340 Japanese did board the *Gripsholm* and sail from New York.[62] These Japanese genuinely represented the Western Hemisphere (see table 6).

Those from Latin America, totaling 737, represented 55 percent of the New York passenger list. Consequently 737 Americans won release from Japanese custody because an equal number of Japanese, as pawns, redeemed them. Although a rumored American desire to exchange additional Japanese civilians for American POWs did not materialize, the U.S. government did willingly use as trade bait hundreds of hapless Latin American Japanese, especially those from Peru, who represented 36.1 percent of this total exchange.[63]

For most, early arrival in the United States and early petitioning had paved the way to early repatriation. Of the 141 men who had disembarked from the *Etolin* in April 1942, 126 now embarked on the *Gripsholm*. The single-purpose patriotic fervor of that group is shown in the fact that, after the *Gripsholm* sailed, only two men of the *Etolin* contingent, one of whom was dead, remained in the United States. The 342 Japanese who had arrived on the *Shawnee* in June 1942 proved equally insistent on repatriation. Increased by two births in Texas, their number boarding the *Gripsholm* was 344. Fewer than 3 percent of those leaving for Japan had arrived in the United States after June 1942. Among them were the family of Naonobu Senoh, who, flown out of Peru in December 1942, had been joined by his wife and five children (passengers on the *Aconcagua*), the three men recently on the *Aconcagua* whose repatriation the Japanese government had requested, and school official Matao Daigo and his wife, the latter's arrival on the *Imperial* coming five months after his on the *Puebla*.

While the desire of the 1,340 was being fulfilled and others awaited a similar opportunity, the United States was indicating that it "would like to make another exchange with the Japanese Government to cover 1500 Americans for 1500 Japanese."[64] As before, American hopes faced stern realities that dampened prospects of another wartime exchange.

TABLE 6
The *Gripsholm*'s Passengers

| Home | Number |
|---|---|
| Peru | 484 |
| United States | 390 |
| Panama | 160 |
| Hawaii | 151 |
| Canada | 61 |
| Costa Rica | 36 |
| Mexico | 34 |
| Nicaragua | 6 |
| Ecuador | 6 |
| Cuba | 5 |
| El Salvador | 5 |
| Guatemala | 1 |
| Alaska | 1 |
| Total | 1,340 |

# 5

# Grinding to a Halt

Month after month in 1943 no ships moved Japanese deportees between Latin America and the United States and none moved internees toward Japan, but the operation of the internment camps and related activities in Washington and Latin America continued. In fact a survey of alien enemy control in all of the Latin American countries, completed in late summer by Ickes and Bell of the AECU, promised to increase those activities. Because no country of Latin America, with the exception of Brazil, had undertaken effective control measures on its own initiative, the AECU considered United States participation in the control programs imperative and urged the conclusion of additional deportation-internment agreements, especially with Chile, Uruguay, Paraguay, Venezuela, and Colombia. As an alternative, for countries that objected to sending dangerous Axis nationals to the United States for internment, they proposed that the United States support financially internment programs within those countries. Attorney General Biddle indicated that the Justice Department had already approved the internment of "283 persons in Chile, 130 in Bolivia, 92 in Paraguay, 23 in Uruguay, and 24 in Venezuela," and he hoped that the Army Transport Command would provide the necessary shipping.[1]

### Complaints, Requests, and Techniques

While some men thus bandied ideas concerning general programs, the specifics of life and death for individuals busied others. Complaints and protests took varied forms. The treatment accorded Alejandro Ouchi, one of the Panamanian Japanese, and his death at Fort Sill produced a barrage of exchanges. Military authorities insisted that his death less than one month after his arrival in Oklahoma was the result of inoperable cancer of the tongue. A Department of State circular instructing all missions in Latin America to obtain the services of reputable doctors to examine every individual immediately before deportation stemmed from this and other cases involving communicable or dangerous diseases, physical and mental.[2]

At Crystal City soaring temperatures elicited a request by certain Japanese that they be allowed to install air cooling units. Both temperature and need had lessened by the time Washington decided to deny such privileges for a few, if not available to all. More general appeals from Crystal City poured in, one seeking an eye, ear, nose, and throat specialist and—free to the needy—such dental work as bridges and false teeth. One complaint emphasized the smallness of living quarters that had not been planned for families with six, eight, and more children. Also, in the wake of the departure of hundreds of Japanese on the *Gripsholm*, a disproportionate number of Germans were being moved in, into areas beautified by Japanese. "Please allow as many Japanese as Germans to come to this Camp," begged the Japanese spokesman.[3]

While government agencies were planning to enlarge the internment program and internees urged improvements within the camps, one American organization had blasted the entire program. "Be it Resolved," read the resolution adopted at the national convention of the American Legion, "That we condemn the practice of importing into the United States aliens from other countries for detention in enemy alien relocation centers and request its discontinuance at once."[4]

Nevertheless, as the year drew to a close, the rising hopes of American, Spanish, and Peruvian officials centered on the likelihood of more deportee-internees moving toward the United States. In Lima the number of women and children who had informed the Spanish embassy of their desire to go to the United States kept growing, and Count de Bureta of that embassy personally thought that between three thousand and four thousand Peruvian Japanese would avail themselves of any repatriation opportunity.[5]

Proceeding apace were diligent efforts to oust individuals designated dangerous, of whom Yoshitomo Yamamoto was one. The FBI file on Yamamoto, established by the legal attaché in Lima, rested on four informants: "A" (a confidential source within the Peruvian police), "B" (a confidential source in the Peruvian Foreign Office), "C" (a Lima credit-reporting source), and "D" (a completely unidentified source). The case against Yamamoto included: (1) his service as secretary of the Asociación Japonesa de Comercio e Industria del Perú, (2) his employment by a company on the Proclaimed List, (3) his fidelity to Japan, and (4) insistence that he was one of the most fanatic Japanese in Lima. Supportive of informant D's statement that "it is well known that Dr. Caesar Cárdenas García, Director of Government, has been taking money from the more important Japanese and Germans in return for 'protection,' " some of which aided Yamamoto, was the report that Yamamoto had escaped expulsion on the *Shawnee*.[6]

The case study provided by the Yamamoto file not only shows how much information was gathered and the kind of information it was, it also raises questions about that intelligence-gathering process. Because informants were paid for information, did not their desire to get paid affect their information quantitatively? Knowing, too, that the Americans wanted to oust Japanese, did they not, on occasion, tailor information accordingly? No FBI personnel in Peru possessed a command of the Japanese language, and their informants suffered the same handicap. The Americans and Peruvians shared another handicap, an irrational hatred of the Japanese. Neither the FBI agent nor the informant ever confronted a suspect, a circumstance that promoted acceptance of unsubstantiated rumor, suspicion, and speculation. Given the participants and the absence of firm criteria for identifying "dangerous" enemy aliens, it is no wonder that life became a nerve-racking experience for countless Japanese.

At Kenedy thirty-eight Japanese asked that their families be allowed to come to them from Peru. At Missoula fifty-eight internees identified by name, age, sex, and precise home address the members of their families they wanted to join them. By the Christmas season the Spanish embassy in Washington had supplied the Department of State with eight lists of prospective voluntary internees, all of which fitted nicely with diplomat Muccio's suggestion from Panama that the U.S.A.T. *Madison* be used to transport enemy aliens from Peru and Ecuador to the United States.[7]

## Men First, Then Others

On January 18, 1944, the U.S.A.T. *Madison* cleared Callao with a passenger list that included thirty-nine Germans and twenty-nine Japanese.

Beginning in the closing days of December the latter—one sizable group of whom were seized at a birthday party—had been picked up and lodged in Lima's No. 6 jail. In an unhealthful, damp atmosphere, and forced to sleep on the cement floor, many spent more than two weeks. During that time no charges were lodged against them and the Spanish ambassador was denied access to them. Ranging in age from twenty-six to seventy-two, they came from Lima (seventeen), Callao (four), Tacna (two), and one each from Ica, Arequipa, Huacho, Huancayo, and Barranco. Included were eleven merchants, eight farmers, a dairyman, a clerk, a journalist, a coal dealer, a ship chandler, a barber, a student, and an office worker. Twenty-four were Japanese citizens, three were naturalized Peruvians, and one was a Peruvian Nisei. The names of eight had appeared on the Proclaimed List.

Trucked to Callao the night of January 17, the men and their baggage underwent two inspections, ashore by Peruvian custom authorities and aboard the *Madison* by Americans. In the rush of embarkation the men had no opportunity to protest, much less fix responsibility for the disappearance of money, razors, pencils, and numerous other items.

The five-day voyage between Peru and Panama these alien enemies spent below deck under guard with portholes closed. Daily respites did allow each man thirty minutes out on deck. As usual, too, they had to prepare and serve food and do general cleaning. At Balboa the men shouldered their baggage and disembarked through a throng of jeering soldiers and marines.

An hour's ride in U.S. Army trucks brought them to two wooden barracks in a detention camp in a desolate area of the Panama Canal Zone. There, for forty-one days, they knew one routine: out of bed at 5 A.M., assembly at the main gate to salute the American flag as it was raised, breakfast, work under guard with machetes and picks in groups of eight to ten, lunch at 11 A.M., work from 1 to 4 P.M., supper, assembly at the main gate to salute the American flag as it was lowered, into bed by 9 P.M.

Almost all of the men were ill-equipped for the work in terms of age, physical condition, prior occupations, and climate. Despite the terms of the Geneva Convention of 1929, they received no compensation for their labor. Other complaints centered on the nature of their food, lack of recreation, and inadequate hygiene and medical services. All this ended, however, on March 6, when, trucked back to the port, the men were surprised, on boarding the U.S.A.T. *Cuba*, to join hundreds of their countrymen.[8]

A week earlier, on March 1, the *Cuba* had sailed from Callao with 339 Japanese—more than half of whom were children, a lesser number of Germans, and a few Italians. The Japanese represented four categories: unmarried men, married men whose families were either in Japan or Peru, wives and children who were joining heads of families, and whole families. At least one passenger, Nisei accountant Pedro Minoru Hashimoto, like Arturo Shinei Yakabi earlier, believed that he had been framed.

Among the unmarried men were Victor Kazuki Tateishi, Jorge Hisao Fujii, and Shuhei Katsuro. Tateishi, a twenty-six-year-old Nisei law student at the University of San Marcos, had served the Spanish embassy for a year as liaison in Japanese matters. Twenty-eight-year-old Shuhei Katsuro had been a clerk for the cotton-trading company Peru Menka during his short two-year residence in Peru. Fujii was the thirty-three-year-old nephew of Sadajiro Yumoto whose deportation on the *Shawnee* had left him in charge of a chicken farm. Fujii was absent the day, February 11, that the police had left a note for him. When he promptly reported to the police station, he was instantly jailed. During his three weeks incarceration before the sailing of the *Cuba*, Fujii heard one Peruvian official insist that the United States, not Peru, was to blame for what was happening to him. Aboard ship the chicken farmer turned dishwasher.[9]

Some men, alone aboard ship, had families elsewhere. Dry goods merchant Hikoichi Hamamura of Huancayo had sent his wife and four children to Japan before the outbreak of war. Takichi Kaneshige, twenty-four of whose forty-five years had been spent in Peru, had left his native Peruvian wife and their five children in Lima. There, too, were the wife and two children of Sentei Yaki, a Peruvian citizen for the last sixteen years and a leader among fellow Okinawan immigrants for more than thirty-five years. Another naturalized Peruvian, Tadao Taniguchi, once untouchable because of influential Peruvian friends in high places, had sailed away from wife and children.[10] All had poignant personal tales to tell, but that of Hajime Kishi was exceptional.

Following his 1913 arrival, Hajime Kishi had delivered milk for a time in the Miraflores section of Lima. One of his customers, who became his fast friend as well, was the young diplomat Alfredo Benavides. With money borrowed from his wealthy lawyer-uncle in Japan, Hajime soon leased and operated about four thousand acres of cotton-producing land and established the Sociedad Agricola Retes Ltda., which he served as president. The company sold its cotton primarily in Japan and Great Britain.

During the May 1940 rioting the Kishi home was invaded and ransacked. Nothing of value was left. Even luggage packed for a trip was carried off and never recovered. A policeman who finally entered the house encouraged the departure of the rioters when he told them, "There's nothing more here." After a six-month trip to Japan, Hajime and the two oldest children, sons Masao and Katsumi, returned to Peru. Family matters detained Mrs. Kishi, who kept the three youngest children with her in Japan.

About October 1941 Alfredo Benavides returned to Lima from diplomatic duty in London, advised Hajime of the inevitability of war between Japan and the United States, and suggested that he delegate control of the Sociedad Agricola Retes Ltda. to someone with Peruvian citizenship. Kishi did so, and in this way the company continued operations for a couple of years after the outbreak of hostilities before its assets were frozen.

Meanwhile Hajime, on the Proclaimed List since March 1942 and considered a community leader, repeatedly had gone into hiding, joined by his sons, whenever deportees were being shipped out. On one occasion, however, Katsumi did not hide, and when police found him at home, he was seized and jailed. Turning to influential Peruvians, Hajime retrieved his son when his Peruvian spokesman chided the police for jailing a minor who had broken no law.

For the three Kishis—Hajime (fifty-nine), Masao (twenty-two), and Katsumi (nineteen)—time finally ran out. When friend Benavides went to Foreign Minister Alfredo Solf y Muro and tried to block deportation once again, he was told nothing could stop it, "The American Government has given us orders."[11]

Thanks to the *Cuba*, some long-separated families faced reunion. Otari Kaneko had not seen her husband Kakuaki for fourteen months when she and ten-year-old Shoichi, nine-year-old Shuji, six-year-old Momoko, and four-year-old Tsuneyo boarded that vessel. For widowed Aiko Yatomi and her two preschool children reunion meant claiming the ashes of Ichiroku.[12]

Anxieties accompanied all the deportees of March 1944 as they ventured into the unknown, but least anxious, surely, were those who traveled as whole families. Their economic interests might be total losses and the years in Peru shrouded in disappointment, but it was something for husbands and wives, parents and children, to be together. Juan Hiroshi Hachiya of Huancayo had fewer worries because his wife and four children accompanied him. So it was for Kensho Kishimoto, whose wife and five children were with him, and for dairyman Kengo Masaki, whose wife and six children were also on the *Cuba*.[13]

That day at Balboa thirteen of the twenty-nine men who had been hacking Panamanian underbrush for six weeks were surprised when they encountered families they had left behind in January. Masakado Hosokawa, sixty-three-year-old ship chandler from Callao, was reunited with his wife Tomiko. Lima farmer Takeo Sakairi embraced his wife and seven children. Also that day bakery-owner Junken Kamisato rejoined his wife and eleven-year-old Chiyeko, four-year-old Motoko, and two-year-old Yasuo. Fear of enemy submarines caused the trip through the canal, across the Caribbean, around Cuba (after a stop at Guantánamo), through the Gulf, and up the Mississippi to New Orleans to take fifteen days—time spent in cramped and ill-ventilated quarters.[14]

Despite previous experience, careful plans, and a battery of men representing the Department of State, Customs, Immigration, Border Patrol, Public Health, and the military, disembarkation proved tedious and time consuming. Instructions distributed as the ship approached New Orleans had alerted the passengers to the baggage inspection system, their meeting with INS men, the check by Public Health personnel, and the disinfestation procedure to which all individuals, clothing, and baggage would be subjected. A sick child sent one family to a hospital; all others boarded the waiting special trains. The men traveling alone headed for Kenedy, while the others set out for Crystal City. Late on March 21, as the trains moved across Louisiana into Texas, the weary, much-hassled, and bewildered Peruvian Japanese were fed for the first time in twenty hours. By the time they had settled into their Texas internment camps, their rising anger was triggering protests.[15]

Passengers, camp spokesmen, and the Spanish embassy voiced these complaints. The twenty-nine men originally on the *Madison* complained about that voyage and the food, forced and unpaid labor, the housing, and much more at the Canal Zone detention camp. Concerning the voyage on the *Cuba*, all complained about excessive crowding (as many as eleven persons had shared a four-berth cabin), distasteful meals noteworthy for shortages of fruit, vegetables, and bread, and the fact that Japanese women had been compelled to clean the toilets and bathrooms.

Specific personal complaints came from a number of enraged women. Kino Ikeda, traveling with four children, reported that as she boarded the *Cuba* in Callao a woman inspector had seized her money belt containing $500, of which she had recovered only $300, the sum one was entitled to have. Kimi Abe also had money troubles. Her $219 somehow became $119 in the hands of ship personnel. Tomiko Hosokawa declared that she had received a receipt for $45 instead of $105 for money deposited with a ship's officer.

These and other complaints received short shrift at the State Department, where it was established that the *Cuba*, a troop ship, had no laundry facilities and never issued bed linens, that the ship traveled blacked out in convoy, that "protest against such accommodations has no validity as they are voluntarily internees," which many were not. Officers and men aboard the *Cuba* were quoted as saying, "The group of Japanese transported on this voyage were the dirtiest and literally the lousiest bunch we had ever carried." A parting blast insisted that two hours out of New Orleans the Pullman cars carrying the Japanese "looked and smelled like pig pens." Additional reply was left to the INS.[16]

Later, forty-seven families reported the value of enumerated articles that were either missing or damaged during the trip aboard the *Cuba*. Kazaemon Ikeda listed face cream, toothpaste, a lady's nightgown, and a Panama hat—total value $27.20. The solid gold watch chain of Masakado Hosokawa, valued at $40.00, was missing. Some losses revealed a lot about the individual: consider forty-five-year-old Junichi Inayoshi's tools for sculpturing, two fountain pens, six bottles of hair oil, and six bottles of face cream. Even among doting mothers, Fumiko Kitsutani's loss of ten kilos of chocolate candy must have raised eyebrows, and Kensho Kishimoto's two dozen jars of face cream hinted at either excessive vanity or a budding commercial operation. In addition to all else, dozens of suitcases and trunks had sustained damage when customs officials used tools rather than keys to open them.[17]

These complaints were more rapidly formulated and more vigorously presented than those of earlier internee contingents. For one thing, these complaints fell into American administrative and Spanish diplomatic channels that by now were well known. The outspokenness of the Japanese women, contradicting their usual quiet and self-effacing demeanor, possibly derived from moral and psychological reinforcement their husbands provided. Furthermore, from both the earlier examples of demanding European Axis internees and their own widening awareness of provisions of the Geneva Convention, the Japanese had become more insistent on their rights. Camp operations had also demonstrated that internee spokesmen suffered no penalties for pleading the cases of their colleagues. To all else, the seemingly interminable internment before them and the basic injustice of their involvement must have provoked increased indignation.

### Program and Prospect

As the fighting in Europe and the Pacific intensified, complications arose. But the Department of State did give the problem of the deportee-internees some attention. Recognizing that this group probably faced internment until the end of hostilities, and then Axis nationals would be reluctant to be repatriated to devastated home countries, the State Department conceded that "the United States Government did not plan to repatriate enemy aliens against their will." But at the same time it avoided any discussion, much less agreement, with Peru and the other states about the prospect of returning the least-liked Axis nationals, the Japanese, to their former places of residence. Apparently a common problem posed by Germans and Japanese might produce different solutions. The internment program had started in 1941–42 with a minimum of firm agreement between governments; in 1944 it continued as something to be "played by ear." Meanwhile Secretary General of the Ministry of Foreign Affairs Javier Correa Elías revealed one aspect of the developing problem and the Peruvian position regarding it when he expressed "the desire that those nationals who are married to Peruvian women, have Peruvian children, or have legally adopted Peruvian citizenship, remain in the United States until the end of the war without being sent to their country of origin, save in the case of their expressing concretely their wish to the contrary."[18]

Finding the Peruvian government "more cooperative than ever before," the embassy in Lima anticipated and planned more deportations. In addition to the stifling effect of wartime trends on previously pro-Axis sympathizers, the established channels of intelligence gathering were also proving more productive. FBI reports bristled with information from "a high source within the Peruvian Extranjería," "a reliable source within the Peruvian Police Department," "a reliable Peruvian official," "a Peruvian thought to be reliable," and even from "a second-generation Japanese."[19]

Long in charge of German issues and heir to the Japanese problems after Emmerson's departure, Rolland Welch summarized the deportation program (see table 7).[20]

In every instance the national totals included diplomatic and consular personnel. Deducting them, the Japanese deportations numbered 1,367. Welch hoped that future deportations would include fifty-six dangerous Japanese males and 364 women and children left behind by men previously deported. Elsewhere in Latin America, official American estimates called for the deportation of fewer than 560 persons. The earliest reduction of any of those numbers occurred April 1 when a U.S. Army transport plane left Lima and headed for the Panama Canal Zone with six Germans and five Japanese.

## Second Voyage of the *Cuba*

While various agencies in the United States were reacting to the complaints of the *Cuba*'s Japanese passengers of March, that vessel called at Callao for more Axis nationals. Of the 377 passengers who left Peru June 17, some 347, or 91 percent, were Japanese who reflected the continuing desire of all concerned to reunite families, there being eighty-one women, 257 children, and only nine men in the group. Two of the men were traveling alone, as were nine women.

The seventy-two women, for each of whom accompanying offspring

**TABLE 7**
**Deportation of Axis Nationals from Peru**

| Nationality | Men | Women | Children | Total |
|---|---|---|---|---|
| Japanese | 727 | 197 | 469 | 1,393 |
| Germans | 401 | 120 | 122 | 643 |
| Italians | 26 | 12 | 11 | 49 |
| Total | 1,154 | 329 | 602 | 2,085 |

ranged from one to eight in number, would reunite (1) twenty-one families of men deported January 10, 1943, (2) forty families of men deported February 24, 1943, and (3) eleven families of men deported January 18, 1944. Unaccompanied, but led by fifteen-year-old Alfredo Minoru, were the seven children of Kotoku Yamashiro, a deportee of February 1943. The wife and mother in this Trujillo merchant family, a native Peruvian, had died in 1941. For almost eighteen months a Peruvian family had cared for the youngsters.[21]

Victoria Nakamura, thirty-six-year-old Nisei born in Supe, and her five children (ages sixteen, fourteen, ten, eight, and five), anticipated reunion with Katsue, formerly a photographer in Trujillo but then experiencing his second hot summer at the Kenedy Internment Camp. He was one of the deportees of January 1943 who would soon join his family at Crystal City. From the February 1943 group of internees, Taijiro Tochio and Mitsutaro Tarawa would soon shift from the all-male facility to the one for families. With thirty-year-old Luisa Villanueva Tochio, the Peruvian wife of sensitive and outspoken Taijiro, had come three children (ages seven, four, and three). From Cañete Kiwa Tawara, a forty-seven-year-old citizen of Japan, brought her five Peruvian-born children to rejoin husband and father Mitsutaro. Joining highly respected Ichitaro Morimoto, the seventy-two-year-old naturalized Peruvian who as the oldest member had suffered most among the twenty-nine tormented by their springtime in Panama, was his sixty-six-year-old wife Ko, another naturalized Peruvian. The Monma family promised a three-generation reunion, because with Kumayo, wife of January-deportee Eisaburo Monma, had come daughter, son-in-law, and four grandchildren.[22]

While this second voyage of the *Cuba* was still under way, authorities in Lima had rounded up seventeen men, eight Germans and nine Japanese, whom they considered immediately expendable. Another plane despatched them. Among these expellees was Nakataro Aray, of whom it was sufficient for the authorities to say, "Subject has long been prominent as a leader of the Japanese colony in Peru." With assets of $16,800, this father of six was a conspicuous success story, the kind that endlessly irritated many Peruvians of less energy and ability. Aray had arrived in Peru in 1908, and in 1915 had established the first Japanese bazaar in Lima. On rented land his success as a cotton farmer led to managerial posts with Sociedad Agricola Retes Ltda. A founder of the Central Japanese Association and a member of the Third Sunday Club, a reputedly elite group of the most influential Japanese, Aray was admired by some, feared by others. "He is reported," one investigator concluded, "to have at one time paid 10,000 soles [$1,600] to a Peruvian official to escape deportation."[23]

Another expellee in this group was Jiro Hasegawa of Lima. There the fifty-six-year-old Hasegawa, a resident of Peru for twenty-three years, a citizen since 1929, had operated the light bulb factory Fábrica Nacional de Lámparas Eléctricas "Diha," S.A., which the United States had speedily consigned to the Proclaimed List. Also a member of the influential Third Sunday Club, he reportedly had avoided deportation for two years owing to protection by powerful Peruvians.[24]

## Life in the Camps

Because the two family-laden voyages of the *Cuba* had prefaced the transfer of scores of men from the Kenedy camp to the one at Crystal City, the INS concluded that a few more shifts would enable them to close the Kenedy operation. Even before the *Cuba* had left Callao on its second trip, and before the seventeen men were flown out of Peru, the INS had canvassed internees at Kenedy to learn if any wished to volunteer to go to Kooskia, Idaho, to work on a road project. Among those responding were seventeen Peruvian Japanese.[25]

Neither the road project nor internee identification with it was new in mid-1944. Under the general direction of the Public Roads Administration the wartime construction of the Lewis and Clark Highway, in need of workers, had turned to the INS and its internees in 1943. That move was the first American experiment in the use of Japanese alien internee labor on a government construction program. That September twenty-one-year-old Arturo Shinei Yakabi and his friend and fellow internee of February 1943 deportation twenty-eight-year-old Seiho Inamine had volunteered for the roadwork. They had spent five weeks at Missoula, and their youthful energy and curiosity was combined with an urge to get outside the internment camp. Yakabi, Inamine, and scores of others moved to Kooskia, where they lived at an old CCC camp. From that base the workers went daily by truck to blast and clear the route of the projected highway.

Yakabi became a member of a five-man drilling crew. Each man had to drill three feet of the fifteen-foot hole into which a charge of dynamite was inserted. At times a worker with a rope around his waist lowered himself down the face of a slope to do the necessary drilling. For such work an internee received fifty-five dollars per month and enjoyed wonders of nature unknown in Lima and Callao. After four and one-half months of work amid the rocks and snow of the rugged setting, Yakabi and others were called back to Missoula, because the contingent in which they had come was leaving for Kenedy, Texas.[26]

The movement that sent men from Montana to Texas was followed at once, in February 1944, by the shift from Texas to Montana of volunteers from the group that had initially left Peru in January 1943 from Talara. What prompted their volunteering can only be conjectured: accounts of those incoming men who had worked at Kooskia, the monotony of life at Kenedy, the desire to avoid the heat of a second south Texas summer, and so forth. At any rate, the sizable number of Peruvian Japanese in this second Kooskia contingent included men who had been barbers, mechanics, restaurateurs, bakers, merchants, farmers, chauffeurs, cooks, and others.[27]

Then, in May, as many married men were soon to move from Kenedy to Crystal City, the call for Kooskia volunteers was raised again. For Yakabi the recollection might have been sufficient, even if camp monotony and hot weather had not influenced him and others. This time, for him and over a dozen other internees, the months in the Northwest—the housing, the work, the pay—were as before.[28] These men, the last group of Peruvian Japanese at Kooskia, never saw Kenedy again.

After the Kooskia-bound men left Kenedy, the authorities, in late August, transferred the remaining men to an INS facility at Santa Fe, New Mexico, and in September the Kenedy Internment Camp closed out its two-and-one-half-year history.[29] By this time the unity of the contingents as deported, once scrupulously maintained, had completely disappeared.

The Santa Fe Internment Camp resembled some other INS operations—like Seagoville, a former prison property, like Kenedy, possessed of old CCC barracks, like Crystal City, a barbed wire stockade within city limits. L. H. Jensen, the officer in charge when the Peruvian Japanese went there, was soon succeeded by Ivan Williams, an administrator some had known at Missoula and Kenedy.

At this all-male facility the internees slept in barracks heated by pot-bellied stoves, performed all of the maintenance work of the camp, and ate meals consisting chiefly of rice, fish, and green vegetables at thirty-eight cents per day per man. They operated a twenty-acre truck farm that yielded nine thousand dollars worth of produce yearly. They earned ten cents per hour when working at other than assigned duties. One such job, the demolition of a German internment camp at Fort Stanton, found Yakabi, a two-time road builder at Kooskia, active in the work force.

For these much-traveled internees the social and recreational life at Santa Fe was much the same—movies, judo matches, ping-pong, Japanese plays, softball (on four diamonds), cigarettes, and Coca-Cola. As elsewhere, the men elected spokesmen who relayed their requests and complaints to the INS officials.

In several respects, however, the Santa Fe experience proved to be different. For the first time, according to Kunio Takeshita, the INS permitted a camp newspaper. Published in Japanese with a minimum of censorship, the Japanese copy was roughly translated for INS approval prior to printing and distribution free to the internees. One could also subscribe to Japanese language publications from the outside. Saburo Ushida received one that was published in Denver. The internee population, which peaked at twenty-one hundred in mid-1945, included Germans, Italians, and Japanese. The latter included many Japanese Americans, among them former teachers who conducted academic classes, one on Americanism.[30] Eventually the determined struggle by many of the Japanese Americans to win release from internment would bring lawyers to the camp. In time the Peruvian Japanese, hard-pressed by yet another threatened deportation, would need and find legal aid, first at Santa Fe.

As the men moved to Santa Fe and the camp at Kenedy expired, the one at Crystal City entered its peak period. The rapid influx of Peruvian Japanese families, combined with Japanese American and German families already there, meant that after mid-1944 the educational program, among others, had heavy demands on it.

In the spring of 1943 R. C. Tate had resigned as principal of Crystal City High School to become education director at the camp. There it was his duty to establish and operate three schools. Planned to meet the needs of the English-speaking Japanese American children, the American school consisted of grades one through twelve, taught by American citizens, following the Texas curriculum and enjoying state accreditation. The German school, employing internees as instructors, used mimeographed materials conceived to serve the needs of the curriculum devised by the staff. The Japanese school, the one attended by the children from Peru, also used internee instructors and mimeographed materials.

The American school began operations in October 1943. In the launching of the others, shortly thereafter, the Japanese proved much more cooperative than the Germans. In all three schools instruction occupied the children from 9 A.M. to 4 P.M. five days a week.[31]

In and out of school the children, especially the little ones, unconsciously helped to break down blind hatred. An illustrative episode is recalled by Tate. The guards, eight to ten of whom were always on duty, either at perimeter stations or inside the camp, were generally grumpy and given to grumbling about how the internees had it better than American citizens amid shortages of butter and other necessities. But one day Tate saw one of those gruff guards "melt."

A kindergarten class from the Japanese school, led by Tate, was taking a short stroll, termed a field trip, outside the camp. Of course a guard had to accompany the energetic enemy aliens. Babbling, skipping, and flitting one way and another the children fell to picking wildflowers. Everyone gathered flowers. About to reenter the camp ground, one little girl moaned that she had dropped hers.

"Can I go back for them" she asked.

"No, I'm sorry you can't go back now," Tate responded.

But even before the youngster's disappointment could cloud her face, the guard, previously surly and uncommunicative, had turned back to pick some blossoms for the little Japanese girl. Explaining his action to Tate, he said, "You can't hold these little kids responsible for what got their parents here." At higher levels than guard, many at Crystal City did not know what had brought the parents of the children there. One explanation among the INS personnel was that when the United States requested four men, Peru had said, "You will have to take all the others." Speaking from his experience at Kenedy, camp commander Williams once declared, "It seems to me that those heads of governments in Latin America arrested anybody not born in their country and sent them to us as alien enemies. A lot of them don't know what they're doing here. I can't say I do either, but we try to keep their minds off their troubles."[32]

As a teenager, Kiyoko Naganuma, second oldest of the seven children of Iwaichi and Isoka Naganuma of Callao, was old enough to remember the camp well. For two years, time that stretched far beyond the end of the war, she attended the Japanese school where all instruction was in that language. Kiyoko played mandolin in a band that included guitars, saxophones, clarinets, and accordions, and she performed in plays directed by Buddhist priests from Hawaii. Kiyoko entered public speaking contests, in one of which she won a medal. Her subject was "Heiwa" ("Peace").[33]

A mere four-year-old on her arrival there, Eugenia Yoshiko Kato nonetheless remembers Crystal City. Yoshiko was the third from the youngest of Chuhei and Michiko Kato's seven children when the family left Lima. To her, Crystal City was a small town, where she went to school, kicked cans, went swimming, and talked through the fence with Americans while her father was busy delivering ice in the camp at ten cents per hour and oldest brother Tadahiko was working in the camp commissary at the same wage."[34]

For young children, life at Crystal City presented few, if any, experiences that scarred them. The crowding so distasteful to their parents and others did not disturb four- and seven-year-olds. The compact community pleased them. Their little town was satisfyingly complete, even if on occasion one did look longingly beyond the fence. School and games and play occupied most waking hours in ways pleasant to recall. Toward dusk little ones often played hide-and-seek as they ran among the housing units. Earlier in the evening older brothers played volleyball and baseball.

When it proved impossible to use government funds for something so frivolous—so pampering for interned enemies—as a swimming pool, the camp authorities circumvented regulations by constructing a large circular concrete storage basin of varying depths which doubled as a reservoir for irrigation purposes. German internees built the tank, and in its role as swimming pool it proved an absolute boon to camp life until one hot August day two small Japanese girls, beyond the cable separating the shallow and deep waters, drowned.[35]

For physically active males the camp community offered many opportunities and diversions. Most important, perhaps, was the measure of freedom from responsibility that the baseball diamond, the football field, the billiard table, and the volleyball courts afforded, not to mention the sumo wrestling, *kendo*, and swimming. In sum, the camp presented a wide array of time-consuming activities for energetic persons with lots of time to kill. Few young men or adults seriously concerned themselves with English, the language of the land that had interned them yet denied them the prospect of permanent residence, not to mention citizenship. So completely in a world apart, the Peruvian Japanese easily became the butts of cruel "teachers" outside the classrooms—individuals who enlarged the English vocabularies of unsuspecting internees by introducing them to the vilest words and phrases. When it was not downright dirty, the English often was wildly incongruous. One Nisei remembers being taught to greet members of the opposite sex with the declaration, "I love you."

Amid circumstances strange, artificial, and of uncertain duration, more and more fathers felt a weakening of their authority as head of the family, and parents generally sensed a diminution of the values and unity the family had long treasured. But, from oldest to youngest, camp life did teach the internees to face the uncertain future with increasing adaptability.

Families as units, while viewing life in the internment camp variously, had few carefree moments. Consider the Tawara family. It was Independence Day 1944 when Mitsutaro, who had been deported from Peru in February 1943, joined his family at Crystal City. At Missoula and Kenedy he had disdained work opportunities, but at the family camp he was again head of a family, one that included wife and five children who ranged from six to twenty-one years of age.

Their housing, uncomfortable in both summer heat and winter chill, offered little privacy and bred complaint. Again the provider, in a sense, Mitsutaro took a job in the camp delivering ice. Driving the ice truck about four hours daily was nineteen-year-old Victor, who like his father was earning ten cents every working hour. Mitsutaro alone knew how much his working was an example, to impress that much-respected work ethic on sons attaining manhood. While the two doubled as icemen, the eldest son, twenty-one-year-old Toshiharu, performed office duties that brought him into daily contact with many internees, along with their hopes and complaints. He and other young men of eighteen and older received three dollars monthly for incidentals, usually cigarettes.

While father and two sons were at work and three subteenagers attended school, Kiwa Tawara busied herself not only with familiar household routines but with some strange ones as well. Like the housing at the WRA camps for Japanese Americans, Crystal City housing allowed unwanted dust and dirt easy entry around ill-fitting windows and doors and up through faulty floors. Keeping the place as clean as a tidy Japanese housewife insisted it should be demanded constant attention. Also, while learning to cope with the allowances—the coupons for clothing, food, and so forth—the women entered a strange new world that frightened and challenged them. Family conferences preceded trips for supplies, expeditions which, in concert with others, became social occasions. Later, with change of seasons and mounting desires, families with funds brought from Peru, and dollars earned in camp, leafed through the mail-order catalogues that camp authorities had obtained.[36]

More important, for many families, than surmounting the problems of physical survival was the cultural side of their fractured lives. Insisting on their identity as Japanese—many looking forward to repatriation to Japan—they wanted their children to emphasize their study of Japanese in order to minimize any penalty accompanying their transfer to Japanese schools. This emphasis on their Japanese heritage, reinforced by the production of Japanese-language plays, speaking contests, movies, and more, simultaneously repudiated the prospect of Americanization. But try as they might, many traditional Japanese families saw their values losing the battle in the prolonged presence of democratizing, Americanizing forces.

Internee complaints continued in the established channels: by way of the Spanish embassy to the Department of State and finally to the INS, which, in turn, looked to the camp administration for answers. When internees complained about concrete floors, they were told they could add any covering they wanted, at their own expense. When internees asked for "maternity houses," they were informed that the request was "very much out of order," for there was no such kind of housing available. Claims pressed by the men who had spent unpaid days laboring in Panama and by those who had sailed on the *Cuba* induced continuing investigations. One claim was different: Shigeru Kawakami's loss of part of a finger while working in a camp laundry led to a request for compensation under the Geneva Convention of 1929.[37]

## Influence and Bribery in Peru

For some time, unknown Peruvians had thwarted American efforts to expel designated Japanese from Peru. But as the war continued the veil of secrecy was gradually parted, revealing the identity of many individuals who through influence, connivance, or outright bribery—sometimes a combination—had delayed or staved off completely all expulsion efforts.

Pivotal in the racket that enabled Axis nationals to evade deportation was a ring led by Director of Government César Cárdenas García, Chief of Investigations Moises Mier y Terán, Prefect of Lima Gonzalo Becerra, and Chief of the International Department of Police Carlos Aguirre. A reliable informant insisted that Mier y Terán, whom Emmerson once described as "an energetic, blustering roly-poly little man," planned to grab the lion's share of the protection money paid by Japanese. Learning of this, Cárdenas García forced Mier y Terán to divide the booty equally. The operation of the ring included use of the rented Hacienda Cueva as the hide-out for the "lucky" Japanese. On one occasion four leading Japanese reportedly on the deportation list—Nakataro Aray, Hajime Kishi, Seigoro Kawamoto, and Genichi Araki—were approached and victimized. Each paid 10,000 soles ($1,600) to Cárdenas García to escape deportation. Informed of this incident, Minister of Government and Police Ricardo de la Puente secured affidavits from the four Japanese, which contributed to the undoing of some of the ring. Eventually the utterly unscrupulous Cárdenas García was removed from office, Mier y Terán became ex-chief, and Becerra ex-prefect.[38]

At many other levels and in numerous ways, powerful individuals, often well paid to exercise their influence, stayed the deportation of moneyed Japanese. In 1943 a Huancayo grocer, Koichi Manuel Kawai, warded off apprehension and deportation for a year through the intervention of local officials and the payment of 5,000 soles. That same year, when Lima merchant Yoshisada Shiga was arrested for deportation, he won release and hid out for a time. Protected by a prefect and a subprefect outside Lima, his escape cost him 10,000 soles. Senator Ismael Ganoza Chopitea of the Department of La Libertad blocked numerous deportations, among them that of Pedro Kishinosuke Yoshimoto, a naturalized Peruvian. Deputy R. Morán interfered to enable Nakataro Aray to evade deportation. Police Commandant Humberto López Rubio ordered the release of several men arrested for deportation, among them two brothers, Onishiki and Ikiro Okada. Victor and Raúl Zapata served as go-betweens for their uncle Colonel Arturo Zapata Veiez, director general of the Guardia Civil y Policia, who reportedly sold safe conduct passes, generally for 100 soles ($16) each. Alejandro Barrios, President Prado's secretary, reportedly received "protection" money from Seigoro Kawamoto. Alberto Noriega Calmet, son of the director of Banco Minero and an employee of the Superintendency of Economy and one handling the liquidation of Axis firms, was suspected of having transferred the firm of T. Kurotobi and Company to his wife.³⁹

In Mexico a noteworthy episode attested that neither Peru nor Peruvian officials had a monopoly on the irregular handling of Axis nationals. In May 1944 all the German and Japanese residents in the state of Chiapas were ordered by Lic. Eduardo V. Ampudia, Jefe de Investigaciones Políticas y Sociales de la Secretaría de Gobernación, to travel to distant Mexico City, presumably to be restricted within the Federal District. In Mexico City, however, a shakedown commenced. Following payment of approximate $100–$150 (500–750 pesos), an individual was permitted to return to Chiapas, where he remained as long as he continued to pay 100 pesos monthly. For some wealthier persons the initial charge was as much as $300. All arrangements were conducted orally through Lic. Enrique Lozano G., a former partner of Ampudia's. These Mexican bribes were termed lawyers' fees.⁴⁰

On occasion the Peruvian *quid pro quo* for help was not clear, as when Luis Miró Quesada, director of Lima's *El Comercio*, saved his former butler, Seijiro Tabata, from deportation and when wealthy lawyer José de la Riva Agüero interceded and won release for Tomiji Koizumi. Questions also concern others: was it friendship or professional counsel that Javier Arias Schreiber, a legal adviser of police headquarters, gave barber Furuya?⁴¹

Some Japanese scheduled for deportation, such as Seigoro Kawamoto and Genichi Araki, remained in Peru, usually at a price. Others, such as Luis Sadaichi Ishikawa, the possessor of considerable land and commercial interests in and around Ayacucho, apparently were never even threatened. Was it his friendship with the prefect of the Department of Ayacucho, his leadership in Rotary and the Chamber of Commerce, his $1,600 donation to a Eucharistic Congress, his marriage to a Peruvian woman? Just what was it that guaranteed his immunity?⁴²

Still others, such as Hajime Kishi and Nakataro Aray, apparently exhausted their pocketbooks, their influence, and their patience, for they eventually suffered deportation. From the standpoint of certain deep-seated characteristics of the Peruvian way of life—the small payments (*coima*) expected by ill-paid police and other functionaries and the not-infrequent bribery of higher government officials—what happened was not unexpected by the Japanese. Nor from the standpoint of those Japanese, eager to salvage business, maintain family unity, and escape the humiliation of undeserved internment, are their efforts to save themselves difficult to understand.[43]

## The Last Voyage from Peru

As 1944 wore on the Department of State continued to support Peruvian aims of expelling Japanese at the earliest possible moment. Blunting these prospects, however, was Department of Justice policy. Only twenty-one Japanese met the criteria for deportation. Coupling that fact with the remote possibility of a third exchange of nationals, it was held that the Peruvian government's "wishes to expel would seem to present a question for solution after active hostilities are ended. SWP [Special War Problems] strongly recommends that assistance to Peru in this respect be made a definite part of this Government's program for post-war action."[44]

Fortifying official Washington's anti-Japanese stance was forty-seven-year-old Pedro Beltrán, who had presented his credentials in mid-July as the Peruvian ambassador to the United States. At that time, Beltrán insisted, President Roosevelt had indicated that the United States would eventually return the Japanese in this country to Japan. Roosevelt denied having given Beltrán any such assurances; the American government had no plans for returning large numbers of Japanese to Japan after the war. Revealing the intensity of Beltrán's anti-Japanese sentiment was his belief that even those who had been naturalized as Peruvian citizens should be expelled from Peru. His rabid interest in ridding Peru of all its Japanese quickly struck some officials in Washington as the obsession of a "considerable nuisance."[45]

Following the heavy movement of families from Peru in March and June, the desire for more such efforts persisted. Men who had left Kenedy for Santa Fe had listed the family members they wanted brought from Peru. In Lima the embassy soon indicated that 127 Japanese wished to join internees. Anticipating a ship in mid-October, the deportation machinery once more got into operation. However, when Ambassador John C. White reported that only ten Japanese and ten Germans would sail, disappointment was registered in Washington in the single word "disgraceful."[46]

The last ship to deport Axis aliens from Peru to the United States left

Callao on October 11, 1944, after picking up thirty-two passengers, ten Germans, and twenty-two Japanese. In microcosm the twenty-two represented many aspects of the conditions and problems associated with the more than seventeen hundred Peruvian Japanese who had preceded them. Lima was home for most of them. Their occupations included farmer, baker, jeweler, waiter, laborer, and dry goods merchant. They ranged in age from one to fifty-seven. Most of the men were Japanese citizens but one had become a naturalized Peruvian. There were Okinawans and *naichijin* in the group. Two of the women were native Peruvians, and every family included children.

One family, that of Koho Gushiken, included his wife, four children, and his father-in-law. Oddly it was his wife's role as teacher rather than any activity of his that led to their departure. Reminiscent of those wives and children on the two voyages of the *Cuba* was Micaela Kage's sailing with her eight children to join the head of family they had not seen for twenty-one months. Only three of the seven men in the group were on the list that the AECU had approved for deportation. For more than two and one-half years two of the men had been on the Proclaimed List. Matsu Ishikawa, a fifty-six-year-old farmer, readily admitted to American authorities that his employment on the estate of a relative of President Prado's had prompted Peruvian officials to try to revoke the order for his deportation.

When the passengers, both German and Japanese, were asked why so many had declined the opportunity to join internees, it was said that the feeling was widespread that the Axis powers were about to lose the war and most did not want to return to defeated homelands. To avoid a repetition of past problems, the baggage searches were conducted only in the presence of representatives of both nationalities. By the time the *Frederick C. Johnson*, earlier the carrier of two all-male contingents between Peru and Panama, had transited the Panama Canal, it carried 134 internees, from Bolivia, Costa Rica, and Ecuador as well as Peru.[47]

Since numerous shiploads of internees from the west coast of South America had generated hundreds of complaints, one would expect considerable expertise in such operations after two and one-half years. However, the October voyage of the *Frederick C. Johnson* was freighted with unlimited potential for increased, not diminished, complaint.

The one-time Hudson River vessel, converted to troop carrying, failed miserably when men, women, and children were involved. The enemy aliens occupied two holds. The women and children were quartered in the afterhold, a space approximately fifty by forty feet with bunks in tiers of four. Lacking guardrails of any kind, those bunks were exceedingly dangerous for small children. To reach this afterhold one had to pass through the area occupied by the men. To enter the only latrine on the ship for their use, the women and children had to go through the men's quarters. Scheduling use of the latrine by both sexes, plus the necessarily frequent closing of the area for cleaning, posed extremely unsatisfactory conditions. Drinking water was unavailable between 9 P.M. and 7 A.M., and during the entire voyage there was no fresh water for bathing or washing.

For part of the trip neither hold had a single chair, bench, or stool. The aliens either sat on their bunks or on the deck. The absence of tables forced the passengers to juggle their mess kits and eat in their chairless quarters amid oppressive odors from the latrine. Lieutenants Cottrell and Casey of the Escort Guard tried to relieve the situation by getting the aliens out on deck as often as possible. There, however, one had to stand, because more than 130 persons were restricted to an area six by ninety feet.

Atrocious neglect characterized the medical care of the internees. The ship lacked both medicines and medicinal supplies, and medical officer Captain Philip Orlando demonstrated neither interest nor initiative. At Panama Lieutenant Casey felt compelled to go ashore in search of a doctor.

The embarkation at Panama of sixty-seven repatriated seamen from the Pacific war zone compounded these problems. All the way to New Orleans, an around-the-clock guard was posted to prevent the seamen from attacking the Japanese.

Finally the ship docked, on October 21, and the usual checks and disinfestation procedures took place. The following day the internees departed New Orleans, the family elements for Crystal City, the single men for Santa Fe.[48]

## While the Fighting Continued

Those Axis aliens in Peru who had declined the opportunity to join interned heads of families because of the deteriorating military position of the Axis powers had correctly interpreted the news from the war zones.

## Grinding to a Halt

The crest of Axis expansion had passed. By mid-1944 the Normandy landings had started the challenge in the west that Germany was never able to halt. Soon, in the south, the northward sweep captured Rome and Leghorn. Off to the east Rumania and Bulgaria were eliminated militarily by the Russians, who pressed toward Belgrade on one front and broke into Czechoslovakia on another. Paris and Antwerp had fallen. While German fighters were falling back on all fronts, German civilians in Peru and elsewhere lost their earlier enthusiasm for repatriation.

In the Pacific more and more engagements were resulting in Japanese defeats. The naval blows dealt Japan in the Battle of the Philippine Sea followed closely on the American invasion of Saipan, and one island in the Marianas led to others as marines and soldiers stormed onto Guam and Tinian. Soon American fleets were pounding Okinawa and Taiwan, and invading forces had secured the Palau Islands. After dealing Japan another naval defeat, Americans had invaded the Philippines. Meanwhile Mariana-based B-29s were bombing Tokyo and other Japanese cities. Like Germany's Europe, Japan's western Pacific had shrunk sufficiently to discourage many would-be repatriates. Peru's declaration of war against Japan in February 1945, a political move, altered neither the course of the war nor Peruvian treatment of the Peruvian Japanese.

For some families births and deaths made life in the internment camp during the second half of 1944 a succession of beginnings and endings. Babies arrived at Crystal City at the rate of about two a month. Among the mothers were four women who had come in July 1943 on the *Aconcagua,* one who had come that month on the *Imperial,* and at least a half dozen from the *Cuba,* most of whom were pregnant when they boarded in March. The birth of a third or a fifth child, however joyous the occasion, carried limited social impact compared with the death of a head of family. In July 1944 Isamu Watanabe died at Crystal City. A month later Eiichi Suzuki's death at Brooks General Hospital, San Antonio, left his wife Kin with five children to care for. In September the wife of Jiro Hasegawa died at Crystal City, and the following month forty-seven-year-old Hikoichi Hara, a baker from Trujillo, died at Santa Fe from peritonitis due to a gangrenous appendix.[49] In 1945 such vital statistics would be appreciably higher.

As winter settled in and the tempo of fighting slackened, those removed from theaters of operations knew a brief calm before the fury renewed. Men at desks in Washington and Lima, parties to this watchful waiting, urged no roundups of "dangerous" enemy aliens, much less their deportation and internment. In Crystal City the welcome release from summer heat soon yielded to unwelcome chill. Some new complaints arose, joining old unfinished business.

The Spanish government, soon to surrender its role as protecting power, doggedly pursued the remaining claims that stemmed from the unpaid work of Japanese in the Panama Canal Zone in 1943. Another set of claims that persisted, those filed by passengers on the *Cuba* concerning money and property, rambled beyond the civilian agencies into military circles and additional delay.[50]

From out of the west the spring of 1945 brought additional Japanese to Crystal City. Eleven family groups of Japanese Americans came from Hawaii. From Tule Lake, the relocation center that had become segregation center, came a few more.[51]

The baby boom at Crystal City continued, at an accelerated pace. In 1945, down to the mid-August surrender of Japan—which had absolutely nothing to do with such matters in Texas—little Japanese American citizens were born to Peruvian Japanese parents at the rate of four to five a month. For the Kakumi Kaneko and Masao Saiki families the children were first-born. For José Kiyoto Makimoto and his wife it was the seventh child. Three families must have acknowledged their multiple births with special celebrations—the Maekawas, Nakachis, and Oyamas all welcomed twins in Texas. The third child of Takeji and Nobu Hiramine entered this world the same day that so many departed it in the bomb blast over Hiroshima. The Hikozo Izumi family represented graphically the kinds of tangled citizenship to which internment was contributing. Hikozo held Japanese citizenship, his wife Masako was a Peruvian Nisei, one child was Peruvian-born, and now their second child was American.[52]

Meanwhile, on widely separated fronts, the Axis powers were being beaten into submission. In the Pacific area this year of decision brought landings on Iwo Jima, carrier attacks preliminary to the ground assault on Okinawa, a steady rain of fire bombs on Japanese cities, and the last-gasp madness of the kamikaze counterattacks. In Europe the East-West pincers squeezed more life out of Hitler's Germany as Warsaw fell in January, Budapest in February. Americans and others crossed the Rhine in March, and the Russians occupied Vienna in April. Germany, reduced to less than the Germany that had initiated warfare in 1939, was getting smaller by the hour when unconditional surrender in May brought an end to the European hostilities.

Less than a month before, at a moment when fighting was fiercest on Okinawa, the last Peruvian Japanese to be deported was hurried by plane to San Antonio, then on to Santa Fe. In Peru since 1908, fifty-five-year-old Carlos Ichitaro Matsuda had succeeded in stock-raising, fruit and cotton cultivation, and wine production. Prominent in affairs of the Central Japanese Association, this naturalized Peruvian citizen reportedly had boasted of his influential Peruvian friends.[53] A measure of uncertainty clouds the reason for his belated ouster from Peru, but quite possibly it was a parting shot at all those whose influence had stayed their deportation.

# 6

# Beyond War's End

The surrender of Germany brought peace in the Atlantic, a greater intensity to warfare in the Pacific, and a prompt reminder from the Peruvian Foreign Office that the deported Germans interned in the United States could not be sent to Germany against their will. American officials wondered whether the Peruvian attitude regarding the interned Japanese would also change. A month later, however, while American forces were consolidating their position on battle-torn Okinawa and sending successive waves of heavy bombers against the main islands of Japan, the embassy in Lima reported, "The Peruvian Government has shown no interest whatsoever in any disposition that may be made of these Japanese and all officers of this Embassy heartily agree that all the Japanese should be returned to Japan." At midyear the INS reported holding 1,333 Japanese from Latin America, the overwhelming majority from Peru. The closing of the Seagoville Internment Camp (June 1945) had also concentrated the Peruvian Japanese at the Crystal City and Santa Fe camps.[1]

In anticipation of the approaching peace, President Truman, three weeks before the first atomic bomb hit Japan, had issued Proclamation 2655 concerning the removal of enemy aliens. It provided that all such persons "deemed by the Attorney General to be dangerous to the public peace and safety of the United States ... shall be subject upon the order of the Attorney General to removal from the United States and may be required to depart therefrom in accordance with such regulations as he may prescribe."[2] The Department of Justice, having played a limited role in bringing the internees into the country, presumably would control their departure.

In the meantime, while American authorities appeared to be gearing up for deportations, the wartime channel of communication for the Peru-

112

vian Japanese was temporarily disrupted when Switzerland succeeded Spain as the protecting power for Japanese interests, a move dictated when Madrid severed diplomatic relations with Tokyo. The atomic bombs dropped on Hiroshima and Nagasaki compounded confusion among the internees and inspired numerous Peruvian Japanese to petition once more for their return to Peru.[3]

The Japanese continued to goad American officials, but the German internees were the ones then receiving attention. Longer in Latin America, better known and more highly regarded, the Germans commonly possessed economic clout, political influence, and social acceptance foreign to most Japanese. Peru illustrated this fact of life when the American desire to implement Resolution VII of the recent Mexico City Conference by completing the deportation of dangerous enemy aliens from the Western Hemisphere encountered Peruvian insistence that the United States could not unilaterally ship German internees to Germany. One Peruvian cabinet member had a German wife, another had a brother-in-law among the German internees, and the sister-in-law of newly elected President José Luis Bustamante Rivero, married to a German, had died during an American air raid on Hamburg.

Similarly high-placed pressure emanated from other Latin American leaders whose wartime cooperation had sent Germans to the United States. In Costa Rica the American ambassador accepted President Teodoro Picado's demands regarding German internees and urged the United States government to do likewise or face diplomatic tensions. Buttressing Picado's position was a writ of habeas corpus issued by the Costa Rican Supreme Court, which demanded that the president produce a certain German then interned in the United States. Related problems concerning American desire to deport German internees and official Latin American opposition thereto took shape in El Salvador, Ecuador, and elsewhere. As this U.S.–Latin American chasm developed, a Department of State memorandum which suggested that the United States should "acquiesce in any requests that the Peruvian Government may make for the return to Peru of individual internees," concluded with the thought, "Whatever attitude this Government may adopt, it would seem more politic to proceed with the repatriation program only after full and frank consultation with the Peruvian Government on a case to case basis."

Complicating the matter further, certain German internees scheduled for early deportation had filed habeas corpus suits as one means of staying their deportation orders. Meanwhile the Department of Justice, secure in its legal right to detain them, was not certain it had authority to remove internees from the United States. Likewise troubling to the Justice Department was the probability that some internees might present prima facie evidence that they were not enemy nationals, in which case they could not even be held in custody.[4] For the time being such matters as preferential treatment, full and frank consultation, case by case consideration, and habeas corpus proceedings were wasted on the more docile, less powerfully connected Peruvian Japanese. But the time would come when they and their counsels would profit by the furor initially raised by and on behalf of German internees.

Now a new set of differences appeared within the American bureaucracy. For many months the differences between the willingness of the Department of State and its agents to accept and act on the official Peruvian desire to deport any and all of the Japanese and the insistence by the Department of Justice that legal norms attend the resultant internment program had affected relations between those departments. But the combination of circumstances that lessened, then ended, the deportation program had rendered the internment of the Latin American enemy aliens manageable, and State–Justice friction had dissolved. The end of warfare, however, signaled new differences.

Weary of its increasingly dubious internment operation, the Department of Justice's INS speedily sought to rid itself of every internee. When some of them instituted habeas corpus and other legal actions, the department envisioned the problem as the resolution of legal issues. The Department of State and its overseas diplomats, on the other hand, viewed quite differently the opportunities afforded by the end of hostilities. Their implementation of a grand strategy which aimed at the long-term removal of German, Japanese, and Italian influences even suggested the desirability of stepped-up investigations that might result in more deportations, more internees. Putting the postwar world into the political and economic shape desired by the State Department did not coincide with the single-track and legalistic outlook of the Justice Department. Indeed the State Department's willingness to continue and expand certain wartime practices had another not so subtle purpose. The more complete the harassment and removal of late enemy nationals and their operations, the more complete the economic void to be filled by Americans, their products and capital. After World War I and heavy losses in Latin America, Germany had nonetheless regained economic importance there. This time the German defeat should result in a more complete removal of German economic strength. Consequently, at war's end the single-purpose, short-range, legal considerations of the Department of Justice and the multifaceted, long-range, political and economic considerations of the Department of State invited no harmonious outlook regarding internees, either Peruvian Japanese or German.

By late August questions concerning the handling of the remaining alien enemy internees provoked a meeting of Justice and State Department officials. Assistant Attorney General Herbert Wechsler explained the reluctance, on legal grounds, of the INS to deliver German internees to the State Department for repatriation to Germany. In reply A. E. Clattenburg of the Special War Problems Division declared that although the original intention of speedily repatriating the internees had not materialized, the Department of State never intended to allow such persons to remain in this country indefinitely. Nonetheless, both a legal adviser and a visa officer readily admitted that the State Department had no authority to remove the internees. Consideration of ways to establish that authority prompted the suggestion that the State Department might secure a proclamation from the president. A draft proclamation went off almost immediately to the White House.[5]

A few days after the Japanese surrender ceremonies aboard the battleship *Missouri*, President Truman willingly obliged. Proclamation 2662 declared, "All alien enemies now within the continental limits of the United States (1) who were sent here from other American republics... and (2) who are within the territory of the United States without admission under the immigration laws are, if their continued residence in the Western Hemisphere is deemed by the Secretary of State prejudicial to the future security or welfare of the Americas... subject upon the order of the Secretary of State to removal to destinations outside the limits of the Western Hemisphere...." In less than two months the main responsibility for removing the Latin American internees had been shifted from the Justice to the State Department. However, this latest proclamation did direct the Department of Justice and all other American agencies to assist in this matter. As the Justice Department's Alien Enemy Control Unit suffered eclipse and the Department of State prepared to establish an Alien Enemy Control Section (AECS), past practices and future prospects were being studied.⁶

Searching for a viable policy that could be implemented within parameters set by the Alien Enemy Act of 1798, the resolutions of the Rio de Janeiro Conference of 1942 and Mexico City Conference of 1945, and the presidential proclamation of September 8, the Department of State first noted the human dimensions of the problem (see table 8).

A proposal of the Special War Problems Division of the department insisted that all internees be considered for deportation to Japan, Germany, and Italy. This raised the issue of orderly procedure, something that had not troubled the same officials when the deportation from Latin America had occurred. The additional suggestion that the decisions regarding deportation to the Axis homelands be based simply on a review of the files, rather than hearings, fostered indignation within the department. "It is not too much to say," declared a memorandum, "that this crowning disregard of basic notions of fairness and decency would earn for this program an equal place with the Mitchell Palmer raids and the anti-alien crusade that followed the first World War."

Preliminary assessment of the problem led to these conclusions: (1) a painstaking administrative review of the cases should occur within the department, (2) hearings should be provided, if requested, and (3) those whose removal from the hemisphere is judged unnecessary should be (*a*) assisted in their efforts to return to the Latin American countries from which they were deported or (*b*) allowed "to regularize their residence in the United States." By coincidence, at the same time these recommendations were emerging within the Department of State, Roger Baldwin, who had founded the American Civil Liberties Union in the early 1920s

TABLE 8
The Internees from Latin America, as of July 1, 1945

| Nationality | Interned in Camps | Interned at Large | Voluntary Internees | Total |
|---|---|---|---|---|
| Germans | 415 | 243 | 157 | 815 |
| Italians | 17 | 32 | 4 | 53 |
| Japanese | 454 | 0 | 849 | 1,303 |
| Total | 886 | 275 | 1,010 | 2,171 |

partly because of the Mitchell Palmer raids, was urging fair and humane handling of the internee issue.⁷

Established on October 24, the Alien Enemy Control Section, under Assistant Secretary for American Republic Affairs Spruille Braden, was charged with "the initiation of policy and action with respect to all matters concerning the disposition of alien enemies...."⁸ Adherence to the earlier recommendations suggested that considerable time would elapse before action became the order of the day.

## Looking Toward Japan

In the same season, the dramatic finale of the war in the Pacific had not unexpectedly injected anticipation and activity into previously dormant men and matters. Hundreds of Japanese desirous of going to Japan could do so, some believing they were going to a victorious homeland, others facing the bleak reality. At any rate, ships would be available and shipping lanes safe. Hundreds insistent on returning to Peru also considered their future free of obstacles. Beginning with the last week of August and continuing into mid-October, eager internees and equally anxious internment officials faced one another.

Once again the officials asked each family head if he wished to petition repatriation to Japan. For numerous reasons those signifying their desire to do so signed the appropriate forms. The most frequently stated reason was loyalty to Japan. Bunsei Yamashiro, a thirty-eight-year-old former teacher in Lima, declared, "As a loyal subject of Japan, I wish to return to Japan." A mechanic from Huacho, forty-three-year-old Yoshio Okinaga, put it quite simply, "I am a Japanese so I am going back to Japan." Perhaps it was exultation over a presumably victorious Japan, perhaps deep-seated disgust over internment when farmer-baker Fumio Endo snapped, "I want to go back and live." Former importer Tokumatsu Otani, exuding more caution and curiosity than assurance, said, "I wish to be repatriated to Japan because I know I would not be relieved until I see it."⁹

Along with unquenchable love of country, loyalty to family prodded many toward Japan. This tie could be doubly strong, involving both love for wife and children and love for aging parents. Kengo Masaki, a Callao dairyman, had brought his wife and six children with him to the United States and now, on September 5, 1945, he was insistent, "I wish to return to Japan with my family." For Saju Takaki, a one-time Chiclayo merchant, family figured differently. The presence of his wife and three children in Japan led him to say, "I deem it my duty to be repatriated to Japan and take care of them." For his wife as well as himself Luis Masaru Muroy, a fifty-year-old laundry owner from Lima, declared, "I desire to see my mother and my two children who are in Japan." Sometimes the magnet drawing a man back to Japan was his special relationship as eldest son. Fifty-one-year-old Niichi Chiba, whose wife and five children were in Japan, said, "I am the first son of our family and it is my duty and obligation for me to return to do my share at this time." Even as he indicated that as eldest son he wanted to support his parents in Japan, Kensho Kishimoto found his loyalties in conflict as he asserted, "but if the Japanese Government says for all persons formerly living in Peru to return to Peru, I would like to return there." The call to duty posed by aging parents also affected merchant Hachiyoshi Nakamura, importer Hikozo Izumi, and merchant Noboru Mizuta, among others.[10]

While, for many, going to Japan was completely desirable, for others it became a lesser of evils rather than a positive choice. Such was the case with Kamei Kobashigawa, who lamented, "I have lost practically everything in Peru and have no future in Peru." The same sentiment permeated hacienda administrator Zenkichi Oda's statement, "I have nothing left of my properties so I am forced to go back to Japan." Plaguing many, and propelling them toward Japan, was an awareness that they were unwanted in Peru. October 12, 1945, Piura merchant Kunio Haraguchi bluntly said, "I do not desire to go back to the country where I am not wanted." Three days later Yoshihisa Muto, an engineer from Arequipa, declared, "as I have been interned from Peru, I think there is no place to go but to my native country." Pedro Minoru Hashimoto, a Nisei accountant who insisted that foul play had accounted for his deportation and internment, said, "Though I am a Peruvian citizen, I have been interned in this camp. I wish to be repatriated to Japan because my wife is a Japanese citizen." Unmarried Nisaburo Inaba, a Cañete barber, decided on repatriation "now the Peruvian Government made it clear that they do not want us back there." Still another lesser-of-evils statement came from factory worker Shigezo Matsubayashi when he declared, "Since I am interned I haven't anything else to do except to be repatriated to Japan."[11]

Others going to Japan with limited enthusiasm included sixty-two-year-old Kurata Moriyama, who confessed, "I am old and cannot work." The unmarried men, a group that included Hisao Shibukawa and Toshiaki Muto, often admitted that they had no ties in Peru. Occasionally, too, the reason for going to Japan was not completely clear. Such was the case of the fifty-year-old teacher from Supe who announced, "Although I have my family consisting of wife and child living in Peru, I would like to be repatriated all by myself."[12]

## Looking Elsewhere

Those wanting to return to Peru offered some of the same reasons, including love of country and family. Saburo Ushida, a Chiclayo merchant whose twenty-two years in Peru had not altered his Japanese citizenship, declared, "My loyalty is to Peru, where I have substantial property. I have no property in Japan. Since the children are still young, I desire to be permitted to return to Peru and support and educate them." Carlos Ichitaro Matsuda, a naturalized citizen for twenty-two years, asserted, "I wish to return to Peru and support and educate my children." Manuel Enrique Ikari, a Nisei who had spent all of his twenty-nine years in Peru, insisted, "I am a Peruvian citizen by birth and have never been in Japan." Another Nisei, baffled by his internment and determined to return to Peru, twenty-three-year-old Arturo Shinei Yakabi told the officials, "My parents and brothers and sisters all are living at Hacienda Bocanegra, Lima, Peru. My home is at no other place but in Peru." Banemon Takahashi, who had not seen Japan since his arrival in Peru in 1915, declared, "My property is mostly in Peru. I am loyal to Peru and wish to be permitted to return to my family there." Zensuke Shiroma and Ricardo Kanashiro, both unmarried, sought to return to Peru because their fathers were there.[13]

Economic prospects had encouraged every immigrant to forsake Japan for Peru initially and now served to draw some back there. Bakeryman Shizuo Taura, many of whose fifty-two years had been spent in Cañete, fortified his request to return with these words, "I have enough funds to start bakery business again in Peru without asking financial aid from any one." For Shogoro Nakamura, who had grown cotton in the Huacho district for twenty-three years, it was simply a matter of saying, "I am a cotton grower ... I wish to go back to Peru and engage in the same occupation." Uncertainty plagued others but still the urge was there, witness

Koshiro Mukoyama, a forty-three-year-old importer-merchant, who said, "I could only live in Peru because I know its language well.... Furthermore my children are majoring in the Spanish language."[14]

Still others desirous of returning to Peru mingled shock and bewilderment. Ricardo Toshiaki Nakagawa, a Catholic dry goods merchant with a native Peruvian wife, declared, "I am unable to understand why I was removed by Peru," to which he added, "the American authorities are very nice to us." Both Genji Nimura and Sentei Yaki, naturalized Peruvian citizens of long standing, although confused and bitter, were nonetheless loyal to their adopted country and eager to rejoin their families. Sorrow and frustration continued to be the lot of Aiko Yatomi. More than twelve months after her arrival she declared, "I came to the United States to get the ashes of my husband to take them to Japan with me. But as yet I have not received them. As I have never been to Japan ... I do not wish to go to Japan. I was born in Peru ... [and] we feel that Peru is our country."[15]

A few Peruvian Japanese, declining repatriation to Japan and not mentioning return to Peru, surely surprised the officials. Believing that his beloved "Okinawa was left in ruins," thirty-nine-year-old Yoshiharu Oyakawa hoped that he could take his wife and five children—one a Texan—to Hawaii. Ryusuke Oshiro, the ailing member of the 119-man contingent of 1943 who later returned to a hospital, unabashedly declared, "I desire to stay in the U.S.A." Yuzo Shibayama, having read letters from internees that reported that they were well treated, had gladly come to the United States. Even as he expressed a desire to return to wife and family, he concluded that he was "better off to leave Peru." Possibly the most forceful Peruvian Japanese statement in this vein came from Seiichi Higashide. The thirty-seven-year-old merchant of Ica, whose Nisei wife and five Peruvian-born children were with him at Crystal City Internment Camp, declared, "I wish to stay in the United States with the whole family and I wish to educate my children in the United States."[16] In 1945, however, the mood of Americans and the laws of the land did not brighten that prospect for any Peruvian Japanese.

### Internee Dissension

Now, as peace beckoned, dissension increased among the internees. Years earlier, when they were being deported and interned, a common tragedy, the fracturing of their way of life, had tended to unite the internees. Then common misery had diminished, if it had not eliminated, previous divisions, and well-to-do and sophisticated citizens of Lima had been almost as one with rustic provincials from small towns. Even that air of superiority indulged by *naichijin* as they looked down on Okinawans in their midst in Peru had lessened. In the long interval between the *Gripsholm*'s sailing of September 1943 and the end of the war, unity and camaraderie had characterized the Peruvian Japanese internee community.

Now the opportunity for dissension had provoked dissension. As heads of families thought about and discussed their Peruvian experiences, their American internment, and their postwar hopes and prospects, the peace that sped the realization of some hopes split the internee community. Some of those desiring repatriation were pro-Japan for many reasons: the superiority of Japanese culture had impelled the retention of their Japanese citizenship and the education of their children, the invincibility of Japanese arms had led many to believe that the American version of the outcome of the war was a monstrous lie, and family ties had fortified inclinations to turn away from Peru. On the other hand, many who wanted to return to Peru felt as they did because they had families there and because they remembered that meager economic opportunity in Japan had impelled migration from that country.

The leisure time of camp life increased the opportunity for debate, bitter remarks, and name calling. "How can you, a member of the Yamato race, turn your back on your homeland?" "How can you possibly want to return to a country whose government callously deported you—you with decades of residence in the land, you without an encounter with the police until that moment when they swept down on you, jailed you, and put you aboard a ship for an unknown destination?" Emotion and logic locked in verbal combat, the outcome of which was an ever-widening chasm between the pro-Japan and pro-Peru internees. Even less understandable, to those wanting to go to Japan, was the pro-United States position of a few. "How can you look with favor on a country at war with the mother country?" "How can you forget that American pressure led to your deportation, the upset of your family, the wrecking of your business?" "How can you forgive the Americans for putting you within barbed wire enclosures where armed guards occupy watch towers?" This was not the dichotomy of Issei with their love of traditional Japanese values versus the love of the new land by the Nisei. Rather it was Issei versus Issei.

The desires, whatever they were, of the generally preadult Nisei sons and daughters were totally subordinated to the desires of their fathers.[17] As men reached decisions for themselves and their families, the unity of the internees, however temporary and artificial it had been, shattered. Nor was it merely the bitterness of brief moments, because unfortunately the first postwar shipping available to take anyone to Japan did not begin to separate these bickering factions until the closing days of November.

## Sayonaras by the Shipload

One young internee who had an unusual opportunity to observe the results of the factionalism within the Peruvian Japanese community inadvertently compiled a record of some of it. Toshiharu Tawara, the twenty-two-year-old son of Mitsutaro Tawara and the eldest of the five children who, along with their mother, had voluntarily left Peru in 1944 to be reunited with the head of the family, held a clerical position in the camp office at Crystal City. At his desk he witnessed the uncertainty plaguing so many. His work included rendering assistance to those who elected repatriation to Japan as they completed the related paperwork. Many persons filed the petitions that offered them expense-free travel across the Pacific. Later, sometimes a matter of days, on other occasions after weeks, even months, men rushed back to him and asked, "Do you still have my request for repatriation? I wish to withdraw it." If told it was already being processed, the next words were, "How can I cancel it?"[18]

In January 1945, when the Department of State publicized the possibility of a third repatriation voyage to Japan, a rush of requests had ensued. Later, when Okinawa fell to the Americans, daily air raids blasted the main Japanese islands, and atomic bombs hit two populous centers, the trickle of requests to withdraw petitions for repatriation turned into a torrent.[19]

On and off his job affable Toshiharu had numerous contacts within the community, and when the autumn opportunity for repatriation did materialize, many of his friends said their good-byes in an autograph book he had recently purchased. For some, the last words were of fun remembered. Kentoku Higa, whose Japanese greeting mentioned their good times together in the classroom and on the baseball diamond and the football field, added in Spanish, "I will not forget you ... so long." Some farewells, often those of female acquaintances, were cast in traditional sentiments, as when fifteen-year-old Atsuko Uchiyama and Tomiko Uozaki wished Toshiharu health, happiness, lots of luck, and the determination to struggle hard. Others, heading Japanward with parents and brothers and sisters, spoke wistfully of Peru, with more than a trace of nostalgia. Takeshi Sugiyama and his sister Shigeko did so as they readied for the voyage that found their father turning his back on Peru after thirty-three years there.[20]

The teasing tone of a friend crept into Fumiko Yoshinaga's greeting when she interrupted her Japanese with Spanish to say, "How are you Cañete?"—a reference to Toshiharu's hometown down the coast from Lima. Most entries in the autograph book simply closed "in the American wartime internment camp" or "in the Crystal City Internment Camp," but a bitter note occasionally sounded, as when seventeen-year-old Kimiko Watanabe mingled her hope that Toshiharu would realize his dreams in his "future" country with the reminder that they were then "in the internment camp of the enemy country."[21]

Some of Toshiharu's youthful well-wishers eagerly anticipated their voyage to Japan. Michie Matsubayashi had cherry blossoms on her mind as she and eight other members of her family, one a Texas-born sister, prepared for the long trip. One evening "in the Japanese dining room of the internment camp," Shintaro Nakashima embellished the greeting he had stroked in Japanese with a sketch of a ship approaching Fujiyama. Cherry blossoms and Mount Fuji, romantic symbols of traditional Japan, symbols learned at home and in the Japanese schools they had attended in Peru and Texas, beckoned youngsters who had never seen Japan.[22]

One Nisei whose identification with Peru was doubly evident, in his name Francisco and the language he employed, wrote, "I hope that you may be happy all your life together with your very dear family." For young unmarried internees the sense of family unity, deep in their culture and presently reinforced by close confinement in hostile and alien circumstances, repeatedly revealed itself. How many were proceeding farther into the unknown out of a sense of duty to family cannot be established.

Another Nisei, writing, as he put it, "just before my departure for Japan," typified the affection and the torment that beset parting friends. Lucho Kenji Maeoka unburdened himself in Spanish, "I know you value me as I value you, joined together in studies and games. Now as I part from you I leave this writing and picture as my only record. God grant that in the future you will not come to forget this camp at Crystal City.

If we meet a second time, let us remember our youth. Before I close I wish for you and yours a way full of happiness. Tawara is is an unforgettable name for me."[23]

These farewells were penned between November 28 and December 1. One week later, 660 Peruvian Japanese from the Crystal City Internment Camp, aboard the S.S. *Matsonia* as family units, were sailing toward Japan.[24]

The families varied greatly in size. Lima tailor Kohei Gushiken had only his wife, while Yasuo Tsuchiya and his wife Harue had a brood of nine, the oldest scarcely of working age, the youngest a three-month-old Texan. Merchant Masaji Watanabe, separated from $14,080 worth of assets in Peru, had his wife Shima and seventeen-year-old Kimiko beside him. Three children accompanied Rensuke Higa and his wife, but a fourth, son Renyu, became quite the exception when he remained behind at Crystal City. Ex-Lima merchant Shigeru Sugiyama, after spending thirty-three of his fifty-four years in Peru, faced toward Japan with his wife Hideko, four Peruvian-born children, and an infant whose birth certificate read "Crystal City." The families of Shozo Uozaki and Sakutaro Maeoka, the former a Lima merchant, the latter a carpenter from Trujillo, each had eight members. Shigezo and Natsuko Matsubayashi were shepherding their seven children, the youngest an American by birth.[25]

In every instance, among those families aboard the *Matsonia*, the future required adjustment to Japanese life by two generations under the stress of the unusual postwar conditions. The dispersal of these returnees rendered impossible any study of their acculturation, but concerning the children one thing seemed certain: because of their stronger sense of tradition, and stronger language training, the Peruvian Nisei were better prepared for entry into Japanese life than most Japanese American renunciants.

In the meantime, another reduction of the number of Peruvian Japanese internees had taken place in New Mexico at the all-male Santa Fe Internment Camp. The passenger list of the U.S.A.T. *General Randall*, which had lifted anchor on November 25 for Japan, included 138 Peruvian Japanese, men whose ages ranged from the low twenties to the seventies. Most of them were merchants—former owner-operators of groceries, bakeries, restaurants, and stores specializing in dry goods, glassware, coffee, clothing, hardware, poultry, and fish. Next most numerous were the barbers—old and young men from Lima, Trujillo, Cañete, Paita, Huancayo, Callao, Pisco, and other Peruvian towns and cities. The *Randall* was also transporting farmers, clerks, waiters, importers, salesmen, teachers, watchmakers, masseurs, printers, cooks, and others—an occupational cross section of the Peruvian Japanese community. All were Japanese citizens, even though many had spent decades in Peru.

The motives for their return to Japan varied and frequently involved more than inextinguishable loyalty to the land of their birth. Approximately one-third were married. Most of them were rejoining wives and children who had preceded them to Japan before the outbreak of the Pacific War. Such was the case with Lima farmer Niichi Chiba, Callao merchant Takeo Gibo, Lima merchant Ryohei Koike, Lima merchant Heiji Miyakawa, Lima bakeryman Toshio Shimura, Lima printer Kaneichi Takahashi, and others.[26] The precise reasons for the early withdrawal of the families of these men are not known, but it seems logical, since most of them were businessmen of the Lima-Callao area, that the anti-Japanese riots of May 1940 prompted numerous heads of families to send their wives and children to Japan for safety. For childless husbands who were rejoining wives, as for those with children, the repatriation voyage was a matter of reuniting families, of facing up to responsibilities.[27]

For a few, however, the *Randall* afforded escape from responsibility. A barber from Trujillo opted for Japan although his native-born Peruvian wife and their three children remained in Peru. Another selfish internee, a teacher from Lurín, had left his Japanese wife and their two children in Peru.[28] But these were rare exceptions, and probably reflected the disintegration of families.

Like those board the *Matsonia*, the Peruvian Japanese males crossing the Pacific on the *Randall* were both eager and despondent, hopefully looking ahead and confusedly recalling the past. One was Kamei Kobashigawa—Japanese citizen, salesman, age thirty-seven, apprehended by Peruvian police December 19, 1942, jailed in Lima, sent by truck to Talara, put aboard the *Frederick C. Johnson* January 10, 1943. Concerning his deportation, unsure American embassy personnel could only say, "Appeared on no previous list." Was he seized merely to fill a quota? Or was he the unprotesting replacement for a more important person who had forestalled deportation by making a deal with Peruvian authorities?

Internment for Kobashigawa meant eighteen months at the Kenedy Internment Camp and fifteen months at the Santa Fe Internment Camp—thirty-three months of detention, for what? When he petitioned repatriation, he declared, "I have lost practically everything in Peru and have no future in Peru." Sailing for Japan he could wonder whether he had a future there.[29]

Another was Samatsu Uema—Japanese citizen, cook, age forty-seven, seized by Peruvian authorities in Piura, January 7, 1943, and seventy-two hours later put aboard the *Frederick C. Johnson*, his deportation recommended by the U.S. embassy because he was "resident in strategic area (near Talara)." His Peruvian home was a hundred miles from the American installation; his American internment was thirty-three months, at Kenedy, and Missoula, and Kooskia, and Santa Fe. Now the widower could at last rejoin his children, who were in Japan.[30] Along with Kobashigawa and Uema many others of the group of 168 who had sailed from Talara were now en route to Japan aboard the *Randall*.

In February 1943 the Peruvians and Americans had arrested and deported 119 men. After months of internment and hard labor in the Panama Canal Zone they had reached the United States in June. Now, after twenty-nine months at internment camps in California, Montana, Texas, and New Mexico, more than two score of them were aboard the *Randall*. Among them were Nisaburo Inaba, a fifty-nine-year-old unmarried barber from Cañete, Masao Mochizuki, a forty-eight-year-old teacher whose family remained in Supe, and Tetsuo Suwa, a thirty-three-year-old merchant from Ica whose wife awaited him in Japan.[31]

In March 1944 the *Cuba* had deposited 368 Peruvian Japanese, many as family groups, at New Orleans. Only a few, therefore, traveled with the all-male contingent aboard the *Randall*. Among them were Jorge Kinsaku Fujishima, Haruemon Oguchi, and Kinsuke Tamashiro. Fujishima, a fifty-five-year-old merchant from Lima, was the father of four children living in Peru. Rationalizing his request for repatriation to Japan, he had said, "I feel that it is no use to apply for nonrepatriation and try to go back to Peru at present." Oguchi, a brilliant twenty-six-year-old economics student at the University of San Marcos in Lima was unusual in that he was identified by a fellow internee as a Japanese espionage agent. Behind Alberto Bunken Tosa, in Peru, were thirty-five years of hard work and assets valued at $109,600. As a farmer Katsuo Nakasone faced his bleak prospects, "All of my property are confiscated by the Peruvian Government." Forty-seven-year-old Tamashiro, after fourteen years in Peru and twenty months in American internment camps, anticipated reunion in Japan with his wife and family.[32]

A few men who had been deported in the late summer and early autumn of 1944—men who had spent between thirteen and seventeen months in internment camps in Texas and New Mexico—also were aboard the *Randall*.[33] They were as confused and uncertain as fellow passengers who had endured internment twice as long. The *Randall* carried many kinds of men, but the prevailing mood aboard it was somber, made more so by the complete absence of comforting women and playful children.

During the postwar weeks before the departure of the *Randall*, the Peruvian Japanese at the Santa Fe camp had experienced the same factional strife that had flared up at Crystal City. Matching those for whom love of family, loyalty to Japan, and disgust over the treatment accorded them by Peru and the United States were uppermost were scores of others whose emotional, social, economic, and other ties with Peru superseded all else. Later the men at Santa Fe who yearned for Peru would fight verbal battles with American authorities, but in the late summer and early autumn of 1945 emotional outbursts, interminable arguments, and bitter name calling had separated the pro-Japan and pro-Peru factions there. Once again some Issei stood for traditional Japanese values while other Issei demonstrated a transcendent identification with an adopted country.

By year's end the December 29 sailing of the U.S.A.T. *General Gordon* from Portland, Oregon, with 4,258 passengers, only seventeen of whom were Peruvian Japanese, enabled the INS to report that 7,159 Japanese, chiefly Japanese Americans, had departed for Japan since VJ Day. The feelings of one of those seventeen from Peru, Hisao Shibukawa, rang in his words, "I have no interest in Peru." At Crystal City lower temperatures and reduced dissension made life a bit more tolerable. For the Peruvian Japanese males at Santa Fe it was much the same, except for those whose lengthening separation from families in Peru meant increasing despair. The all-male facility bred a gnawing loneliness which may, in part, have contributed to the relatively high death toll there. Kakichi Takahashi, a forty-five-year-old barber from Pisco, died in August, and widower Kosuke Asato, another barber, in October. In November Nakataro

Aray's death spelled hardship for his wife and six children in Lima, and word of Segoro Kawai's death had to be conveyed to wife and children in Japan.[34]

## Straws in the Winds

Among American officials, the INS eagerly looked forward to closing every internment camp and the Department of State focused on certain internee-inspired litigation. In several instances German internees from Costa Rica and El Salvador had filed habeas corpus petitions in federal district courts, claiming that they were not natives or citizens of an enemy country and therefore not alien enemies as defined by the Alien Enemy Act. The United States, possessing insufficient evidence, did not even contest some cases; others were pending. Some writs of habeas corpus had also been filed by persons who were admittedly citizens of an enemy country in order to contest the authority of the American government to hold them in internment.[35] Court decisions, more than administrative will, promised to determine the future for many internees, Peruvian Japanese among them.

Meanwhile, the American government had shifted its position and, adopting the policy that the Peruvian foreign minister had insisted on six months earlier, informed its embassies throughout the Western Hemisphere that it "could not repatriate alien enemies brought from other American republics without the full consent and cooperation of the countries from which they came" for two reasons: (1) unilateral action by the United States would damage relations "with the other American republics," and (2) "the Alien Enemy Act ... seems clearly to require that the alien be given an opportunity to 'depart' from the country before he can be 'removed,' which would mean that if he were able to obtain a visa to the country from which he came (or to any other country) he would be able to escape removal to Germany." After explaining the reasons for the changed policy, the State Department indicated, "The plan now is to review all the evidence on the individual cases and to prepare lists of those who appear to fall within the standards for repatriation and those who do not."[36]

Even as the State Department began to review the cases (once again an initiative prompted by German internees would affect the Latin American Japanese), the department prefaced that endeavor with an attempt "to review the nature of our understandings with Peru" regarding the ultimate disposition of aliens deported from Peru to the United States. In his memorandum of December 13, Jonathan Bingham reached four conclusions: (1) "There was never any clear understanding as to the eventual disposition of the aliens after the war, primarily because at the time they were deported from Peru no one was thinking about the postwar period," (2) "The United States never made any commitments in writing or ... orally that the aliens would be returned to Peru upon Peru's request after the war," (3) "At all times the Peruvians were obviously of the opinion that the aliens were theirs to control.... The United States never contradicted this view, and on various occasions appeared to acquiesce in it," and (4) "The Peruvians could properly assert that, from early 1944 on, it was their understanding that the aliens were being held in this country only for the purpose of internment during the war, and that certain persons in whom Peru had a particular interest would not at any time be repatriated to Germany (or Japan) against their wishes. (The United States did not expressly confirm this understanding but it did not seek to correct it.)"[37]

Countless questions might be asked about the loose, informal deportation-internment program that for years had disrupted the lives of thousands. It would seem that American authorities, because they were concerned about a war of indefinite duration and magnitude, and had to deal with so many countries that similar, firm, and precise agreements were impossible to formulate, preferred an open-ended approach that tackled the problem through successive ad hoc cooperative measures. Also it would seem that Peruvian authorities, and those of eleven other cooperating Latin American governments, were sufficiently jealous of sovereign rights, and insufficiently impressed by the urgency of the war, that they agreed to these ad hoc cooperative arrangements that momentarily served their purposes and those of the United States. Beyond the war, however, these mutual interests ceased to exist.

"If it is decided to accede to Peru's request without further argument," Bingham continued, "I believe we should insist that Peru also take back all the Japanese sent here from Peru.... Peru states that it is willing to have us repatriate the Japanese to Japan on the ground that they are all 'indigent.' ... Furthermore, unless we can get Peru to take the Japanese back, we shall be forced to repatriate all of them to Japan, since we have no information which would enable us to make a case-by-case review. In the very great majority of the cases, the Japanese were sent here only on the say-so of the Peruvian Government."[38]

This statement is interesting on several counts. It hints strongly that exploitation of Peruvian aversion for the Japanese—and American desire for consistency—might give the United States leverage regarding all the internees. By placing the responsibility for the ouster of the Japanese almost completely on Peruvian authorities, it implies that the legal attachés (FBI agents), Emmerson, Welch, the military, naval, and commercial attachés, and the visiting representatives of the Department of Justice's Alien Enemy Control Unit had made no significant contribution toward the deportation of the Japanese. It also promises ("since we have no information") that any case-by-case review of the Peruvian Japanese internees will be perfunctory and pro forma.

In the course of the next half year, sporadic sailings to Japan included additional Peruvian Japanese. On February 23, 1946, more than eighty were among the 626 persons who sailed from Los Angeles for Japan aboard the U.S.A.T. *General Ernst,* and more than fifty Peruvian Japanese embarked on June 13, 1946, aboard the U.S.A.T. *General Meigs.* Almost without exception these were family groups. More than half of them had one or more American-born children. Often the dates of birth, in the closing months of 1945 and early in 1946, accounted for the tardy departures. Among those on the *Ernst* the six children in the Mankichi Nakachi family included twin sons born in 1945 at Crystal City. On board the *Meigs* the seven offspring of Katsutaro Horiba counted two Americans, one born in 1944, a second in 1946. During internment many Peruvian Japanese couples maintained and fulfilled the desires for large families that they had entertained in Peru.[39]

At this time, although the number of Japanese internees greatly exceeded the Germans and Italians, American policy decisions primarily responded to circumstances involving Germans. Their filing for writs of habeas corpus and other court actions posed domestic legal problems, while on the diplomatic front the insistence of Peru, Ecuador, and El Salvador that certain German internees be returned to them added international problems. Beyond the Latin American assertions of jurisdiction—something the United States had assumed it alone would exercise once the aliens were in this country—the return of the Germans endangered the American intention of using Resolution VII of the Mexico City Conference to oust Axis aliens from the hemisphere.

Sensing all this, the Department of State hoped (1) to persuade the governments to withdraw their requests for individuals whom Washington deemed "clearly dangerous," (2) to persuade the governments to take back those aliens judged not dangerous, and (3) to persuade any government that insisted on the return of any of its internees, to which the United States would accede, to agree to accept all of them. Assistant Secretary of State Dean Acheson, reacting to these recommendations, wrote, "I agree but these countries should take the Japs too. I understand that we have no evidence against them and don't want to be stuck with them."[40]

By this time many of the Peruvian Japanese at the Santa Fe Internment Camp, having expressed their desire to return to Peru, were banding together to petition the Department of State. Their appeal, led by young Victor K. Tateishi, included the following information about each man: name, age, birth date, birthplace, status (citizenship), names of family members, and addresses of same. The status of wives, which was not indicated, might have advanced the prospects of any who were married to Nisei or other native Peruvians or to naturalized citizens of Peru. Of the eighty-six petitioners, five were from Bolivia, eighty-one from Peru. Of the latter, two were naturalized Peruvians, seven were Peruvian Nisei, and seventy-two were Japanese Issei.[41] Unless Peru altered its previously stated criteria for readmission, only nine of these men had any real chance of returning to Peru.

# 7

# Challenging Human Endurance

Months beyond the close of hostilities, as 1946 dawned, competing views and prospects emerged regarding the Peruvian Japanese internees. As both Washington and Lima scrambled for firm postwar policies to replace strained and fuzzy wartime arrangements, irreconcilable differences surfaced. Washington, wishing to terminate the internment program, hoped for a speedy resolution of the problem, but Peru was less inclined to rush matters. Washington wanted to use Resolution VII of the Mexico City Conference to facilitate mass deportations to Germany and Japan, but Peru, less concerned about the American concept of hemispheric security, was demanding jurisdiction over the internees. But if the United States accepted the Peruvian position, which Ecuador and El Salvador also shared, and guaranteed the return of many Germans to those countries, she faced a new problem, that of consistency, since the internment program involved twelve Latin American states.

More potential confusion attended the Peruvian response to a major American proposal. The United States expected Peru to select one of two alternatives: accept the return of all internees or allow the United States jurisdiction in the resolution of the internee problem. But the Peruvian reply straddled the issue. Unwilling to yield jurisdiction and equally unwilling to readmit every internee, Peru wanted to exercise a selective policy that would be lenient for Germans and highly restrictive for Japanese. Lima's willingness to admit Germans, whom the United States considered dangerous, and unwillingness to admit many Japanese, all of whom the American government had come to consider harmless, troubled Washington. Already, in late November, a Peruvian note had illustrated the selective process regarding the readmission of the Japanese.

Listing certain internees eligible for reentry, that Peruvian note not only included individuals who had elected to go to Japan, and had already done so, but also Japanese who were not Peruvian citizens. Incidentally, Peruvian willingness to consider the readmission of noncitizens raised the question: was the readmission of Japanese, like their expulsion, to be accompanied by instances of favoritism, bribery, and other irregularities? Washington had even more reason to wonder about the eventual disposition of the hundreds of Japanese who had refused repatriation to Japan and were being denied readmission by Peru.

The United States, pressing for Peruvian acceptance of one of the alternatives in toto, knew that either one would allow those Japanese to return to Peru: Peru would accept all of them, or the United States would exercise the right to dispose of the matter. Appreciation of the fact that the United States had stacked the diplomatic cards probably stiffened Peruvian resistance. Ahead lay an indefinite period of bureaucratic tedium and diplomatic secrecy.[1]

While this diplomatic congeries was developing, the Department of State was establishing its hearings procedure for alien enemy cases. This followed a January 10 decision in the Federal Court of the Southern District of New York that the internees brought from Latin America were "alien enemies" within the meaning of the Alien Enemy Act of 1798.

If it was decided, after the review of an alien's case, that he should be held for further proceedings in anticipation of his repatriation, the alien was to be informed of that decision and of his right to request a hearing within one week. In the absence of such a request he would be subject to repatriation after a final review of his case. In the event of a hearing, which would take place at the internment camp, the alien would be given at least one week's notice of the scheduled date and place. For the three-man hearing board, the department turned to James D. Bell, formerly of the AECU, and Louis Henkin and Daniel Tenney, attorneys in the AECS. At a hearing, informal in nature and with the rules of evidence not applying, the alien would have the right to counsel. At the close of a hearing the board was expected to render its decision immediately.

The German cases, two-thirds of which had been subjected to preliminary review, would begin about mid-February. "Because of the complete lack of information on them," Bingham wrote, "we have done nothing yet about reviewing the 650 Japanese (317 cases) remaining."[2] The resultant potential for hearings, set forth in table 9, indicates that in peacetime, as in wartime, the Japanese problem pivoted on Peru.[3]

In addition to being told the details of the alternatives the United States had presented to the Latin American governments, the internees were informed that (1) the hearings, without which no one would be deported, would begin soon after February 1, (2) no released individual could remain in the United States, (3) a lawyer would not be required in order to obtain release, (4) filing a petition for habeas corpus to win release would not be productive in view of the recent decision in New York regarding the legal right of the United States to detain enemy aliens, (5) in general, paroles would not be authorized pending a decision regarding an individual, and (6) anyone to be returned to the country from which he had come would "probably be out of the internment camp within two months."[4] These unduly optimistic statements soon generated disappointment and disgust among the Peruvian Japanese. In the meantime many pursued their individual objectives as best they could.

From Crystal City, correspondence directed to Lima and Washington sought information and advice for fifty-one families desiring to return to

**TABLE 9**

**Alien Enemies from Latin America in U.S. Custody, January 31, 1946**

| Country of origin | Germans | Italians | Japanese |
|---|---|---|---|
| Bolivia | 61 | 1 | 18 |
| British Honduras | 11 | ... | ... |
| Chile | 5 | ... | ... |
| Colombia | 21 | ... | ... |
| Costa Rica | 145 | 5 | ... |
| Dominican Republic | 18 | 1 | ... |
| Ecuador | 111 | 3 | ... |
| El Salvador | 27 | 3 | ... |
| Guatemala | 79 | ... | ... |
| Haiti | 25 | ... | ... |
| Honduras | 68 | 4 | ... |
| Nicaragua | 54 | 10 | ... |
| Panama | 130 | 5 | ... |
| Panama Canal Zone | 4 | ... | ... |
| Paraguay | 15 | ... | ... |
| Peru | 123 | 5 | 495 |
| Total | 897 | 37 | 513 |

Peru. Despite the announcement regarding paroles, one was sought to attend school in the United States, another for temporary residence in Hawaii, and a number of families ignored the "not wanted" sign written in American law and petitioned to stay in the United States.[5]

## The Pawley Recommendations

In Lima recently arrived William D. Pawley, an aeronautical executive whose campaign contributions had probably propelled him into his ambassadorship, was demonstrating a disconcerting combination of political gullibility, cultural prejudice, and humanitarian unconcern. Basic to his conclusions and proposals was the idea that the unsettled internee issue "may affect adversely our present excellent relations with Peru." Accepting the often mouthed but never documented statements of Haya de la Torre that the return of the Japanese would be politically disastrous, Pawley added, "this alien population in Peru has reverted to its nonmoral Asiatic cunning, unchecked by self-respect." Urging a compromise regarding the internees, he advanced four recommendations: (1) return to Peru those Axis nationals Peru wants to readmit, (2) subject the remaining Germans and Japanese unwanted by Peru to further review, looking forward to their repatriation to Germany and Japan, (3) subject those Japanese and Germans remaining in the United States to further negotiations between the United States and Peru, looking forward to the chartering of vessels to enable Peru to effect their repatriation, and (4) subject the issue of the Japanese in Peru to negotiation between the United States and Peru.

Pawley's suggestions were radical, naïve, and callous. His first point, radical in terms of the either-or alternative previously established, nonetheless proved acceptable to the department. His second point ignored both the completeness of the departmental review of the Germans and the total lack of significant information regarding the Japanese. His third proposal was calculated to shift from Washington to Lima the onus for repatriations that callously disregarded internee refusal to accept those destinations. Pawley's final recommendation, on continuing U.S.–Peruvian negotiation, indicated that (1) he shared the Peruvians' blind hatred of the Japanese and supported their desire to remove all of them from Peru, and (2) he brought to the embassy in peacetime less levelheaded intelligence regarding the Japanese issue than his wartime predecessors. Secretary of State James Byrnes accepted the idea that compromise with Peru was necessary, killed the chartered ship proposal as "cumbersome" and "probably not feasible," and ignored the suggestion that the United States help to oust all of the Japanese.[6]

## Action and Reaction

Uncertainty, widespread among the internees, diplomats, and policy makers, dissipated somewhat when Acting Secretary Acheson, referring to approximately 425 Peruvian Japanese, informed Attorney General Tom Clark, "In no case is there clear evidence that the individual's continued residence in this hemisphere would be prejudicial to the security and welfare of the Americas. I am therefore requesting you to inform these persons that they are no longer subject to restraint as dangerous alien enemies." As he shifted responsibility from State to Justice, Acheson continued, "you will presumably wish to take steps looking toward their departure from the United States within a reasonable time."[7] For the internees, horns of dilemma had replaced clouds of suspicion.

Six months after the termination of hostilities the mentalities of American and Peruvian officialdom deservedly provoked wonder. For the United States the discontinuity involving three secretaries of state, countless shifts within the Department of State, three ambassadors, and numerous staff changes in Lima had contributed to changed outlooks. Indeed, in 1946 the American ambassador was sufficiently removed from the issue that he could and did repeatedly misspell the names of ships used in the deportation program. As the embassy saw matters increasingly from the Peruvian viewpoint and the Department of State surrendered the internee burden to the Department of Justice, much seemed to stem from a frustrating weariness—a desire to get away from it, to close out wartime matters. On the other hand, Peruvian officials, however much their personnel changed —a different president, four foreign ministers, and different officials in the Foreign Office and in the embassy in Washington—had not changed their outlook. Whereas the Americans, war weary and peace hungry, had altered their stance regarding Japanese in general, the Peruvians were clinging stubbornly to their prewar and wartime anti-Japanese outlook.

Prompt notification of the internees of their changed status inspired a flurry of communications. Sixty-eight Peruvian Japanese at Santa Fe sent a telegram and a letter to President Truman. They mentioned the fact that there had been no hearings, and set forth claims of Peruvian citizenship, long law-abiding residence, and the hardships that repatriation to Japan would impose. They appealed for a show of democracy, justice, and fair play in the handling of their cases.[8] Similar appeals went to Secretary of State Byrnes, Chief of the AECS Bingham, the INS, and the International Red Cross. Simultaneously ten telegraphic appeals went to Peru to the following: President José Bustamante Rivero, Foreign Minister Enrique García Sayán, the presiding officers of the Senate and Chamber of Deputies, the president of the Supreme Court, the papal nuncio, the archbishop of Lima, and the presidents of the Peruvian Red Cross, the Círculo Militar del Perú, and the Sociedad Entre Nous. Lengthy letters followed the telegrams.[9]

The Department of State asserted that since no action against the Japanese was contemplated under Resolution VII of the Mexico City Conference, hearings would serve no purpose. Further negotiations were skirted by citing the negative results of previous ones. As if to free itself, the department asked the INS to indicate that the internee cases were completely in the hands of the Department of Justice.[10]

From Crystal City, at the same time, an internee committee made an appeal on behalf of "approximately 50 Japanese families." They sought the following: (1) fulfillment of the Department of State memorandum that stated that Japanese nationals not considered dangerous and married to native Peruvians or Nisei and/or had children born in Peru could return to Peru, (2) the promised hearings, (3) renewed negotiations with Peru regarding readmission, and (4) negotiations with the INS for the postponement of deportation proceedings during U.S.–Peruvian negotiations. In support of their petition the internees cited these facts: they had no desire to go to Japan; they had resided in Peru for many years; all of their children had been born in Peru and the United States; and many were married to native Peruvians, Spanish or Nisei. In a final note of desperation, if denied reentry into Peru or permanent residence in the United States, the internees asked for assistance in gaining entry into other Latin American countries.[11] At both Santa Fe and Crystal City such activity reflected not only the desperation and desires of the internees but also the cohesiveness they had attained.

Few of the many appeals had reached their destinations when Department of Justice officers in San Antonio and El Paso executed the anticipated arrest warrants. For the arrest of Iwamori Sakasegawa, one of the men at Santa Fe, the warrant asserted, "he was an immigrant not in possession of a valid immigration visa and ... he did not present an unexpired passport ... and he is an alien ineligible to citizenship and was not entitled to enter the United States."[12] What irony those few words contained—that a permanent resident of Peru shanghaied by Peruvian and American authorities and thrust against his will into the United States should be termed "immigrant"; that the lack of a visa stemmed directly from orders to consular officials in Peru not to issue visas; that the lack of a passport derived from the confiscation and nonreturn of passports and other documents; that the illegal entry of internees ineligible for citizenship had been fashioned and executed by officials sworn to enforce American law. The damning warrants afforded only one ray of light, a hearing.

### Marshaling Support

Their fright mounting as the warrants for their arrests arrived, despairing men grasped any opportunity and made any appeal that might help them. From Santa Fe the results of a survey of the religious affiliations of sixty-eight Peruvian Japanese and their families were forwarded (see table 10).

**TABLE 10**

**Religious Affiliation of Internees at Santa Fe**

| Internees | Catholic | Buddhist | Protestant | Unspecified | Total |
|---|---|---|---|---|---|
| Men | 38 | 28 | 1 | 1 | 68 |
| Married | 27 | 10 | ... | 1 | 38 |
| Wives | 31 | 7 | ... | ... | 38 |
| Children of Catholic mothers | 105 | ... | ... | ... | 105 |
| Children of Buddhist mothers | 21 | ... | ... | ... | 21 |

SOURCE: Compiled from "List of the Denominations of Religious [sic]" (copy), April 1, 1946, 1946 File, WMC Papers.

Although the list simply stated the religious affiliations of individuals and their families, it prompted certain conclusions: (1) the passing of generations and the mounting Catholicity of the Japanese attested to their Peruvianization, and (2) the internee appeals to church authorities and agencies, more of which would come, derived from more than simple desperation; they represented a cry of the faithful.

Detailed general appeals, each signed by sixty-four internees, went from Santa Fe to the president, the secretary of state, the attorney general, and the Peruvian ambassador. From Truman they asked understanding and pity, from Byrnes immediate action, "since we are racing with time."[13]

At this time the sixty-eight men at Santa Fe were in the following categories: (1) four desired repatriation to Japan, (2) sixty-four sought readmission to Peru, but (3) only thirteen of them claimed Peruvian citizenship. At Crystal City sixty-one families represented 301 internees, of whom 108 had been born in Japan, 170 in Peru, and 23 in the United States. At least nine of those born in Japan possessed Peruvian citizenship. Since the authorities had routinely divested the internees of legal papers and documents before their departure from Peru, efforts to prove civil status invited time-consuming delay and complete dependence on Peruvian officials. If, however, Peru persisted in its announced refusal to readmit noncitizens, considerable social chaos was in store for these families, because although some native Peruvian wives promised to accompany their Japanese husbands to Japan, others planned to say good-bye to their husbands and return to Peru with their children. Some children, approaching adulthood, elected separation from family in order to return to Peru.[14]

As hearings approached, many internees whose hearts were set on Peru executed INS Form I-255, "Application for Departure in Lieu of Deportation and/or Preexamination," checking the section marked "permission to depart from the United States at my own expense in lieu of deportation." Anything to forestall deportation. But the maze of laws, regulations, and accompanying documents increasingly confused the Peruvian Japanese, and those at Santa Fe concluded that they needed legal counsel. Because the camp included Japanese Americans whose problems frequently brought lawyers there, it was not difficult to develop the desired contact.

On April 4, a contract executed on behalf of sixty-two of the internees obtained the services of the law firm Wirin, Maneo and Tietz of Los Angeles. For the sum of five thousand dollars, to be paid over a five-month period, the lawyers were to advise and help at the hearings, do everything possible to defeat the threatened deportation to Japan, negotiate with the Departments of Justice and State, secure congressional or presidential aid, and take court action, at their discretion, in one or more United States district courts. Unspecified additional payment was pledged for work in the U.S. Circuit Court of Appeals and the U.S. Supreme Court.[15] The internees would go to any legal length in their fight.

To fortify their counsels' arguments, sixty-one men compiled a list of their family ties in Peru. The wives of the thirty-seven married men included twenty-five Peruvians, eleven Japanese, and one American citizen. The deportation of the men had left 137 children, twenty-two of them motherless, in Peru. Unable to list dependent wives and children, the unmarried men maximized their identification with Peru by listing parents, brothers, sisters, nieces, nephews, and cousins resident there—a labor inspired by the Department of State pronouncement that it was giving "great weight to the factor of native American family ties."[16]

While internees prepared to do battle with American authorities, some of the latter altered the prospects facing the Peruvian Japanese. Because released Latin American German internees were given ninety days to effect their departure when they signified a desire to depart to a destination of their choosing at their own expense, Acheson conceded that the Japanese should be accorded similar opportunity. "If, instead," he wrote to the attorney general, "legal proceedings are instituted to effect their prompt deportation to Japan, the result will be in effect the same as if they had been found dangerous and removed to Japan under the Alien Enemy Act." Attorney General Clark considered the following procedure devoid of discrimination: (1) deportation proceedings would be promptly instituted against all of the Japanese, but (2) they would be notified that those able to show that any country is open to them or that there is a reasonable possibility that negotiations would lead some country to receive them would have ninety days in which to effect the necessary arrangements, but (3) all others would be deported "as soon as the usual procedures are completed."[17] On some internees the American authorities had lengthened the leash slightly.

Another potentially humane gesture came from Peru. Reopening the internee issue, the Foreign Office requested the temporary suspension of deportation proceedings for fifteen men, pending fuller investigation of their alleged family ties in Peru. Article 7 of Peru's alien law 4145 held that provisions for deportation from Peru would not be applied to "foreigners married to Peruvian women with whom they have been living normally nor to widowers of Peruvian women." How much this Peruvian move derived from simple adherence to law and how much from the special outlook of recently appointed Foreign Minister Enrique García Sayán is impossible to determine. However, as a trained economist and as a person who had carefully observed life in Japan and was grandson of naval Captain Aurelio García y García (the Peruvian who had signed the treaty of 1873 with Japan), García Sayán was in a position to render a more dispassionate assessment of the economic value of the Japanese to Peru than most Peruvian leaders.[18]

Since neither the Peruvian authorities nor the embassy had lists of the men with Peruvian wives and children, and the men themselves held few if any convincing papers, a period of delay and diplomatic activity loomed. Within the week Peru, acting on the claims of eight others, denied the Peruvian citizenship of five of them on technical grounds related to the registration of births.[19]

While administrative decisions in Washington and Lima, of which they were not immediately aware, appeared to improve their prospects, the men at Santa Fe were changing legal counsels. One way and another, financial considerations dictated this move. As if the promised five-thousand-dollar fee was not worry enough, the internees also had to face the following: (1) changed circumstances might reduce the number of men burdened with that payment, (2) the vague expenses attending appeals up to and including the Supreme Court staggered their imagination, and (3) some of the internees, presently enthusiastic, might prove to be either impoverished or simple "deadbeats." Even as such thoughts were troubling them, the leaders of the Santa Fe group learned of the generous offer of legal assistance by San Francisco attorney Wayne M. Collins that would relieve them of much of their anxiety. Immediately they terminated their contract with Wirin, Maneo and Tietz.[20]

Like Wirin, Wayne M. Collins was one of those courageous civil liberties-minded California attorneys who in both their private practices and their association with such bodies as the American Civil Liberties Union (ACLU) and the Japanese American Citizens League (JACL) had identified themselves with the pursuit of justice for Japanese Americans. At the end of the war Collins's interest in groups subjected to wartime abuses included both the Peruvian Japanese and the American renunciants.

Earlier, as counsel in the Korematsu case, wherein the basic issue was the constitutionality of the American evacuation program, Collins had argued that case before the Supreme Court. The 6–3 decision of mid-December upheld the constitutionality of the evacuation that Korematsu had defied, but the same day another Supreme Court decision gave displaced Japanese Americans a notable victory in a case that forecast the pattern for some of Collins's approaches to the Peruvian Japanese issue. Mitsuye Endo, evacuated from Sacramento in 1942 and petitioning for a writ of habeas corpus, had asked that her liberty be restored. The petition cited her law-abiding nature, the lack of any charge against her, and her unlawful detention under armed guard against her will—precisely the experience and position of every Peruvian Japanese internee. In this case Collins had filed a brief on behalf of the Northern California chapter of the ACLU. Apparently the American government was anticipating the Supreme Court decision that provided Endo her unconditional release, because just a few hours before the decision was handed down the West Coast exclusion orders were revoked.[21]

Both the psychological impact of the judicial victory and the precise nature of the case brought hope to the Peruvian Japanese a year later as Collins prepared to spearhead legal battles on behalf of the men who were being transferred from the Santa Fe Internment Camp, which was being closed, to the San Pedro INS facility in the first of the government's deportation moves. To counter the action Ernest Besig of the ACLU of Northern California filed stays of deportation.[22] While Collins was acquiring and studying the files supplied by his new clients, Washington and Lima directed attention to lists of Japanese eager to return to Peru.

Although the Japanese citizenship of most internees dimmed their chances of readmission by Peru and gave momentum to deportation proceedings, Peruvian willingness to consider the return of those Japanese married to Peruvian-born women brightened the prospects of others. "No deportations to Japan at present imminent," Byrnes informed the embassy in Lima as the effort to clarify family ties continued. In addition to cases already being investigated by Peru, Washington reported that twenty-six men were married to Peruvian citizens and fifty-two men had families in Peru. Related lists went to Lima to speed the work there. At the same time Peruvian consideration of the readmission of internees with Peruvian-born wives led the Department of State to hope that the Justice

Department would "suspend for the time being any steps looking toward the deportation to Japan of those Japanese with Peruvian families." The attorney general's office, in agreement, so advised the commissioner of immigration and naturalization.[23]

Among the internees at Crystal City the need for assistance had also led to contacts with the ACLU through Besig and Collins. From Crystal City information was channeled to the attorneys by the spokesman of the Peruvian group, forty-four-year-old Koshiro Mukoyama, a former Lima importer of dry goods whose wife and five children, one a Texan, were with him. Away from Texas a Japanese American, Gongoro Nakamura, who had been at Crystal City, not only supplied Besig and the ACLU with information but also plied the Department of State with messages concerning the desire of the Peruvian Japanese to return to Peru.[24] In this same period, however, Director Roger N. Baldwin's correspondence indicated that the national office of the ACLU in New York was neither as involved in nor as knowledgeable about the issue of the Peruvian Japanese internees as Besig, Collins, Wirin, and the ACLU chapters in California were.[25]

Additional efforts on behalf of the internees came from a variety of sources, including Catholic agencies and clergymen. One wide-ranging effort started when the International Committee of the Red Cross in Geneva appealed to Monsignor Howard J. Carroll of Washington in poignant terms, asking his kind consideration of "the case of these unhappy Japanese whose deportation to Japan must be avoided." Supported by Cardinal Stritch, Monsignor Carroll sought the good offices of Apostolic Delegate Amleto Cicognani, hoping that "the Holy See might make representations to the Peruvian Government." The apostolic delegate quickly despatched a radiogram to the Vatican, "suggesting that the Holy See contact the Government of Peru on behalf of the Japanese-Peruvian internees."[26]

This agitation continued work that had interested the Immigration Bureau of the National Catholic Welfare Conference (subsequently the United States Catholic Conference) and its director, Bruce M. Mohler, for months. Later in May Mohler would appear before the Board of Immigration Appeals to request that the deportation orders be stayed. Possessed of less clout regarding this issue but a stubborn fighter for the rights of Japanese Americans, the Japanese American Citizens League urged the Department of State to extend "justice and humanity to an unfortunate group of human beings," the Peruvian Japanese.[27]

While lawyers studied individual files and national and international organizations protested the plight of the internees, the men whose transfer to the Terminal Island INS Station at San Pedro had brought them face to face with the threatened deportation continued to marshal information supportive of their individual and collective cases. As of May 1, 1946, eighty-one men stood as follows: one Nisei had won clearance to return to Peru, and six others were seeking to do so; four naturalized Peruvians had won clearance to return to Peru, and two others were seeking clearance; and of the sixty-eight Japanese citizens only three, a number reduced two weeks later to one, desired to return to Japan.[28]

"I do not expect any of you to be deported to Japan," Attorney Collins informed the internees at Crystal City. While the INS was suspending deportation proceedings and the Department of State awaited further word about Peruvian policy, Collins believed that, even if Peru refused to permit reentry by the internees, American courts would block their deportation and order their release from custody.[29]

### The Ordeal of Iwamori Sakasegawa

Any comfort afforded by Collins's words quickly gave way to renewed fears when notification of warrants of deportation went to the group at Crystal City. Again the ninety-day delay would be permitted "if you are able to secure permission to enter some country other than Japan." In the meantime Collins, preparing test cases in habeas corpus for the group at Terminal Island, had selected Chika Yamasaki as representative of the unmarried men and Iwamori Sakasegawa as representative of the married men with relatives in Peru. As a preliminary, the men were to answer a thirty-five-item questionnaire formulated by Collins.[30]

The torment of the moment gave Sakasegawa reason enough to fight. Behind him were thirty-four years of law-abiding residence in Peru, a marriage of twenty-two years, and a family of seven children ranging from one to twenty-one years of age. Like every other internee he could say, "I know of no reason why I was apprehended and moved to the United States." More so than most interned family heads, Sakasegawa could declare, "my wife has a long, gloomy way to go with heavy burden on her shoulders.... She is already about to sink under the weight of responsibility in bringing up those children." Sandwiched between his appeals to the Departments of State and Justice, a warrant for his arrest had been issued. On three counts—lack of a valid immigration visa, lack of an unexpired passport, and lack of eligibility for citizenship at the time of his entry into the United States—the Justice Department ordered its Santa Fe representatives to take Sakasegawa into custody "and grant him a hearing to enable him to show cause why he should not be deported."

April 6 was Iwamori Sakasegawa's day. For some it had come earlier, for others it would come later, but this day a baffled mechanic who spoke no English had to state his case to officials who knew no Japanese. To preside over the hearing, W. J. Waterson had come out from Santa Fe to the Santa Fe Internment Camp. With him came interpreter Kay Kamada, without whom the effort at communication would have collapsed completely, and secretary Audrey L. Lawrence, who would neatly type the answers directly onto the standard hearing forms. However much he had prepared for the ordeal by rehashing in his mind the events of two years and his unproductive appeals to various authorities, Iwamori stood alone, his Los Angeles lawyer, J. B. Tietz, having waived his presence at this hearing.

As the graying 5-foot 3-inch fifty-two-year-old alien faced his accuser, the United States government, the contest was an unequal one, but even the stacked-deck approach of his opponent did not blunt his quest for justice. Asked when and where he last entered the United States, Sakasegawa replied, "I was brought into the United States...," clearly punctuating the record with the truth that the action was not of his own free will and accord. He was asked—it was question no. 18, "For what purpose did you last enter the United States, what was your destination and how long did you intend to remain?" Considering that he had been shanghaied and shipped into the United States by American officials in violation of American law, the question was irrelevant, but he answered it.

"As I was brought into the United States by the American authorities," he replied, "I did not know where I was going or how long I was going to stay." Repeatedly he put the onus for his being in the United States on American authorities, but, as the questioning continued, Waterson blithely ignored that reality.

Yet the presiding officer, seemingly interested in the troubled human being before him, politely asked, "Please explain the circumstances leading up to and including your last entry into the United States." One could not easily compress the events of years into a few words, but the internee tried.

"I was arrested by Peruvian detectives on April 24, 1944, in Puerto de Huacho, Peru and held in jail one night," Sakasegawa related. "I was then taken to Lima, Peru where I was held until May 20, 1944 when I was put on an American airplane and taken to Panama. I was in Panama until June 20 and I was put on a boat and taken to New Orleans where I was immediately put into an internment camp and I have remained in an internment camp since that time." It was not the tale of an eager immigrant, this account of arrest, jailing, deportation, confinement. Not a single step in a sequence that put him in a barbed wire enclosure in a strange land had been initiated by Sakasegawa.

As the hearing droned on, officer Waterson learned that Iwamori's second son, Ernesto, was serving in the Peruvian Army, that he himself, at the time of his apprehension and deportation, had no savings, that he did not know how his family was faring. But nowhere among the fifty-three questions did American officialdom, insistent from beginning to end that the alien alone was guilty of wrongdoing, meet this internee fairly in quest of elementary justice. Apparently American law and regulations could not possibly be wrenched and violated by American officials. Steeped in pathos and insensitivity, the hearing concerned a man who, strong in the right, was insistent that he be returned to his home and family. Asked, "In the event of your deportation what will be your final destination?" the unbowed victim replied, "Puerto de Huacho, Peru."

Next, for Sakasegawa, had come the application and petition for the writ of habeas corpus filed by Wayne M. Collins in the Federal Court of the Northern District of California. This led to a changed place of detention, San Francisco. Legal maneuvering and delay set in, the stipulation and order of early September continuing until mid-December the hearing to show cause.[31]

While most internees teetered between fear and hope, joyous relief came to a few. Aided by Attorney A. L. Wirin, frequently a cooperating attorney for the ACLU in Los Angeles, a thirty-seven-year-old farmer, accompanied by a sister, her children, and a nephew, was fortunate to have a brother in Denver who along with former Governor Carr of Colorado served as their sponsors and won their release to Denver. Sponsored by a Japanese American in Los Angeles, a forty-four-year-old merchant, his wife, and child, once of Lima, moved to California, aided by Gongoro Nakamura. A forty-six-year-old Lima watchmaker and his wife had a sponsor in Long Beach and hoped to post bond and head westward.[32] Since all these men were Japanese citizens, one wonders: were these concessions to illegal "immigrants" a recognition that negotiations with Peru about them might prove very lengthy, an admission that the United States had no legal grounds for holding them, or simply a move to reduce government expense by helping the INS close its last internment camp? Wayne Collins was on the verge of quietly helping others out of Crystal City, but first the critical plight of the men at Terminal Island prompted a publicity campaign.

Deportations previously scheduled for May had been rescheduled for June, to the accompaniment of efforts to get the House Immigration and Naturalization Committee to prevent deportations to Japan by reporting favorably on a bill that would grant a stay of deportation for Japanese in "hardship" cases. On this matter the ACLU of Northern California focused attention. Earlier certain complaints of the Japanese at Terminal Island—denial of access to baggage, a shortage of chairs (four for eighty-one men), and the penniless plight of many while their funds remained at Santa Fe because the INS had no finance officer at San Pedro—had been remedied by the intervention of the same branch of the ACLU.[33]

A leading West Coast newspaper pointed out editorially that the United States government, after forcibly interning the Peruvian Japanese, was degrading itself by proceeding against them on charges of evading immigration rules. Late in June the ACLU, represented by Collins, filed in the U.S. District Court of Northern California the test suits that sought to prevent the deportation to Japan of Chika Yamasaki and Iwamori Sakasegawa. More publicity ensued.[34]

The filing of these two cases promised indefinite delay, and the INS countered by shipping the entire group from Terminal Island to Crystal City. Almost at once the INS also considered a proposal that would enable it to close the Crystal City camp, its last internee operation. Meanwhile, at midyear, Washington had closed out its odious "blacklist."[35]

## Seabrook Farms

Nine months after the cessation of war in the Pacific Wayne M. Collins was not only buoying up the spirits of one-time Santa Fe, one-time Terminal Island men whose deportation he was fighting, he was also tendering an interesting proposition to the expanded internee group at Crystal City. It concerned employment at the Seabrook Farms in New Jersey. During the life of the by then defunct War Relocation Authority, the Seabrook Farms, a large truck-farming and food-freezing establishment that embraced sixteen corporate entities, had recruited many Japanese Americans as wartime workers. Allowed to relocate but not permitted to return to the West Coast, numerous Japanese American farmers and others had seized the Seabrook opportunity in order to escape the relocation centers. By December 1945 the personnel records at Seabrook had included 1,024 evacuee men and women whose diligence had highly commended them. The Seabrook management entertained a fine opinion of the Japanese.[36] When the lifting of legal restraints hurried most Japanese Americans to their prewar locales, that management readily welcomed other Japanese.

Aware of the westward migration of the released Japanese Americans and of the frustrations of the tormented Peruvian Japanese, Collins had urged American authorities to allow the internees from Latin America to join the Seabrook work force. Informed of the New Jersey prospect, internee spokesman Koshiro Mukoyama buttressed word that the proposition had "aroused marked interest" with a list of 160 interested individuals. At the same time the business sense of the forty-four-year-old former Lima importer prompted him to say, "I consider it necessary to have a responsible representative of the Seabrook Farm call on this camp to explain full details before a final decision can be reached by us."[37]

Mukoyama's wishes coincided with the practice of the Seabrook Farms. As the leading nongovernmental recruiter of evacuee workers, the New Jersey operation routinely, between 1943 and 1945, had sent agents to the WRA centers to describe working conditions and to sign up workers. Their willingness to hire aliens and the promise of group living facilities heightened interest among the Peruvian Japanese. Mukoyama's tentative lists of interested parties included twenty-two families totaling 106 persons, in addition to fifty-four individuals who are either unmarried or whose families remained in Peru.

When the Seabrook representative visited the Crystal City Internment

Camp in midsummer, the selection, centering on males and females between the ages of eighteen and fifty-five and allowing up to one child per adult chosen, resulted in the acceptance of 110 persons. Nonacceptance was attributed to certain characteristics, described by Mukoyama: "either invalid, old age, female, families with many children or those who desire to relocate to their chosen localities on parole."[38]

Disappointment assailed the heads of several large families. One such was Seiichi Higashide, a thirty-eight-year-old clothing store operator in Ica in prewar years, whose family had five preteenage youngsters. Former Lima glass merchant Kakuaki Kaneko could not join this New Jersey-bound group because his five children, none of whom was a teenager, included a diaper-clad Texan. Seven children with only one parent barred the Kotoku Yamashiro family from early consideration. Size of family also blocked spokesman Mukoyama, one of whose five young children had been born in Texas. But not every large family desirous of going to New Jersey was denied that opportunity, witness the Yoshisada Shiga and Mitsutaro Tawara families, both of which counted numerous teenage and older children—potential workers.[39]

At Crystal City, mid-August 1946 resembled late November 1945 in one respect, as a time for good-byes. In November those with overriding loyalty to Japan had headed west to waiting ships. Now a much smaller group, adamantly insisting that they be returned to Peru, would travel east, lured by an interim work opportunity. In August, as in November, friends and acquaintances of young Toshiharu Tawara penned farewell sentiments in his autograph book.

Nami, at nineteen the eldest of importer Rokuichi Kudo's three children, admonished Toshiharu to put forth his maximum effort. Teenager Isamu Shibayama, thinking that they might never meet again, wanted to be remembered as the pitcher on a championship baseball team. Elisa Fusako, Isamu's younger sister, wished Toshiharu health and happiness and added, "don't forget we played tennis together." Two of the four fatherless Suzuki girls, Atsumi and Suzuko, were conscious of parting. To all else Atsumi added that she considered Toshiharu a "nice boy"—words drawn from a language growing less strange. Sister Suzuko recalled two years of camp life—of play and studies she had shared with Toshiharu and could not forget. Tadahiko and Luisa Fumiko, son and daughter of Lima merchant Chuhei Kato, wished Toshiharu health and happiness, both adding, "until we meet again." For all it was a bittersweet farewell, a moment when the buoyance of youth tempered tragic confinement.[40] Most did meet again, at Seabrook Farms.

Led by Peruvian-born twenty-seven-year-old Enrique Isamu Kurotobi, the group of 110 men, women, and children, "paroled" to the Seabrook Farms, left Crystal City for that distant place. "With the deepest gratitude ever felt by man," young Kurotobi soon wrote Wayne Collins and Ernest Besig, "I, on behalf of the group of the Japanese from Peru who were recently paroled from the Crystal City Internment Camp and presently working at the Seabrook Farms, N.J., wish to express our appreciation for your untiring efforts."[41] Kurotobi's words were an indication of the boundless thanksgiving of shipwrecked souls who had finally set their feet on solid ground.

Their Peruvian lives wrecked by the whims of Peruvian and American officials, the 110 nurtured more than a flicker of hope in their changed circumstances. No longer would they face the interminable heat of south Texas; no longer would they look up to see guard towers; no longer—if lucky enough to work eight hours—would essentially piddling jobs put eighty cents a day into a man's pocket. Every ex-internee now termed parolee fervently longed to get back to Peru. The revitalization of a dormant business, or the reestablishment of a confiscated one, would require working capital. Seabrook Farms presented an opportunity to earn needed money. Nonetheless, questions and uncertainty accompanied this shift from Texas to New Jersey. In a group that included numerous barbers, merchants, importers, grocers, and restaurateurs, not one of the sixty-five men could be described as a dirt farmer. Could such adults adjust to agricultural work? Age, prior economic endeavor, and way of life in internment prompted another question: were they, however short their stay, up to the demands that Seabrook Farms would place on them? In addition, the sense of community that had developed at Crystal City and their shared desire to return to Peru made this August contingent realize that their experience would greatly affect the prospects of those who remained in Texas.

Meanwhile Collins was heaping sugar sweet praise on Attorney General Clark. "I wish to thank you," he wrote, "for consenting to liberate Peruvian Japanese from Crystal City on parole so that they may be occupied gainfully pending a determination of their re-admission to Peru by the Peruvian Government and the decision of our courts on the deportability of those who may be denied such admission." Collins was viewing the new attorney general as a beacon of reasonableness, hoping for the settlement of pending Japanese issues, American and Peruvian.[42] However, another beginning was canceling out the prospect of concessions in either Lima or Washington regarding most of the Peruvian Japanese still in this country.

### Clouds Over Peru

Sweeping across South America to Peru from the more populous Japanese colony in Brazil was a highly nationalistic, pro-Japan underground movement, the Aikoku Doshi-kai (Society of Japanese Patriots in Peru) modeled on the Shindo Remmei. This Brazilian Japanese "League of the New Way" had repudiated the idea that Japan had lost the war and was exploiting the ignorance and fanaticism of many Japanese in Peru. False photographs and reports were encouraging hundreds, in the Lima-Callao area especially, to believe that Japan would soon send vessels for their expense-free return to the victorious homeland. Duped patriots gladly advanced large sums of money to unscrupulous promoters.[43] Years would pass before some of these gullible Japanese faced reality, but it required less time for Peruvian and American authorities to harden their outlook.

In mid-1946 J. Edgar Hoover repeatedly apprised the Department of State of intelligence reported by an FBI operative (legal attaché) stationed in Lima. The attaché termed the tightly knit clandestine Aikoku Doshi-kai fanatical and terroristic, a threat to those Japanese who resisted its advocates. Ambassador Prentice Cooper, the recently arrived successor to Pawley, accepted and approved the legal attaché's report. The latter's sources included Japanese nationals and Peruvian police. The former insisted that the Aikoku Doshi-kai intended to keep alive the ideals and principles of the wartime Japanese regime as it moved to form a mutual-aid society, a not uncommon operation among the Japanese. The petition to form a mutual-aid society, which, incidentally, would have accorded the Aikoku Doshi-kai a legal front, so to speak, was denied by Peruvian authorities. Occurring when it did, the denial seemingly stemmed from the continuing anti-Japanese sentiment of Peruvian officialdom, rather than from any real knowledge of the pro-Japan fervor of the clandestine leadership. More than once the lengthy FBI report circulated in influential sectors of the State Department.[44]

What, for a time, was disquieting only in official Peruvian and American circles soon had a wider public and a reinforcing influence. Early in August Peruvian police had arrested two Japanese nationals, Kenzo Abe and Takeshi Torigoe, both from Brazil. At the time of their arrest in Huaral, the police also seized films, a projector, and a quantity of Japanese-language material considered to be propaganda. The Lima police quickly arrested more Japanese. These events prompted a succession of articles and editorials in the Lima press. The account sent to Washington by the embassy indicated that "Abe . . . admitted that he had come to Peru on a 'mission' to organize the Japanese in this country, following which he intended to proceed to the United States for the same purpose. He planned to visit Colombia and Venezuela and other places en route to the United States." Not unexpectedly an American official wrote, "it is very likely that a request will be made by the Peruvian Government for the assistance of the United States Government in effecting the deportation of these Japanese."[45]

The sweep of Shindo Remmei across South America and the outcropping of Japanese fanaticism in Peru, through the Aikoku Doshi-kai, produced long-lingering effects. For many months, official Washington and official Lima had been drifting apart regarding the issue of the Peruvian Japanese. Peru, regretting that it had not rid itself of all its Japanese, insistently refused to readmit most of those who had been shipped to the United States. Secure in the knowledge that the interned Peruvian Japanese had constituted no security risk to either country at any time, the United States had hoped that Peru would relent and readmit the several hundred who desired to return there. Now, American officials in Lima and Washington increasingly recognized validity in Peruvian reluctance. To FBI men who had never uncovered anything resembling a security threat during wartime, the Aikoku Doshi-kai loomed as a sinister threat to the hemisphere. Within the Department of State the Aikoku Doshi-kai scare crystallized a willingness to see the Japanese issue the Peruvian way. American pressure on Peru to allow the Peruvian Japanese to return did not quicken. Only time would tell whether official American interest in the return of the Peruvian Japanese to Peru had lessened, whether the nudgings given Lima by Washington were milder and pro forma, lacking the vigor that yields results.

In the same season the charge that a number of American servicemen based at Talara had molested one or more women whom a Peruvian naval officer was escorting gave rise to a flurry of diplomatic activity regarding the jurisdiction of Peruvian courts that threatened a wave of Peruvian resentment.

### New Destinations for Old Internees

Despite irritating episodes in U.S.–Peruvian relations and the fueling of anti-Japanese sentiment in Peru by such postwar developments as the Shindo Remmei and the Aikoku Doshi-kai, Peru did not alter the conditions to be met for eligibility to return. Eligible were (1) those born in Peru (the Nisei), (2) naturalized citizens, and (3) those aliens married to Peruvians. Already the few internees to win readmission had met these tests. Three of the four men who flew to Peru late in May, Ichitaro Morimoto, the oldest of the internees, Jiro Hasegawa, and Sentei Yaki, were naturalized Peruvian citizens, and Pedro Minoru Hashimoto was Peruvian-born. In mid-June Sansuke Kakutani, a naturalized Peruvian, took his Japanese wife and their three Peruvian-born children back to South America. During the last week of July Nisei Victor Kazuki Tateishi and Genji Nimura, a naturalized Peruvian, had flown to Peru. In mid-August, the day before the 110 persons had left Crystal City for the Seabrook Farms, Carlos Shinkyu Taira, a naturalized citizen of Peru, had flown to rejoin his native Peruvian wife. During May, June, July, and August approximately twenty men, women, and children had left the United States for Peru. More than one of the men had rallied sufficient influence to delay his deportation, and all had marshaled both influence and documents to hasten their return.

Despite the pro-Japan clandestine operations in Peru and the outpourings of hostile Peruvian journalists, official permission to return to Peru soon went forth for fifty-seven persons. Some of the lucky ones in the newly designated group were already at Seabrook, but most remained at Crystal City. For one man, however, the word came late, at least nine months late, because in November 1945 Ichiro Shimizu, a sixty-one-year-old farmer from Arequipa, had sailed to Japan. Of the other twenty-four heads of families—and all were family men—twenty-three were still Japanese citizens. They derived their right to return to Peru from their marriages to women born in Peru. Only six of the twenty-four had their families with them in the United States. For all, transportation remained to

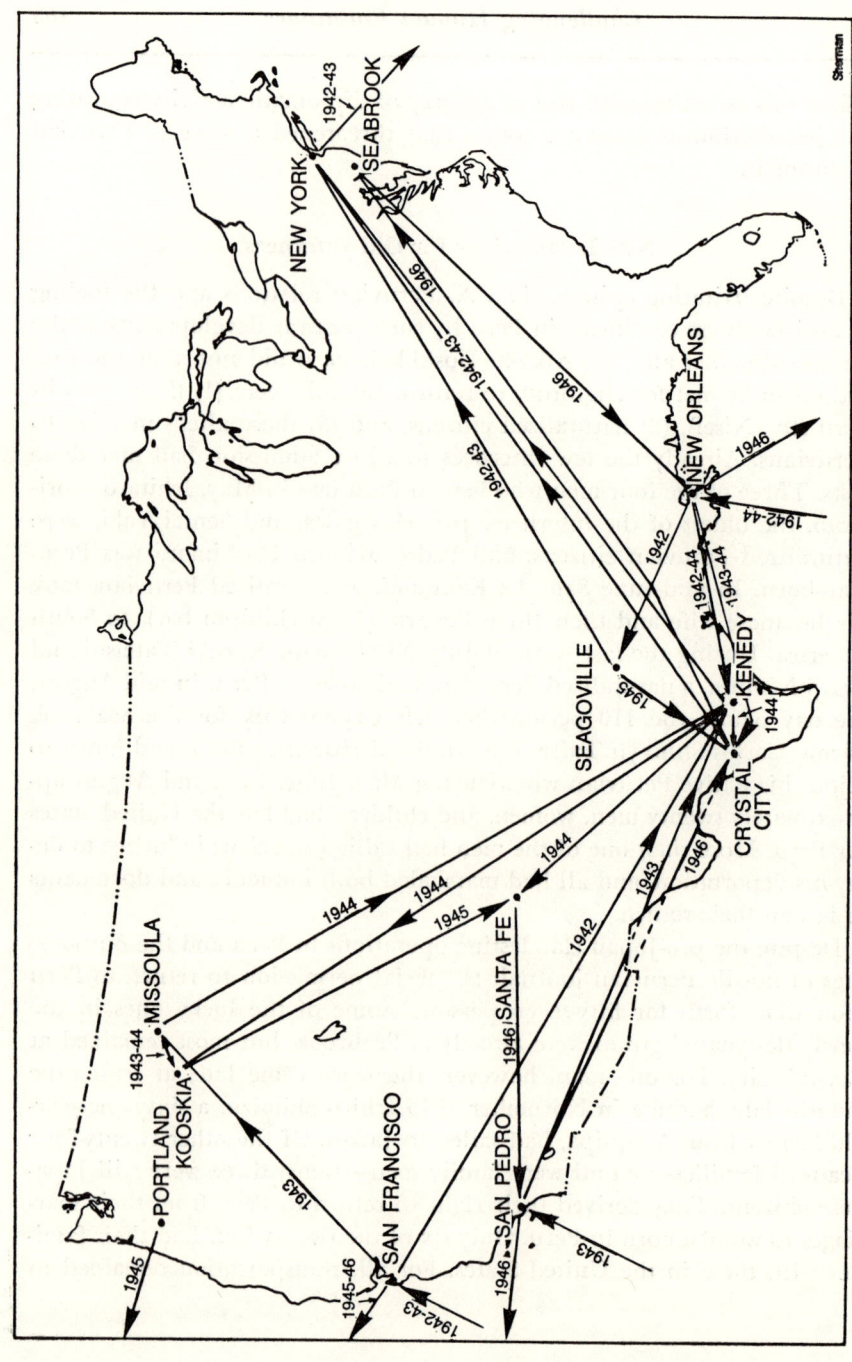

Map 2. Movements of the Peruvian Japanese, 1942–46

be arranged, but the joy that a few knew kindled the hopes of others.[46]

One of the men soon to return to his family was Iwamori Sakasegawa, the mechanic from Huacho around whom Collins had fashioned one of his pending habeas corpus cases. Denied a judicial victory—the case would be dismissed in February 1947—Collins nonetheless knew a humane victory as Sakasegawa prepared to return to his wife and seven children.[47]

Scarcely had the Crystal City internees digested word that Peru was opening its doors to some of them when a second contingent packed and entrained for Seabrook Farms. Exactly three weeks had elapsed between the first Seabrook-bound group and this one—enough time for the New Jersey employers to discover that the Peruvian Japanese were as industrious as their Japanese American predecessors. Meanwhile, labor shortages persisted during a peak production season, and even more worker losses were in the offing. After all, eleven of the adults in the August contingent were simply awaiting transportation to Peru.[48]

In this second group, the Seabrook enterprises virtually eliminated their requirement concerning ratio of children to adults. The September contingent of ninety-nine included only twenty-six family heads, six of whom were slated to return to Peru. Fourteen families totaled eighty-seven members—proof that even large families with numerous young children were now acceptable to the New Jersey employers. This time the families of Seiichi Higashide, Kakuaki Kaneko, Kunikichi Matsuda, and former spokesman Koshiro Mukoyama were welcome. The same was true for the Yuzo Shibayama family of eight, Kin Suzuki's seven, and the motherless eight in the Kotoku Yamashiro family. In this September group almost everyone who wanted to go to the Seabrook Farms did so. The enlarged community in New Jersey, totaling 209, represented two-thirds of all the Peruvian Japanese then in the United States.[49]

Some 105 other individuals were divided between the Crystal City Internment Camp and parole to private parties elsewhere in the United States. Fourteen, by this time, had won parole to individual guarantors, most of whom were in California. The ninety-one men, women, and children at Crystal City looked in various directions for their salvation. The families of Mantaro Kage, Kosuke Kitsutani, and Hideo Ohara, plus two men, tubercular Enzo Minamoto and grocer Ichijiro Yoshizumi, whose families were in Peru, already were on the list of those allowed to return to that country. Certain other families, among them those of Chuhei Kato, Usaburo Maoki, Iwaichi Naganuma, and Taro Ohashi, were seeking guarantors that would permit them to remain in the United States. Shrinking and hopeful, the Crystal City group appeared to be on the brink of extinction.[50]

In October, while the INS sought transportation to Peru, at least one indigent returnee, Mantaro Kage, suffered doubts and fears. Deported in January 1943 because he resided in the general vicinity of the American base at Talara, the one-time restaurateur and barber shop proprietor of Chulucanas, Department of Piura, had lost everything during his internment. Marriage to a native Peruvian facilitated his return to Peru, but how was he going to support nine children, only one of whom could be considered of working age. Before any authorities, American or Peruvian, could be brought to face the problem for which Kage was a glaring but not the sole example, he and his family had departed for Peru.[51]

On October 15 the first airplane ever chartered by the INS to effect the deportation of aliens transported thirty-one Peruvian Japanese to Peru. The flight, which originated at Philadelphia with five men from Seabrook Farms, continued to San Antonio where it picked up twenty-six men, women, and children from Crystal City. Three families were going home intact, the eleven members of the Mantaro Kage family, Kosuke Kitsutani and his five dependents, and Hideo Ohara, his wife, and four children. Every family included young Texans.[52] Their anxieties, however great, were exceeded by those of men returning to families after absences ranging from two to four years. How had Enzo Minamoto's wife, a native Peruvian, managed with three children aged five, two, and one when the authorities had shipped him to America? How would all the Minamotos manage when he, tubercular, returned home? Most of the wives had suffered the wartime barrage of anti-Japanese sentiment and physical loneliness, wondering whether their husbands' loyalty to Japan might exceed affection for families and Peru. Doubts surely assailed the Lima mechanic whose common-law native Peruvian wife was the mother of his two children. Going home was not joy unconfined.

A week later, at nearby Millville, New Jersey, twenty-six more Peruvian Japanese from the Seabrook Farms boarded a second Peru-bound plane. Ten of the thirteen men were returning to families in Peru; three had their families with them. Shoichi Ikeda remembered his former *shoyu* (soy sauce) establishment in Lima as he, his Nisei wife, and their Peruvian and American-born children headed for the land in which he had lived seventeen years. Similarly, fifty-six-year-old Octavio Taijiro Tochio surely looked forward to reestablishing in Arequipa his dry goods store to support his Peruvian wife Luisa, their three Peruvian-born children, and sixteen-month-old Utako, the Texas addition to their family. The third complete family, that of Iwazo Nakao of Lima, also boasted a young Texan. All of the men had been absent from Peru between two and four years. Among those now returning, Iwamori Sakasegawa wrote Collins, "I wish to express my deepest gratitude to you for your kindness and unrelenting efforts to be re-admitted to Peru."[53]

Certain persons on the two flights to Lima harbored a mingled sense of obligation and gratitude as they tried to pick up the threads of interrupted lives. Overwhelmingly Roman Catholic, the returnees had sent a delegation to visit the papal nuncio and Cardinal Guevara, archbishop of Lima. Reporting this to the National Catholic Welfare Conference, which, in Washington, had steadfastly supported the internee cause, the spokesmen for the returnees added, "We dare beg you to aid our compatriots still remaining in your country who are anxious to return to Peru."[54] The fortunate few who returned to Peru in October considered themselves the advance element of a continuing wave. Peruvian authorities, on the other hand, considered this show of official generosity the major, possibly the sole concession to be made to internees. But the dismal prospect of never returning to Peru was not entertained by approximately 180 hopeful individuals as they settled into their routine at Seabrook Farms.

## Life at Seabrook

The housing, schools, and all other considerations, important as they were, ranked below the all-important work that had drawn the internee-parolees to the Seabrook Farms. In view of the extensive acreage, the variety of crops, the planting, cultivating, harvesting, processing, packing, warehousing, and transportation, work assignments varied greatly. In almost every instance, however, the Peruvian Japanese, competing with Mexican-Americans and other unorganized and unskilled workers, faced the reality of relatively low wages.

When the Kakuaki Kaneko family arrived in the September contingent, both Kakuaki and his wife Otari immediately joined the work force, he at an hourly wage of 67.5 cents, she at 55.5 cents. Overtime work was plentiful, but it did not alter the wage schedules. Otari sorted and packed vegetables, and when they were unavailable she cut flowers. The Kanekos were supporting a family that included five children, the youngest an American, and their work lengthened into days, weeks, and months of financial scrambling. Kunio Takeshita, one of the unmarried men in the August group, remembers the many foods produced and processed—the corn, carrots, string beans, beets, potatoes, and spinach, among others. At times the processing plant operated twenty-four hours a day, and it was not unusual for a worker to clock sixty to seventy hours weekly. Saburo Ushida, also in the first group to go from Texas to New Jersey, remembers his wage as 65 cents per hour. Yet a third member of that first group, Hisao Fujii, recalls wages of 52.5 cents an hour. When the Mitsutaro Tawara family reached Seabrook Farms in August, four members immediately set to work. The two boys, Toshiharu and Victor, worked at the dock, receiving produce from the fields. Their days often included twelve hours of labor, at 62.5 cents an hour. Masao Kishi, then the twenty-four-year-old son of Hajime Kishi, recalls picking and freezing many kinds of vegetables. Some work, not directly related to food production, found carpenters, nurserymen, and others in support activities.[55]

Seabrook made many significant changes in the Peruvian Japanese way of life. For one thing, the housing afforded them greater privacy than they had known at Crystal City and helped to restore dignity that had suffered in camp. Many families attained greater unity, and parental discipline reasserted itself. At the same time that Japanese traits and values were reemerging, certain aspects of Americanization also intensified. For adults the purchasing of foodstuffs, clothing, and other necessities thrust them into the American economic system. For children, no longer attending a Japanese-language school, incorporation into the normal local school programs brought numerous influences, as English became paramount in their lives and their Spanish and Japanese suffered. This issue of the rapid Americanization of the youth, coupled with the traditional concern of Japanese parents about the education of children, would, in time, affect fundamental desires and decisions. The longer one was at Seabrook getting acquainted with American life in unfettered fashion, the more Seabrook became something other than a way station to Peru.

Some of the hazards and complications of American life quickly beset the parolees in New Jersey. Under the Internal Revenue Code all the new workers were treated as nonresident aliens and their wages were subject to a 30 percent withholding tax. After a personal exemption of $1.40 per day this 30 percent rate was applied to every parolee's wages. While all were getting introduced to American taxes, Eikichi Sakoda, introduced to the hazards of American traffic, was hospitalized, seriously injured in an automobile accident.[56]

# 8

# Drawn Out Finales

For numerous individuals of Japanese extraction, the American winter of 1946–47 was a season of hoping and waiting. In California and elsewhere Japanese Americans were hoping that the United States would face up to the injustice heaped on them during the war years, and they were waiting for Washington to enact a program that would compensate evacuees for their losses. A slow-growing sentiment worked on their behalf. At the same time the hopes of Peruvian Japanese parolees in New Jersey and Texas were bogging down at the hands of two insensitive bureaucracies, Peruvian and American, neither of which was nudged to action by any concerted public opinion. The autumn of 1946, marked by the novelty of the transition for many from Texas to New Jersey and the anticipated return that planeloads of Peru-bound colleagues had generated, had changed not only to the physical chill of winter but also to an anguished feeling that they were being frozen out.

Early in 1947 some 298 Japanese Peruvians remained in the United States: 178 at Seabrook Farms, ninety-one at Crystal City Internment Camp, twenty-six paroled elsewhere in the country (ten in Colorado, sixteen in California), and three confined to hospitals. All at one time or another, many on numerous occasions, had insisted on returning to Peru. Sixteen months after the conclusion of hostilities their chances of doing so revolved around issues of citizenship, Peruvian willingness to reunite families, and Washington's eagerness to wash its hands of an exasperating wartime legacy.

Assuming that parolee interest in Peru remained high in 1947—something that could not continue indefinitely—their chances of returning varied enormously. Six men, born in Peru, surely entertained strong hopes, despite problems regarding the registration of births. A score of

Japanese citizens counted on the Peruvian citizenship of their wives. In approximately fifty families in which both parents held Japanese citizenship fainter hopes centered on their Peruvian-born children. Almost nonexistent were the prospects of a half dozen childless couples in which both husband and wife were Japanese citizens. Similarly dim were the hopes of almost a score of unmarried Japanese men. But even childless Japanese couples and unmarried Japanese males knew that in Peru influence and money might produce miracles.

A few cases posed special problems. Would Peru readmit the Peruvian-born children and the Japanese wife of a man who had died in internment? Would Peru allow the reentry of a childless Japanese couple with three Peruvian-born stepchildren? What attitude would Peru adopt regarding the Japanese male whose American wife had mothered his three Peruvian-born children? Would Peru allow a Japanese father to rejoin a child whose Peruvian mother had died? Some hopes rode on the belief that stern Peruvian bureaucrats might alter their rigid rules. A potentially competing American interest hovered around those seventeen families that included young Americans and those fortunate few who had savored freedom and opportunity in Colorado and California.[1]

### Attorney at Work: Wayne M. Collins

One man who never wavered in his insistence that Peruvian Japanese would not be deported to Japan against their will, nor in his belief that their return to their adopted South American homeland could be achieved, lawyer Wayne M. Collins did not limit his efforts on their behalf to judicial proceedings. When he launched a multitargeted letter-writing campaign, his patience had worn thin.

His first appeal to Secretary of State George C. Marshall began, "During 1943 and 1944 [he neglected to include 1942] our Government, through the instrumentality of the State Department, in collaboration with the Government of Peru, kidnapped several hundred persons of Japanese ancestry then lawfully residing in Peru and thereafter lodged them in various concentration camps within the confines of the continental United States." He reminded Marshall that many internees were Peruvian citizens, that all had been forcibly removed from Peru, that no charge or evidence of wrongdoing had ever been adduced against them, and that early in 1946 all had been released from any claim of being alien enemies.

Marshall was also reminded of the test cases in habeas corpus proceedings that had halted the deportation program. "Thereafter," Collins wrote, "the State Department informed the Justice Department that the Government could not litigate the issues.... The litigation is held in abeyance in order that your Department and the Peruvian Government might arrange for their repatriation to Peru." Adding that "an undeserved internment is not conducive to anything but the general economic, moral and spiritual deterioration of these hapless victims of international intrigue, connivance and malice," Collins asserted, "the State Department primarily has been guilty of this.... I urge you to take immediate steps to obtain the return of these Peruvian Japanese and their children to Peru."[2]

This was just the opening blast by a man who would not couch righteous indignation in deferential phrasing and pious platitudes. In contrast to the officials and those of Collins's justice-seeking ACLU colleagues who were irritated by his sledgehammer approach, scores of Peruvian Japanese admired him.[3] His tactics demonstrated awareness that an individual who attacks a colossus, in this case national governments, on a relatively unpublicized and emotional issue cannot succeed by indulging customary restraint.

A lengthy letter put the matter before the new Peruvian Ambassador Jorge Prado along with detailed lists of the Peruvian Japanese. If the Peruvian replies, which concluded with the assertion that "this Embassy is not authorized to take any action in these cases," failed to satisfy him, the response of the Department of State proved even less palatable.[4]

Clattenburg's statement that the United States government was anxious to get the Peruvian Japanese out of this country and had no objection to their return to Peru "if the Peruvian Government indicates its willingness to accept them" said nothing about continuing negotiations on the subject, nor did it indicate that any pressure was being exerted on behalf of the Peruvian Japanese. Consequently Collins fired back, "I infer from your letter that our State Department is not very active in endeavoring to hasten their return to Peru.... The problem would seem to merit something more than inaction and indifference."[5]

Irritated by underling Clattenburg's bland generalities, Collins laid some specifics before Secretary Marshall. Among the Peruvian Japanese "abducted from their homes...by our Government and...lodged in concentration camps in this country," Collins cited three "suffering from the ravages of tuberculosis." Each of them—one the mother of three minor children, another the father of seven children, and the third also the parent of seven minor children—had requested and been refused the new streptomycin treatment for arresting the disease. "It would be astounding if our Government which is responsible jointly with the Peruvian Government for the affliction from which they suffer would refuse to supply this drug for them without cost under the circumstances."[6] Collins's efforts to rouse State Department concern and action combined legal and logical appeals regarding all the Peruvian Japanese with humanitarian and emotional appeals concerning individuals.

In a matter of weeks the lawyer informed the Department of State, "I have written to each of the executive officers, senators and deputies of the Republic of Peru urging them to use their good offices for the purpose of enabling the Peruvian Japanese ... to be repatriated to Peru. In addition I have written to the Pope in Rome, the Cardinal in Lima, and other Catholic Church dignitaries. ... What astounds me is that our own Government has been so negligent and callous in failing to impress the Peruvian authorities with the urgency of the matter."[7]

In the meantime the Department of State, in the first quarter of the year, had sent one relevant communication to the embassy in Lima. Acheson informed that mission (1) of the desire to liquidate the Peruvian Japanese problem, (2) that only seventy-two persons had been readmitted by Peru, (3) that the attitude of the American courts dictated that before any deportation proceedings took place individuals had to be given a bona fide opportunity to return to the country of previous residence, and (4) that the INS, busily issuing deportation warrants, planned to seek travel documents from Peruvian consuls. Along with all of this the Peruvian Foreign Office was to be reminded that the Peruvian Japanese were not dangerous within the meaning of Resolution VII of the Mexico City Conference.[8] The extent to which Collins might have inspired this communication is unknown. What is known is that it prompted no action in Lima.

Interspersed with his assaults on the citadels of power were Collins's efforts for his clients, collectively and individually. It pleased him to learn that Peru was considering the reentry of eighteen more of them and that the INS, acceding to a request from him, was permitting the Kakuaki Kaneko family to move to California from the Seabrook Farms. When Yoshisada Shiga voiced the hope that a stepson might be allowed to remain in the United States to complete his high school studies, Collins tendered both advice and assistance.[9]

Suspecting that apathy attended the problem within the Department of State and dissatisfied with the impact of his earlier efforts to provoke concern and action, Collins renewed his battle with an oblique approach. A four-page letter concerning the Peruvian Japanese went to countless members of Congress, among them Congressmen J. J. Allen, F. H. Havenner, and N. Poulson and Senators Sheridan Downey and William F. Knowland, all of California, and Senator Robert F. Wagner and Congressman Emanuel Celler of New York, Senator Alexander Wiley of Wisconsin, and Delegate J. R. Farrington of Hawaii. His letter not only detailed the wartime internment program, it also described the Peruvian Japanese as "the innocent victims of a shocking international plot of Machiavellian nature and proportion.... inasmuch as our Government primarily is responsible for having kidnapped them, impoverished them and wrongfully deprived them of their liberty," Collins continued, "it would seem only just that the Congress seriously consider legislation to compensate them for the losses they have suffered." (Congress was then considering compensation for the Japanese Americans, something it granted in niggardly fashion in 1948). In closing, Collins urged every official to use his good offices on behalf of the people from Peru.[10]

Almost at once the lawyer informed Secretary Marshall that he had directed appeals "to the President of Peru, his cabinet officers, each member of the Peruvian Senate and Chamber of Deputies and others" and "to our President, the Secretary of State, our Ambassador in Peru and to each United States Senator and Representative." Noting that the United States government had recently prevailed on Peru to make oil concessions to the International Petroleum Company, Collins remarked, "it seems to me that it ought to be willing to expend a little effort in persuading the Peruvian authorities to provide for the repatriation of these Peruvian residents in order to preserve their civil rights and liberties."[11] Even as he wrote that, Collins surely wondered whether a humanitarian issue could vie with an economic one in the minds of American officials.

When a deluge of inquiries from congressmen descended on the Department of State, Director of the Office of American Republic Affairs Ellis O. Briggs routinely summarized the wartime program and the meager postwar developments. By way of explaining the existing stalemate, he told each correspondent, in exactly the same words, "To date the Peruvian Government has not indicated its final decision." Looking to the future, Briggs added, "In the event that the Peruvian Government declines to accept any additional Japanese from the group, it will be necessary, under the law, to then issue deportation orders to Japan, unless some special legislation is introduced in Congress in the form of a Bill specifically exempting these Japanese from the provisions of the Immigration laws and thus permitting them to remain in this country. I am not aware, however, that any such legislation is contemplated."[12]

A contemporary opinion by Legal Adviser R. W. Flournoy indicated that Briggs was not alone in the departmental speculation about the uncertain future. "A difficulty which may be encountered in these cases," Flournoy wrote, "if the aliens in question resort to habeas corpus proceedings, lies in the fact that the deportation provisions in our immigration laws contemplate cases of aliens who entered the United States of their own accord." Six months later Flournoy's fear became reality when a U.S. Circuit Court of Appeals, treating the case of Guatemalan German internee Max Paetau, held, "An alien seized by the United States elsewhere, and brought to the United States against his will for internment for security reasons as an alien enemy, cannot be deported as an 'immigrant,' at least not before he has been afforded an opportunity to depart voluntarily."[13]

However clouded the future prospect, the immediate present did brighten momentarily at midyear when Ambassador Prado announced Peruvian willingness to readmit the four members of the family of Shoichi Mishima, who, in February 1943, had bought off his then scheduled deportation from Peru. Prado's statement, "The Peruvian Government has been prompted to take this decision in consideration of the fact that the two children of Mr. and Mrs. Mishima were born in Peru," encouraged both the Department of State and the long-suffering Peruvian Japanese. On two counts the readmission of the Mishima family rekindled optimism among the parolees: because scores of their families also included Peruvian-born children and because neither Shoichi nor Kikuno Mishima possessed Peruvian citizenship. The reply by the State Department reminded Ambassador Prado additionally, "There are also five cases of individuals who appear to have been born in Peru and a group of fourteen who have Peruvian-born wives."[14]

Ten days later Peruvian Foreign Minister Enrique García Sayán arrived in Washington for a four-day visit. He called on President Truman, lunched with Secretary Marshall, and "official Washington left no stone unturned in paying him its respects,"[15] but apparently the visit included no consideration of the Peruvian Japanese issue. If the State Department's failure to introduce it stemmed from belief that the recent concession regarding one family constituted an open sesame to the total problem, time soon disabused it of that outlook.

In October, having received no reply to its note of June, the State Department once more nudged the Peruvian embassy. Again there was no reply, a state of affairs that persisted the remainder of the year.[16] In the course of twelve months Peru had accepted four persons. Twenty-eight months after the end of the war any disappointment felt by American authorities was trifling compared with the dashed hopes of hundreds of Peruvian Japanese.

As 1948 dawned, the principals maintained these stances: hundreds of Peruvian Japanese desired to return to Peru; Peruvian officials continued to ignore their own promise to readmit Japanese with close Peruvian family ties; and American officials, deferring to Peru and ignoring the Peruvian Japanese, were making minimal diplomatic moves and those primarily when pressure forced them. Still the number one applier of that pressure, Wayne M. Collins refused to allow the Department of State to bury the matter. Early in the year he told Marshall that he found it incredible that United States diplomats could not prevail on Peru to allow those people to return. He concluded, saying, "If your office feels that it is helpless and cannot persuade the Peruvian Minister of Foreign Affairs to issue visas to these people kindly let me know by return mail and I shall telephone that Minister and ascertain whether or not he will accede to the request of a private American citizen." Further indicating his willingness to ignore the diplomatic apparatus, Collins asked Ambassador Cooper whether the Peruvian president and foreign minister would understand English in case he telephoned them.[17] Again the amount of inspiration Collins supplied is uncertain, but three days later the department that had learned nothing from the Peruvian embassy in the course of six months returned to the issue, instructing Cooper in Lima, "If for no other purpose than for the record, the Department now requests that you formally approach the Foreign Ministry on this subject." Compounding the State Department's frustration was the admission by the INS that nine months of effort to procure travel documents from Peruvian consuls had yielded not a single visa.[18]

Eight months after receipt of a note from Foreign Minister García Sayán, the embassy belatedly reported its contents to Washington, adding, "it would be inadvisable again to take up the matter with the Ministry of Foreign Affairs." Indicative that official lethargy was widespread, a list of persons eligible to return to Peru which García Sayán had promised in June 1947 had not left his office the following February. Next, when the State Department chided the embassy for withholding information, it announced that it was sending two detailed lists of the Peruvian Japanese, but the embassy was baffled when it received only one list.[19] Someone casting an Alphonse and Gaston act could not have found characters more true to life.

Naturally Wayne Collins was unaware of such depressing detail, but just as naturally he wearied of waiting, and so he proceeded to fire a volley in the direction of the White House. After mentioning the hundreds of innocent victims, two wrongdoing governments, and the passage of five years to President Truman, he wrote, "I urge that you immediately take steps to withdraw our Ambassador from Peru and also to notify the Peruvian Government that, until it authorizes the return of these unfortunates to their Peruvian homeland, the United States prefers that the Peruvian Ambassador to the United States be recalled to Peru."[20]

Even as Washington apparently hoped that some generous action in Lima would resolve the problem, two complex dimensions of the impasse were recognized: (1) the decision in *Paetau* v. *Watkins* made impossible the deportation of the Peruvian Japanese, and (2) "unless Peru or some other government permits their entry it would appear that the Peruvian Japanese may remain permanently in the United States." The thinking of Congressman Emanuel Celler was in the same vein, but when he asked, "Should any of these Peruvian nationals apply for permanent residence in the United States via the Immigration and Naturalization Service, would they be permitted to stay in this country?" he was informed, "The Department is not aware of any such plan."[21]

When Marshall's request for a progress report brought nothing from Lima, the department turned once more to the Peruvian embassy and again learned nothing. As the year ended, Collins wrote the secretary of state and registered his continuing disgust that no solution had eliminated the dilemma of the Peruvian Japanese, but he did so in an unusually restrained manner. He told Marshall that 241 of the parolees still desired to return to Peru, and he urged a renewed approach to Lima in the wake of the October revolt that had toppled the administration of President Bustamante. The others, approximately fifty in number, "because of their prolonged sojourn here, now are applying for a permanent suspension of deportation under the provisions of Title 8 USCA, Sec. 155 (c), with the view to remaining permanently in the United States."[22]

As 1949 dawned, the Department of State instructed its embassy to raise the issue of the repatriation of the Peruvian Japanese with the government of President Manuel A. Odría, adding, "Wayne Collins, Attorney for these persons, indicates new government might be more favorably inclined...." Two months later a highly negative report reached Washington. After reciting some of the delaying tactics of the Peruvian Foreign Office, the dispatch asserted, "it is believed practically all Japanese who were deported from Peru during the war and who have relatives in Peru with sufficient influence to procure their return, already have been brought back to Peru.... The Government of Peru is not interested in the fate of Japanese in question and would prefer that they be sent back to Japan or remain in the United States. Embassy is, therefore, of the opinion that it would be useless to pursue the matter further."[23]

That spring, seven years after the first deportee-internees had left Peru for the United States, extreme frustration dogged both the Peruvian Japanese and the Department of State. Three representatives of the former, Ginzo Murono, Hajime Kishi, and Manuel E. Ikari, detailed their "long years of worry, melancholy and mental agony," stated their worries about the education of their children, and appealed to be released and returned to Peru. Almost simultaneously a State Department memorandum declared that "the obvious solution is to regularize their status in the United States as permanent immigrants legally admitted" and proposed that the Policy Committee on Immigration and Naturalization "draw up or arrange for the preparation of legislation granting these deportees status as permanent lawfully admitted immigrants."[24]

### Resolution Down the Road

In the spring of 1949 the Department of State understood the dilemma —the Peruvian Japanese would not go to Japan and could not return to Peru—and it knew the solution. But five more years were destined to pass before the obvious solution became a reality.

In the meantime the Peruvian Japanese, agonizing over their future, had scrambled as best they could to better their immediate prospects. Consider the case of Taro and Fusae Ohashi and their three children, one an invalid. For months the Ohashi family, aided by attorney Collins, had petitioned parole. On a temporary basis Taro had gone to Chicago to study the plastics industry "to prepare for future life in Peru." But as the moment for their exodus from Crystal City approached, weariness and dismay beset the family. "We are really tired out of the long internment life," Taro wrote. Health problems plagued more than one member of the family.[25]

After more than fifty months of internment, this paroled family moved to San Francisco, sponsored by Wayne M. Collins, who next strove to win institutional care for the handicapped child. Taro applied for suspension of that unceasing torment, the deportation order. Something else that then eluded him was steady employment. Late in 1949 the Board of Immigration Appeals informed the Ohashi family, "It is ordered that the hearing be reopened . . . and It is further ordered that orders and warrants of deportation now outstanding be withdrawn."[26]

Thirty-two months later, in July 1952, that hearing took place. By then the family, having resided in the United States more than seven years, "met the residence requirements for suspension of deportation under Section 19 (c) (2) (b) of the Immigration Act of 1917." A check of local and federal records had failed to reveal any arrest, criminal record, or connection with any subversive groups, and on September 3, 1952, the deportation of the family was ordered suspended, subject to congressional approval. A year later a concurrent resolution of Congress approved the suspension of deportation.[27]

During the late 1940s and early 1950s other Peruvian Japanese, individuals and families, struggled in like fashion, with similar results. In 1948 the family of Mitsutaro and Kiwa Tawara, sponsored by Kiwa's Denver-based Japanese American sister, had left Seabrook Farms for the mainstream of American life, Colorado style. In 1951, Hajime Kishi and his sons Masao and Katsumi were encouraged to exchange the Seabrook Farms for southernmost California in the knowledge that Kakuaki Kaneko and his family had successfully established themselves there. Around Los Angeles and San Francisco others also dotted the California scene.[28]

Chicago came to represent opportunity and home for a considerable number of the Peruvian Japanese. There Kunio Takeshita found a sponsor that permitted his departure from New Jersey, and there he met and married an American Nisei, a step that hastened his Americanization. Leaving Seabrook Farms somewhat later, George Hisao Fujii and his San Diego–born Nisei bride tried Los Angeles, San Francisco, and Denver before settling in Chicago. Along the way the one-time chicken farmer had turned electrician and mechanic. Chicago likewise drew Seiichi Higashide, the father of five who long before had told American authorities, "I wish to stay in the United States with the whole family and I wish to educate my children in the United States." Kin Suzuki, widow of Antonio Eiichi, and her five children also found Chicago an agreeable place to settle. Without his wife and four daughters, all of whom remained in Peru until years later when two of the children joined him, Saburo Ushida also moved to Chicago, beginning a new life at age forty-eight. In time the former owner of four stores in Peru established his own business, this time a dry-cleaning establishment.[29]

The years that injected cultural confusion into the lives of all these Peruvian Japanese, eroded the hopes of the adults of returning to Peru, and confounded the educational prospects of their children proved eventually to have some redeeming features. In the United States, though only rarely did an article focus on the plight of the Peruvian Japanese,[30] a sequence of circumstances unintentionally improved their prospects. For one thing, domestically, the American public, aware of both the extraordinary heroism of Japanese American servicemen during the war and the injustice thrust upon 110,000 Japanese Americans, was undergoing some fundamental changes of attitude about persons of Japanese ancestry. Congress even made an effort, a limited one, to compensate one-time internees of the WRA program. In the same period, internationally, the spectacularly harmonious MacArthur-led occupation of Japan further altered prewar and wartime stereotypes. At midcentury the outbreak of the struggle in Korea converted Japan into supporter and quasi ally of a United States military effort. On a front that combined domestic and international matters, amended American immigration and naturalization laws were making it easier for Japanese, those thousands previously rendered "aliens ineligible to citizenship" as well as the remaining Peruvian Japanese internees, among others. So it was, for the Peruvian Japanese, that as their chances of returning to Peru disappeared, their chances of winning permanent residence status and the related opportunity to apply for American citizenship increased. Finally, on August 31, 1954, a portion of Public Law 751 read, "The first sentence of section 6 of the Refugee

Relief Act of 1953 (67 Stat. 403) is hereby amended to read as follows: 'Any alien who establishes that prior to July 1, 1953, he... was brought to the United States from other American republics for internment, may, not later than June 30, 1955, apply to the Attorney General of the United States for an adjustment of his immigration status.' "[31]

At last every Peruvian Japanese who had been deported from Peru and interned in the United States had found a homeland, many in Japan, a few in Peru, and the remaining hundreds in the United States. Administrative frustration, rather than either understanding or compassion, finally closed a thirteen-year chapter in which fear and hatred had disrupted the lives of innocent thousands.

# Epilogue

Time enough for remembering—almost forty years—has elapsed since the outbreak of the war that twisted the lives of thousands of Peruvian Japanese deportee-internees and tormented unknown thousands who lived those wartime years in Peru under the constant threat of deportation and internment.

During the succeeding decades the one-time Peruvian Japanese who elected repatriation to Japan have once again simply become Japanese. One who reasserted his Japanese loyalty and reestablished his Japanese identity was Okinawa-born Ryosho Taira. In 1934, at age twenty-seven, he had gone to Peru to teach in one of the Peruvian Japanese schools in Lima. Parties to the third deportation, he and his wife Nobuko left Peru aboard the *Shawnee*. Their return to Japan in September 1943 afforded them ample opportunity to experience something more fearsome than deportation and internment, the devastating invasion of their Okinawa by the American military. That, too, Ryosho survived, and thirty-three years later the one-time teacher in Lima and former internee in Seagoville was occupying the office of mayor of the city of Naha.[1]

Generally, however, it is impossible to trace those who returned to Japan. Wartime chaos dispersed many of the earliest returnees. Among those who returned in the postwar period, economic prostration, then economic opportunities, surely moved many from the areas to which family ties had first called them. From all, postwar conditions demanded maximum adaptability; from some who had expected a victorious homeland the strain might have been excessive. Amid the shifting fortunes afforded by decades, one can only wonder whether any of those Texas-born babies, now in their thirties, ever used their American birthright to effect yet another move.

Fewer than 5 percent of the deported Peruvian Japanese—considerably fewer than one hundred persons—were allowed to return to South America. The family of Jorge Koshiro Mukoyama, denied reentry into Peru, started anew in Venezuela. The fortunate few who did return to Peru included the Nisei whose births had been recorded in compliance with Peruvian law, the small number of men who had renounced Japanese citizenship to become naturalized Peruvians, and those Japanese whose wives were Peruvian citizens. By the end of 1946 most were readjusting to Peru. For some, that early period was economically difficult—a struggle to regain property, a struggle to reestablish oneself, a struggle to survive. For some, that early period was socially difficult—a torment for the man who, having dreamed of a happy reunion, had to face the reality of his wife's infidelity.

Nonetheless the returnees resumed their places in the Peruvian Japanese community, again principally in and around Lima. Some of them operated gift shops, sporting goods stores, and bazaars. An occasional returnee practices a profession. They have actively supported the development of the Centro Cultural Peruano-Japonés, the Universidad Católica, the Estadio Japonés, and the Jardín Japonés—a succession of postwar contributions that enrich life in Lima. Jiro Hasegawa, now dead, was sixty-two years old when, in 1950, he played a major role in the reestablishment of the Japanese language press in the Peruvian capital. That newspaper, *Perū Shimpō*, continues its operations today. When returned ex-internee Ichitaro Morimoto died in 1959 at age eighty-seven, he was widely honored for his public-spirited philanthropy and his unselfish and inspiring leadership within the Japanese colony.

When one sits and talks with men of their wartime experiences, neither humor nor malice punctuates their recollection of events of thirty-five years ago. Time has tempered them. Several men who once saw the United States only from behind fences in the shadow of guard towers have seen fit to send children and grandchildren to colleges in the United States.[2]

Unlike the story of the deported and interned Peruvian Japanese, no full account of the wartime experiences of the Japanese community that remained in Peru will emerge. Unknown will be the precise number of men whose pocketbooks and influential contacts enabled them to escape deportation. Unknown will be the total amount of money paid as bribes. Unknown will be the complete record of the property transfers, confiscations, and other maneuvers by which Peruvians eagerly victimized Peruvian Japanese. On every count, officially and unofficially, Peru prefers to forget—better said, ignore—a chapter that lends no distinction to its history.

In the United States during the mid-1950s, men whose tenacious hold on Japanese citizenship had previously barred their return to Peru did not repeat that mistake. Most of them rushed to obtain American citizenship at the earliest opportunity. His United States passport now enables one Nisei who was denied the right to return to Peru to go back there to visit relatives, something he has done repeatedly. Citizenship paved the way for Taro Ohashi's employment in the United States Postal Service. However, in the United States, as in Peru, the one-time internees have tended to become independent proprietors—nurserymen in California, Colorado, and Texas, owners of small shops in Chicago. The most unified group—so conscious of that unity that they founded their own organization, the Chicago Peru-kai—is based in and around the Windy City. There and elsewhere in America, from coast to coast, the contributions of the one-time Peruvian Japanese have been consistently positive. Neither relief roles nor registers of jails carry their names, and their accustomed emphasis on education has been reflected in the lives of their children.[3]

Today, is it enough to remind ourselves that former Secretary of State Acheson, who once blurted out, "we...don't want to be stuck with them," ill appreciated the potential of these accidental Americans? Consider one little girl who came to internment as a four-year-old and grew up to be a medical researcher at a leading New York City hospital. Consider one of her brothers who uses his Ph.D degree in cancer research. Consider, too, the other brother, the one who was born at Crystal City Internment Camp and now serves as a vice president of a major New York bank.[4]

Today, is it enough to remind every American, as has been done by John K. Emmerson, the man who knew it best, that the program of deportation and internment thought so necessary and pursued so relentlessly by countless American officials "was clearly a violation of human rights and was not justified by any plausible threat to the security of the Western Hemisphere."[5]

More than twenty years ago, in the process of applying for American citizenship, Saburo Ushida was asked, "Why do you want to stay in America?" By then well into his fifties, with Peruvian and American experiences that welled up in memory, Ushida replied, "I have received much mistreatment at the hands of American authorities and I disliked the United States but at Seabrook Farms and here in Chicago I have met many friendly people because of whom I have developed a desire to remain here."

"You should not have said those things about America," replied the naturalization officer. But he did not own memories that included apprehension in Peru with the connivance of American officials, transportation to America guarded by American soldiers, being told that he was an illegal entrant into a country whose officials had forced that entry, being fenced in as if he were a vicious animal, and being shifted about almost as if he were an inanimate object.[6]

Is it only for victims such as Saburo Ushida to summon up such righteous indignation? Even as one reflects on certain events of the 1940s and 1950s and concludes that they were unnecessary militarily, inept politically, and inhumane socially, it is no consolation that they are part of the dead past in which the Alien Act of 1798, President Roosevelt's Executive Order 9066, General DeWitt's orders on our West Coast, and Ambassador Norweb's program in Peru fostered gross abuse of elementary human rights. The uncertain future that precipitates other tense and fear-laden moments may unfortunately find American law, an American president, the American military, and American diplomats equally able and willing to violate the human rights of innocent men, women, and children.

# Abbreviations

| | |
|---|---|
| AECS | Alien Enemy Control Section |
| AECU | Alien Enemy Control Unit |
| AmChLima | American Chargé, Lima |
| AmEmLima | American Embassy, Lima |
| AmEmPanama | American Embassy, Panama |
| AmLegBern | American Legation, Bern |
| DC | Department of Commerce |
| DJ | Department of Justice |
| DS | Department of State |
| EW | European War |
| FBI | Federal Bureau of Investigation |
| FRUS | *Foreign Relations of the United States* |
| GPO | Government Printing Office |
| HAHR | *Hispanic American Historical Review* |
| INS | Immigration and Naturalization Service |
| INS Files | Immigration and Naturalization Service series 146–13–2–1 through 146–13–2–2488 of Alien Enemy World War II, Detention and Internment (Accession No. 53A10, RG60). All citations are by the last group of numbers alone (i.e., 1 to 2488). |
| NA | National Archives, Washington, D.C. |
| NCWC | National Catholic Welfare Conference |
| ND | Navy Department |
| PAU | Pan American Union |
| PW | Pacific War |
| RG | Record Group |
| SpEm | Spanish Embassy |
| SS | Secretary of State |
| SWP | Special War Problems Division |
| SwLeg | Swiss Legation |
| USCC | United States Catholic Conference |
| WD | War Department |
| WMC Papers | Wayne M. Collins Papers |
| WNRC | Washington National Records Center, Suitland, Maryland |
| WRA | War Relocation Authority |

# Notes

### Preface

1. INS Files, nos. 376, 1864, and 2148, RG60, WNRC; U.S., DS, *The Proclaimed List of Certain Blocked Nationals*, Supplement 5, December 9, 1941 (Washington: GPO, 1941), p. 12; and Arthur Shinei Yakabi to CHG, Seabrook, N.J., April 1, 1977.
2. *La Constitución del Perú* (1933). Translation by writer.
3. U.S., *United States Statutes at Large*, vol. 1 (Boston: Little, Brown and Company, 1861), p. 577, and *FRUS 1942*, vol. 5 (Washington: GPO, 1962), p. 90.
4. Peruvian and American sources do not agree on the total number of internees. *Zai Peru hōjin 75 nen no ayumi* (*The 75th Anniversary of the Japanese Resident in Peru*) (Lima: Editorial *Perú Shimpo*, 1974), p. 151, lists the total as 1,771, while State Department Memorandum, January 30, 1946, 711.6211 AR/1-3046, RG59, NA, lists 1,799. Neither total includes the dozens of children born in internment.

### 1. The Japanese in Prewar Peru

1. C. Harvey Gardiner, *The Japanese and Peru, 1873–1973* (Albuquerque: University of New Mexico Press, 1975), pp. 24–27; James Lawrence Tigner, "The Okinawans in Latin America," Ph.D. diss., Stanford University, 1956, pp. 584–86; INS Files, no. 2202, RG60, WNRC; conversation with George Hisao Fujii, Chicago, August 29, 1976; Japanese Canadian Centennial Project, *A Dream of Riches: The Japanese Canadians, 1877–1977* (Toronto, 1978), pp. 24, 30–31, 50–51; C. Harvey Gardiner, "The Japanese and Mexico," manuscript; and C. Harvey Gardiner, "The Japanese in Brazil, 1908–1968," paper presented October 30, 1968, at the Southern Historical Association, Washington, D.C.

For details concerning the INS Files, see both Abbreviations and Bibliographical Essay.

2. Gardiner, *The Japanese and Peru, 1873–1973*, pp. 61–64; Perú, Dirección Nacional de Estadística, *Censo nacional de población y occupación 1940: Primer volúmen, Resumenes generales* (Lima, 1944), pp. 522, 528–29; Japanese Canadian Centennial Project, *A Dream of Riches*, p. 78; Gardiner, "The Japanese and Mexico"; Gaimusho (Japanese Foreign Office), *Nippon to Burajiru (Japan and Brazil)* (Tokyo, 1978), p. 17; and Tigner, "The Okinawans in Latin America," pp. 589–91.

3. Gardiner, *The Japanese and Peru, 1873–1973*, pp. 73–77; Perú, *Censo nacional de población y ocupación 1940*, pp. 522–23; Tigner, "The Okinawans in Latin America," pp. 611–16; and Japanese Canadian Centennial Project, *A Dream of Riches*, pp. 18, 24, 30, 64.

4. Perú, Cámara de Diputados, *Compilación de la legislación peruana*, 5 vols. (Lima: Cámara de Diputados, 1950–56), 2:792, 3:1092–93, 1319–20, 1333, 4:1422; Arturo Nieves Ayala, ed., *Los extranjeros ante la ley peruana* (Lima: Talleres Offset "La Confianza," [1961]), pp. 1–23, 72–80; C. Harvey Gardiner, "El desarrollo del sentimiento antijaponés en el Peru, 1899–1941," *Boletín de la Academia de Historia del Valle del Cauca* (Cali, Colombia), 41, nos. 161–64 (December 1973): 811–23; Gardiner, *The Japanese and Peru, 1873–1973*, pp. 38–39, 50–55, 61–80; John K. Emmerson, *The Japanese Thread* (New York: Holt, Rinehart and Winston, 1978), pp. 130–39; Edward N. Barnhart, "Citizenship and Political Tests in Latin American Republics in World War II," *HAHR*, 42, no. 3 (August 1962): 299–300, 309, 318; Edward N. Barnhart, "Japanese Internees from Peru," *Pacific Historical Review*, 31, no. 2 (May 1962): 169–70; INS Files, nos. 361 and 483, RG60, WNRC; Japanese Canadian Centennial Project, *A Dream of Riches*, pp. 30–31, 38–39; Gordon Hirabayashi, "The Japanese Experience in North America," paper presented at the Symposium on Emigration of the Japanese People, Tokyo, December 6–8, 1978; C. Harvey Gardiner, "The Panamanian Japanese and World War II," manuscript; and Gardiner, "The Japanese in Brazil, 1908–1968."

5. Louis G. Dreyfus, Jr., to SS, March 14, 1940, 800.20210/495, RG59, NA; *FRUS 1940*, vol. 5 (Washington: GPO, 1961), pp. 158–59; U.S., *United States Statutes at Large*, vol. 54, pt. 2 (Washington: GPO, 1941), pp. 2344–65, vol. 55, pt. 2 (Washington: GPO, 1942), pp. 1254–62; and *FRUS 1941*, vol. 7 (Washington: GPO, 1962), pp. 524–48.

6. J. Edgar Hoover to Adolf A. Berle, Jr., August 6, 1941, 862.20223/181, RG59, NA. A second translation of the same Aprista memorandum, thought to have been written by Haya de la Torre, was sent by Hoover to Berle September 30, 1941, 862.20223/200, RG59, NA.

7. Dreyfus to SS, March 14, 1940, 800.20210/495, Hoover to Berle, February 24, 1941, 862.20223/157, and February 25, 1941, 894.20223/70, and J. F. McGurk to SS, July 1, 1941, 892.20223/175, RG59, NA.

## 2. Shaping a Deportation-Internment Program

1. J. Irizarry y Puente, "Exclusion and Expulsion of Aliens in Latin America," *American Journal of International Law*, 36, no. 2 (April 1942): 257, 260, 262–64, 267–69.

2. Norweb to SS, April 21, 1942, 894.20223/124, RG59, NA; Roger Daniels, *Concentration Camps USA: Japanese Americans and World War II* (New York: Holt, Rinehart and Winston, 1972), pp. 43–70; *FRUS 1942*, vol. 1 (Washington: GPO, 1960), p. 420; and Japanese Canadian Centennial Project, *A Dream of Riches*, pp. 77–78, 90, 92, 111.

3. Ambassador Edwin C. Wilson to SS, October 20, 1941, 740.00115 PW/1, AmEmPanama to SS, December 18, 1941, 894.20219/112, SS to WD, December 20, 1941, and SS to AmEmPanama, December 23, 1941, 740.00115 PW/13½, Wilson to SS, January 14, 1942, 740.00115 PW/76, RG59, NA; and *La Estrella de Panamá* (Panama), December 8, 1941.

For related U.S.–Panamanian cooperation during World War I, see DS, *Papers Relating to the Foreign Relations of the United States 1918: Supplement 2, The World War*, vol. 3 (Washington: GPO, 1933), pp. 232–34; DS, *Papers Relating to the Foreign Relations of the United States: The Lansing Papers 1914–1920*, vol. 1 (Washington: GPO, 1939), pp. 593, 631–32; and Norman J. Padelford, "Neutrality, Belligerency, and the Panama Canal," *American Journal of International Law*, 35, no. 1 (January 1941): 74–75.

4. U.S., DS, *The Proclaimed List of Certain Blocked Nationals*, Supplement 5, December 9, 1941 (Washington: GPO, 1941), pp. 12–13; INS Files, nos. 2232, 1519, 1383, 1528, and 402, RG60, WNRC; Emmerson, *The Japanese Thread*, pp. 133–34; conversation with Ginzo Murono, Seabrook, N.J., October 7, 1977; and Hiroko Stevenson (granddaughter of Jiro Hasegawa) to CHG, Wilmington, Delaware, March 25, 1978.

5. INS Files, no. 2213, RG60, WNRC. Needless to say, Japanese names related to this study also promoted confusion in other records, including those of the Department of State, the INS, and the FBI.

6. "The War: Third Meeting of Ministers of Foreign Affairs of the American Republics," DS *Bulletin*, 6, no. 137 (February 7, 1942): 128–30.

7. Emergency Advisory Committee for Political Defense, *Annual Report (July 1943)* (Montevideo, 1943), pp. 10, 24–35, 73, 75, 77. A *Second Annual Report* (Montevideo, 1944), covers the work of the committee in the period July 15, 1943 to October 15, 1944. Related documents are in *FRUS 1942*, vol. 5 (Washington: GPO, 1962), pp. 74–107; *FRUS 1943*, vol. 5 (Washington: GPO, 1965), pp. 2–39; and *FRUS 1944*, vol. 7 (Washington: GPO, 1967), pp. 1–26.

8. Military Attaché to WD, December 7, 1941, 894.20223/111, RG59, NA, and *Inmigración japonesa al Perú 75 aniversario 1899–1974* (Lima: Editorial *Perú Shimpō*, 1974), pp. 39–40.

9. Jefferson Patterson to SS, December 15, 1941, 800.20223/40, and Norweb to SS, March 10, 1942, 894.20223/114, RG59, NA.
10. Norweb to SS, February 11, 1942, 701.0023/24, RG59, NA.
11. Norweb to SS, February 3, 1942, and February 12, 1942, 701.0023/18 and 25, DS to AmEmLima, February 13, 1942, 701.0023/24, Norweb to SS, February 14, 1942, 701.0023/32, February 15, 1942, 701.0023/26, March 3, 1942, 740.00115 EW1939/2137, and March 4, 1942, 701.0023/36, RG59, NA.
12. Norweb to SS, March 5, 1942, 701.0023/34, RG59, NA.
13. *FRUS 1941*, vol. 6 (Washington: GPO, 1963), pp. 498–503; *FRUS 1942*, vol. 6 (Washington: GPO, 1963), pp. 664–94; and Stetson Conn and Bryon Fairchild, *The Framework of Hemisphere Defense* (Washington: GPO, 1960), p. 203.
14. Welles to AmEmLima, March 5, 1942, and Norweb to SS, March 7, 1942, 740.00115 EW1939/2137 and 2184, RG59, NA.
15. Patterson to SS, March 10, 1942, 740.00115 EW1939/2341, RG59, NA.
16. L. S. Rowe (PAU) to L. Duggan (DS), March 17, 1942 (includes an undated letter by Larrañaga), 894.20223/119, RG59, NA. A year later Manuel Gallagher of the Peruvian Ministry of Finance shared Larrañaga's view regarding the fire hazard posed by the Japanese in Lima; see *FRUS 1943*, vol. 6 (Washington: GPO, 1965), p. 721.
17. DS Memorandum, March 19, 1942, 740.00115 EW1939/2439, RG59, NA.
18. Norweb to SS, March 19, 1942, 894.20223/115, RG59, NA, and Emmerson, *The Japanese Thread*, pp. 126–27, 139, 142–43, 148 (quotation).
19. Norweb to SS, March 24, 1942, 701.0023/55, RG59, NA.
20. Patterson to SS, March 31, 1942, Allan Dawson to SS, April 1, 1942, 740.00115 EW1939/2588 and 2535, and Boaz Long to SS, Quito, April 2, 1942, 701.0022/29, RG59, NA.
21. Welles to AmEmLima, April 4, 1942, 740.00115 EW1939/2614a, and Norweb to SS, April 2, 1942, 701.0023/56, RG59, NA.

## 3. Coming and Going, by the Hundreds

1. Norweb to SS, April 6, 1942, and April 7, 1942 (includes Rolland Welch Memorandum), 740.00115 EW1939/2590 and 2718, RG59, NA; U.S., Department of Commerce, Bureau of Marine Inspection and Navigation, *Merchant Vessels of the United States 1941* (Washington: GPO, 1941), p. 28.
2. The above information is derived from INS Files, nos. 106, 108, 111–14, 118, 126, 129, 132–35, 137, 140, 143, 145, 154, 157, 161, 164, 166, 167, 178, 184, 187, 188, 194, 195, 206–8, 212, 226–29, 231, 233–35, 247–50, 261–65, 270, 276, 280, 282, 284, 287, 289, 296–98, 300, 308, 315, 319, 320, 322, 329, 340, 341, 344, 346–47, 355–57, 360, 362, 379–82, 395, 398, 406, 407, 413, 417, 431–33, 439, 440, 454–56, 466,

479, 480, 482, 496, 499, 504–6, 514, 520, 526, 529, 531, 533, 546, 548, 554, 559, 576, 580, 596, 608, 615, 635, 637, 646, 648, and 1547, RG60, WNRC; Norweb to SS, April 7, 1942 (includes Auxiliary Section Memorandum), 740.00115 EW1939/2718, RG59, NA; and U.S., DS, *The Proclaimed List of Certain Blocked Nationals*, Supplement 5, December 9, 1941, pp. 11–15, and Supplement 6, December 23, 1941, pp. 12–13.

3. INS Files, nos. 227–29, 231, 296–98, and 514, RG60, WNRC.

4. INS Files, nos. 362, 347, and 134, RG60, WNRC.

5. DS (J. C. Hill) Memorandum, August 26, 1942, 701.0010/555½, RG59, NA; *FRUS 1945*, vol. 9 (Washington: GPO, 1969), p. 279; and Jerre Mangione, *An Ethnic at Large* (New York: G. P. Putnam's Sons, 1978), pp. 321–22.

6. *Kenedy Advance* (Kenedy, Texas), April 2, 9, and 23, and May 21, 1942; and Ivan Williams to Mangione, October 16, 1943, INS World War II Internment Files, General Files, box 5, 104/025, RG85, WNRC.

7. *Kenedy Advance*, April 30, 1942, and DS (Bernard Gufler) Report, May 22, 1942, 740.00115 EW1939/4715, RG59, NA.

8. DS (Edward M. Groth) Report, May 30, 1942, 740.00115 EW1939/4035, RG59, NA.

9. *Kenedy Advance*, May 21 and July 2, 1942, and Williams to Mangione, October 16, 1943.

10. Willard F. Kelly and Gufler Memorandum of conversation, May 6, 1942, 740.00115 PW/746, RG59, NA, and *Kenedy Advance*, June 25, 1942.

11. Williams to Mangione, October 16, 1943, and SpEm to DS, July 29, 1943, 311.9415/477, RG59, NA.

12. DS (Whitney Young) Supplemental Report on Alien Enemy Detention Camp at Kenedy, Texas, August 7, 1942, 740.00115 PW/968, RG59, NA, and *Kenedy Advance*, August 20, 1942. For an appraisal of administrator Williams, see Mangione, *An Ethnic at Large*, pp. 325–29 passim.

13. Williams to Mangione, October 16, 1943.

14. Ibid.; DS (P. W. Herrick) Supplemental Report on Civilian Detention Station, Kenedy, Texas, October 13–14, 1942, 740.00115 EW1939/5373, and Kelly and Gufler Memorandum of conversation, May 6, 1942, 740.00115 PW/746, RG59, NA; and INS Files, no. 261, RG60, WNRC.

15. U.S., DC, *Merchant Vessels of the United States 1941*, p. 9; Norweb to SS, February 11, 1942, 740.00115 EW1939/2023, April 13, 1942, and April 17, 1942, 701.0023/66 and 68, Lemuel B. Schofield to Long, May 4, 1942, 740.00115 EW1939/3059, and DS (Hill) Memorandum, August 26, 1942, 701.0010/555½, RG59, NA; and U.S., DS, *The Proclaimed List of Certain Blocked Nationals*, Supplement 5, December 9, 1941, p. 11, and Supplement 6, December 23, 1941, p. 12.

16. DS (Gufler and Herrick) Report on Civilian Detention Station, Seagoville,

Texas, May 23, 1942, 740.00115 EW1939/4004, RG59, NA, and Mangione, *An Ethnic at Large*, pp. 334-37.

17. DS (Gufler and Herrick) Report; Gufler to DS, May 24, 1942, and DS to Gufler, May 25, 1942, 740.00115 EW1939/3221, and DS (Young) Supplemental Report on Civilian Detention Station, Seagoville, Texas, August 13, 1942, 740.00115 PW/972, RG59, NA; and Joseph L. O'Rurke and Amy N. Stannard, Information Concerning the U.S. Detention Station at Seagoville, Texas, April 6, 1943, INS World War II Internment Files, General Files, box 5, 104/025, RG85, WNRC.

18. ND to DS, April 16, 1942, 894.20223/125, DS (Welles) Memorandum, April 7, 1942, 740.00115 PW/513, and DS (Philip W. Bonsal) Memorandum, April 20, 1942, 894.20223/127, RG59, NA.

19. Jefferson Dennis to DS, March 30, 1942, and DS to AmEmLima, April 16, 1942, 894.20223/121, April 22, 1942, 894.20223/117, and April 25, 1942, 740.00115 EW1939/2768, RG59, NA.

20. Norweb to SS, April 18, 1942, and April 20, 1942, 740.00115 EW1939/2736 and 2768, RG59, NA.

21. Norweb to SS, April 21, 1942 (includes Emmerson's memorandum, April 18, 1942, 894.20223/124; and DS (Seldin Chapin) Memorandum, April 29, 1942, 740.00115 PW/685, RG59, NA.

22. Norweb to SS, May 1, 1942, 740.00115 PW/520, RG59, NA.

23. *El Comercio* (Lima), May 2, 1942, p. 3; "Visit of the President of Peru to Washington," *Bulletin of the PAU*, 76, no. 7 (July 1942): 373-79; U.S. 77th Cong. 2d sess., *Congressional Record*, vol. 88, pt. 3 (Washington: GPO, 1942), pp. 4034-35; and *FRUS 1942*, 6:664-94 passim.

24. Patterson to SS, May 7, 1942, 740.00115 PW/543, and SS to AmChLima, May 19, 1942, 862.20223/256, RG59, NA; and *El Comercio*, May 7, 1942, p. 10.

25. DS to SpEm, May 15, 1942, 740.00115 PW/510, and Rowe to SS, May 28, 1942, 894.20223/153, RG59, NA.

26. Patterson to SS, May 25, 1942 (includes Emmerson's memorandum, May 20, 1942), 740.00115 PW/605, and May 23, 1942 (includes Emmerson's memorandum, May 23, 1942), 894.20210/174, RG59, NA; and Emmerson, "Japanese and Americans in Peru, 1942-1943," p. 46.

27. U.S., DC, *Merchant Vessels of the United States 1941*, p. 60; DS Memorandum, May 11, 1942, 740.00115 EW1939/4003, DS to AmEmLima, May 21, 1942, 740.00115 PW/543, and May 27, 1942, 740.00115 EW1939/3177, Patterson to SS, May 28, 1942, and June 16, 1942, 740.00115 EW1939/3245 and 3482, and DS (Fletcher Warren) Memorandum, May 30, 1942, 740.00115 EW1939/3340 10/11, RG59, NA.

28. The sources for these figures and for those in table 5 and the remainder of this section are: INS Files, nos. 101-5, 109, 111, 127, 128, 130, 131, 136, 138,

141, 144, 146–51, 158, 160, 162, 163, 174, 175, 179–83, 186, 189, 191–93, 200, 209–11, 215, 218, 230, 232, 236, 237, 246, 260, 266, 267, 269, 271–75, 278, 279, 281, 283, 285, 286, 288, 305–7, 314, 316, 318, 321, 339, 342, 343, 345, 348–52, 354, 358, 359, 361, 376, 389, 390, 393, 394, 396, 402, 404, 405, 415, 416, 430, 441, 442, 446; 458, 467, 478, 481, 500, 501, 503, 512, 513, 515–17, 521, 524, 527, 528, 530, 532, 545, 547, 549, 550, 551, 555–57, 564, 575, 577, 581, 585, 588, 599, 601, 602, 607, 609, 616, 621, 636, 1291, 1319, 1325, 1478, 1480, 1500, 1505, 1507, 1513, 1515, 1518, 1519, 1522, 1526, 1533, and 1610, RG60, WNRC; Patterson to SS, June 17, 1942 (includes the passenger list of the *Shawnee*), and June 19, 1942, 740.00115 EW1939/3499 and 3612, DS (G. L. Brandt) Memorandum, June 23, 1942, and William Snow to DS, June 23, 1942, 740.00115 EW1939/3586 213 and 3571, RG59, NA; U.S., DS, *The Proclaimed List of Certain Blocked Nationals*, Supplements 5–6 (December 1941) and Revision II (May 1942) and Supplements 1–5 (May–July 1942) (Washington: GPO, 1941–42); and Emmerson, *The Japanese Thread*, pp. 133–34.

29. *FRUS 1942*, 1:377–435 passim (quotation p. 387); Benjamin C. Corlett to Cordell Hull, January 8, 1944, 311.9415/564, Lee H. Seward to C. Clark, June 12, 1942, 701.0090/318½, and DS to SpEm, June 15, 1942, 740.00115 PW/687, RG59, NA; and Graham H. Stuart, "Special War Problems Division: (c) The Repatriation Unit," DS *Bulletin*, 11, no. 267 (August 6, 1944): 142–45.

30. Norweb to SS, April 7, 1942, 740.00115 EW1939/2718, and April 17, 1942, 701.0023/68, RG59, NA.

31. John J. Muccio to SS, Panama, April 2, 1942, 740.00115 EW1939/2617, and INS Files, nos. 289, 811–14, 829–44, 846–49, 858–64, 870–73, 878, 879, 881, 883–86, 889, 896, 897, 901, 906, 909, 910, 912, 913, 915–17, 921–24, 928, 931, 935, 937, 940, 942–53, 956–58, 961, 962, 1025, 1026, 1028–39, 1041, 1043–62, 1065, 1066, 1077, 1078, 1081, 1082, 1084, 1085, 1096, 1097, 1133, 1149, 1153, 1154, 1188–91, 1195–1200, 1213, 1220, 1224, 1295, 1465, 1476, 1497, 1498, 1516, 1535, 1566, 1609, 1613, and 1619, RG60, WNRC.

32. INS Files, nos. 950, 1048, and 1566, RG60, WNRC, and Muccio to DS, Panama, September 25, 1942, 740.00115 PW/995, RG59, NA.

33. INS Files, nos. 1220 and 1295, RG60, WNRC, and DS (Special Division) Memorandum, August 21, 1942, 740.00115 PW/1000, RG59, NA.

34. Edward J. Ennis to Joseph C. Green, June 6, 1942, 740.00115 PW/687, RG59, NA, and *FRUS 1942*, 1:447–49.

## 4. More Internees, More Repatriates

1. George H. Butler to SS, June 23, 1942, 894.20223/155, Patterson to SS, July 3, 1942, 740.00115 EW1939/3764, and Norweb to SS, September 15, 1942, and August 29, 1942, 740.00115 PW/1002 4/6 and 889, RG59, NA.

2. Norweb to SS, July 20, 1942, and DS (John E. Peurifoy), Memorandum, July 25, 1942, 740.00115 PW/1002 2/6 and 1002 3/6, Patterson to SS, October 29, 1942, 823.00/1595, and DS (Duggan) Memorandum, November 6, 1942, 740.00115 PW/1164, RG59, NA.

3. Patterson to SS, June 24, 1942, 894.20223/160, Norweb to SS, August 5, 1942, 894.20210/194, and Welch to SS, October 19, 1942, 894.20223/179, RG59, NA; and Emmerson, *The Japanese Thread*, pp. 142–43.

4. Norweb to SS, August 18, 1942, 894.20210/198, and L. S. Rowe to DS, July 1, 1942 (includes letter by Larrañaga), 894.20223/163, RG59, NA.

5. DS (Duggan) Memorandum, June 18, 1942, 740.00115 EW1939/3682, DS (Green) Memorandum, July 10, 1942, 740.00115 PW/1002 1/6, Norweb to SS, July 11, 1942, 740.00115 EW1939/3747, DS (J. H. Wright) Memoranda, August 5, 1942, and September 30, 1942, 740.00115 PW/806 and 1002 5/6, RG59, NA.

6. Joseph Grew to Franklin D. Roosevelt, August 8, 1942, DS (J. Daniel Hanley) Memorandum, September 8, 1942, DS (Bonsal) Memorandum, September 8, 1942, DS (Chapin), Memorandum, September 28, 1942, and DS (Wright) Memorandum, September 30, 1942, 740.00115 PW/2791½, 889, 888, 1002 5/6, and 1002 5/6, RG59, NA.

7. DS (Wright) Memorandum, October 19, 1942, and DS (Duggan) Memoranda, October 9, 1942, and October 21, 1942, 740.00115 PW/1140 3/7, 1140 1/7, and 1140 4/7, RG59, NA.

8. DS Memorandum re removal of enemy aliens, November 3, 1942, DS (Albert E. Clattenburg) Memorandum, December 30, 1942, and Hull to Roosevelt, August 27, 1942, 740.00115 EW1939/5835, 5649, and 4476, RG59, NA.

9. Biddle to Hull, June 25, 1942, 740.00115 EW1939/3610, RG59, NA.

10. Charles Fahy to Long, July 9, 1942, 740.00115 EW1939/4307, DS Memorandum, July 7, 1942, 701.0010/514, DS to AmEmPanama, September 14, 1942, and September 19, 1942, 740.00115 PW/1 and 864, Wilson to SS, September 23, 1942, 740.00115 PW/959, and DS to DJ, September 29, 1942, 740.00115 EW1939/3610, RG59, NA.

11. DS (Special Division) Memorandum, November 6, 1942, 311.9415/251, and Biddle to SS, November 9, 1942, 740.00115 PW/1126, RG59, NA.

12. SpEm to DS, June 18, 1942, January 4, 1943, and July 21, 1942 (includes letter by Tatsujiro Kurotobi and Rinuemon Takahashi, July 3, 1942), 740.00115 PW/652, 1289, and 784, RG59, NA; and League of Nations, "Convention Relative to the Treatment of Prisoners of War," *Treaty Series*, vol. 118 (1931–32) (Lausanne: Imprimeries Réunies, 1932), pp. 343–411 passim.

13. SpEm to DS, July 21, 1942, 701.0090/896, DS to SpEm, July 21, 1942, 701.0010/515, and SpEm to DS, November 24, 1942, 740.00115 PW/1200, RG59, NA.

14. WD to DS, July 25, 1942, 740.00115 PW/801, and November 2, 1942,

740.00115 EW1939/5790, and SpEm to DS, January 9, 1943, 740.00115 PW/1282, RG59, NA.

15. DS (Young) Report, August 7, 1942, 740.00115 PW/968, RG59, NA; Williams to Mangione, October 16, 1943; and WD (Lt. Col. Howard F. Breese) to DS Special Division, January 4, 1943, 740.00115 PW/1254, RG59, NA.

16. DS (Young) Report, August 13, 1942, 740.00115 PW/972, RG59, NA; INS (O'Rourke and Stannard) report concerning Seagoville, April 6, 1943 (see chap. 3, n. 17, above); DS to Swiss Legation, December 22, 1942, 740.00115 EW1939/5339, and WD (Breese) to DS Special Division, January 2, 1943, and H. Suñaga to SpEm, October 8, 1942, 740.00115 PW/1247 and 1042, RG59, NA.

17. N. D. Collaer, "The Crystal City Interment Camp," INS *Monthly Review*, 5, no. 6 (December 1947): 75–77; Kelly to Gufler, May 25, 1943, and DJ to DS, November 23, 1942, 740.00115 EW1939/6762 and 5218 1/10, RG59, NA; *Zavala County Sentinel* (Crystal City, Texas), February 19, 1943; Warren Page Rucker, "United States–Peruvian Policy Toward Peruvian-Japanese Persons During World War II," M.A. thesis, University of Virginia, 1970, p. 51; and Mangione, *An Ethnic at Large*, pp. 329–34.

18. *Zavala County Sentinel*, February 19, 1943, and Collaer, "The Crystal City Internment Camp," p. 77.

19. U.S. DS, *The Proclaimed List: Cumulative Supplement No. 3, June 6, 1946* (Washington: GPO: 1946), p. 3, and *The Proclaimed List: Supplement 3, June 19, 1942* (Washington: GPO, 1942), pp. 6–9.

20. *Revista Mensual del Comercio del Perú* (1942), pp. 384, 386–88. For a listing of wartime anti-Axis actions by Peru, see Perú, *Compilación de la legislación peruana*, 5:1693–94.

21. For example, a regulation of June 1942 for Ley 9592 regarding contracts, funds, and the expropriation of Axis properties, which along with Ley 9586 was basic to the wartime control of the interests of Axis nationals, called on "dichos peritos a prestar el servicio sin remuneración alguna" ("said experts to contribute service without any remuneration"); see Perú, *Compilación de la legislación peruana*, 5:1697.

22. Norweb to SS, September 1, 1942, 740.00115 PW/883, and September 5, 1942, 894.20223/169, DS to AmEmLima, September 17, 1942, 740.00115 PW/883, DS Special Division Memorandum, November 3, 1942, 311.9415/222, and Patterson to SS, December 10, 1942, 740.00115 EW1939/5552, RG59, NA. Chief of Staff General George C. Marshall personally intervened in this matter, referring to the men as nine tailors; see Barnhart, "Japanese Internees from Peru," p. 171.

23. Norweb to SS, December 23, 1942, 800.20223/117, and DS (Sidney K. Lafoon) Memorandum, December 10, 1942, 740.00115 EW1939/5532, RG59, NA; and INS Files, nos. 1536 and 1354, RG60, WNRC.

24. DS (James H. Keeley) Memorandum, December 1, 1942, 740.00115

EW1939/5844, and DS to AmEmLima, December 3, 1942, 740.00115 PW/1171b, RG59, NA.

25. Biddle to SS, December 5, 1942, and DS (Keeley) Memoranda, January 6 and 7, 1943, 740.00115 PW/1172, RG59, NA.

26. Patterson to SS, December 10, 1942, 740.00115 EW1939/5552, and December 12, 1942, 740.00115 PW/1214, RG59, NA.

27. Welch to SS, January 5, 1943, 740.00115 PW/1291, RG59, NA, and INS Files no. 2218, RG60, WNRC.

28. Conversation with Ginzo and Seiki Murono, Seabrook, N.J., October 7, 1977; INS Files, no. 1383, RG60, WNRC; and Butler to SS, enclosure 3, January 19, 1943, 740.00115 PW/1368, RG59, NA .

29. Conversation with Taro and Fusae Ohashi, San Francisco, May 5, 1977; INS Files, no. 1367, RG60, WNRC; and Butler to SS, enclosure 3, January 19, 1943, RG59, NA.

30. Conversation with Kakuaki and Otari Kaneko and their daughter Momoko (Mary), Lemon Grove, California, May 15, 1977; INS Files, no. 1393, RG60, WNRC; and Butler to SS, enclosure 3, January 19, 1943, RG59, NA.

31. Conversation with Saburo Ushida, Chicago, August 29, 1976; INS Files, no. 1284, RG60, WNRC; and Butler to SS, enclosure 3, January 19, 1943, RG59, NA.

32. The foregoing passenger analysis is derived from the following: Norweb to SS, January 12, 1943, Patterson to SS (includes Emmerson's memorandum re Talara operation), January 16, 1943, and Butler to SS (enclosure 3 of which is an annotated list of the Japanese deportees), January 19, 1943, 740.00115 PW/1302, 1344, and 1368, RG59, NA; INS Files, nos. 229, 290, 379, 1607, 1828, 2287, 2299, and 1275–1538 passim, RG60, WNRC; U.S., DS, *The Proclaimed List* (through Revision IV, Supplement 2, December 18, 1942), passim; and Arequipa "Luz y Libertad" to DS, January 11, 1943, 740.00115 PW/1445, RG59, NA.

33. Conversation with Kakuaki Kaneko, May 15, 1977. Saburo Ushida, who graphically recalls this sequence of events, concluded his conversation with the writer (August 29, 1976), by saying, "Tell it all. It is the truth." The camp was described by DS (Gufler) Report, May 28, 1942, 740.00115 EW1939/4030, RG59, NA.

34. Biddle to SS, January 11, 1943, DS (Keeley) Memorandum, January 12, 1943, and Biddle to Long, February 6, 1943, 740.00115 PW/1276, 1276, and 1392, RG59, NA.

35. Welch Memorandum, January 16, 1943, 740.00115 PW/1343, and Norweb to SS, January 27, 1943, 800.20223/125, and January 30, 1943, 740.00115 EW1939/5934, RG59, NA.

36. Norweb to SS, February 21, 1943, DS to AmEmLima, February 22, 1943, and Norweb to SS, February 27, 1943, 740.00115 EW1939/6153, 6197n, and 6247, RG59, NA.

37. The foregoing summation regarding the 119 is based on the following: Norweb to SS, February 27, 1943 (includes the passenger list), 740.00115 EW1939/6247, RG59, NA, and INS Files, nos. 137, 146, 2160, and 1743–1886 passim, RG60, WNRC.

38. Conversation with Mitsutaro and son Victor Tawara, Englewood, Colorado, September 27, 1976, and INS Files, no. 1793, RG60, NA.

39. *Perū Shimpō* (Lima), October 9 and December 9, 1976, and INS Files, no. 1820, RG60, WNRC.

40. Conversation with John Kunio Takeshita, Chicago, August 28, 1976, and INS Files, no. 1790, RG60, WNRC.

41. Arthur Shinei Yakabi to CHG, Seabrook, N.J., April 1, 1977, conversations with Yakabi, Ionia, Michigan, October 1–2, 1977, and INS Files, no. 1864, RG60, WNRC.

42. Norweb to SS, March 2, 1943 (includes R. W. Ickes's memorandum, February 26, 1943), and March 12, 1943, 740.00115 EW1939/6277 and 6247, RG59, NA, and *FRUS 1943*, 6:731–33. Aided by James D. Bell, Ickes continued this role of the AECU throughout Latin America: see Muccio to SS, Panama, April 2, 1943, 740.00115 PW/1522, RG59, NA; R. W. Ickes to CHG, Berkeley, California, November 8, 1976; and James D. Bell to CHG, Santa Cruz, California, April 15, 1977.

43. Biddle to SS, April 3, 1943, and Henry L. Stimson to SS, May 14, 1943, 740.00115 EW1939/6484 and 6684, RG59, NA.

44. SpEm to DS, January 22, 1943, DW to DS, February 26, 1943, DS to SpEm, February 27, 1943, WD to DS, April 13, 1943, and DS to DW, May 5, 1943, 740.00115 PW/1348, 1434, 1332, 1604, and 1604, RG59, NA.

45. Nikumatsu Okada to DS, January 12, 1943, DS to AmEmLima, February 15, 1943, and Julian Greenup to DS, March 25, 1943, 740.00115 PW/1311, 1311, and 1521, and Welch to DS, May 12, 1943, 740.00115 EW1939/6740, RG59, NA.

46. DJ to DS, February 24, 1943, and SpEm to DS, April 2, 1943, 740.00115 PW/1439 and 1540, RG59, NA.

47. DS (E. L. Eslinger) Memorandum, March 4, 1943, DS (Lafoon) Memorandum, March 5, 1943, Welles to AmEmLima, March 11, 1943, and Norweb to SS, March 25, 1943, 311.943/63, 64, 65n, and 66, DS (Lafoon) Memorandum, March 6, 1943, and Ennis to DS, April 8, 1943, 740.00115 EW1939/6395 and 6663, RG59, NA; and INS Files, no. 2301, RG60, WNRC.

48. The Panama experience of the 119 is derived from the following: conversation with John Kunio Takeshita, Chicago, August 28, 1976, conversations with Arthur Shinei Yakabi, October 1–2, 1977; conversation with Laura Yakabi, Seabrook, N.J., October 6, 1977; INS Files, nos. 1790, 1793, 1820, 1853, and 1864, RG60, WNRC; and *Perū Shimpō*, December 9, 1972.

49. Keeley to Captain E. Zacharias (ND), June 3, 1943, 311.9415/527a, RG59, NA.

50. Conversations with Arthur Shinei Yakabi, October 1–2, 1977; conversation with John Kunio Takeshita, August 28, 1976; and Edwin A. Plitt to Kelly, May 13, 1943, 740.00115 EW1939/6688a, RG59, NA.

51. DS to AmEmLima, June 3, 1943, and June 15, 1943, 740.00115 EW1939/6277 and 6860, and Keeley to Col. L. M. Mathewson (WD), June 22, 1943, 740.00115 PW/6–2243, RG59, NA.

52. Norweb to DS, June 15, 1943, and DS to AmEmLima, June 21, 1943, 740.00115 EW1939/6874, RG59, NA.

53. This segment concerning the *Aconcagua* group is based on the following: Taro Ohashi to CHG, San Francisco, September 24, 1976; Ginzo Murono to CHG, Seabrook, N.J., September 29, 1976; conversation with Taro and Fusae Ohashi, May 5, 1977; INS Files, nos. 1281, 1283, 1301, 1305, 1307, 1317, 1330, 1348, 1354, 1367, 1368, 1370, 1372, 1377, 1379, 1383, 1390, 1391, 1397, 1417, 1438, 1536, 1788, 1835, 1891, 1892, and 1893, RG60, WNRC; Norweb to SS, June 16, 1943, June 28, 1943, and June 29, 1943, 740.00115 PW/1679, 1694, and 1680; conversation with Margaret Nan Williams, Crystal City, Texas, May 20, 1977.

54. Norweb to DS, July 2, 1943, DS to AmEmLima, July 3, 1943, Norweb to DS, July 5, 1943, Norweb to SS, July 10, 1942, and Butler to DS, July 10, 1943, 740.00115 PW/1684, 1684, 1688, 1700, and 1728, RG59, NA.

55. This segment regarding the *Imperial* group is based on the following: Norweb to SS, July 1, 1943, July 6, 1943 (includes list of passengers), and July 10, 1943, and Butler to SS, July 10, 1943, 740.00115 PW/1692, 1703, 1700, and 1729, RG59, NA; and INS Files, nos. 551, 1282, 1300, 1306, 1316, 1318, 1321, 1323, 1324, 1333, 1345, 1349, 1350, 1355, 1360, 1371, 1373, 1376, 1408, 1414, 1423, 1429, 1430, 1449, 1474, 1538, 1822, and 1823, RG60, WNRC.

56. Keeley to Mathewson (WD), July 7, 1943, 740.00115 PW/6–2243, RG59, NA.

57. Emmerson, *The Japanese Thread*, p. 147, and Norweb to DS, July 7, 1943 (includes Emmerson's "Memorandum on the Control of Japanese in Peru," which was intended to help those who were then planning a control system for the Japanese in Paraguay), 740.00115 PW/1706, RG59, NA.

58. Patterson to DS, October 9, 1943, and August 11, 1943, and DS Memorandum, November 2, 1943, 894.20223/196, 193, and 11–243, RG59, NA. J. F. Normano and Antonello Gerbi's *The Japanese in South America* (New York: John Day Company, 1943) was the latest of a spate of kindred volumes which included Carleton Beals, *The Coming Struggle for Latin America* (New York: J. B. Lippincott Company, 1938), John Gunther, *Inside Latin America* (New York: Harper and Brothers, 1940), and Reginald W. Thompson, *Germans and Japs in South America* (London: Faber and Faber, 1942). As widely circulated contributions to

the climate of opinion, they smacked of colorful, sensational journalism rather than documented research, and featured gross exaggerations and wild imaginings.

59. DS Memoranda, November 2, 1943, and January 25, 1944, Butler to SS, March 27, 1944, DS Division of Research and Publication, April 4, 1944, and John Campbell White to SS, February 20, 1945, 894.20223/11–243, 1–2544, 220, 2–1444, and 2–2045, RG59, NA.

60. DS to DJ, July 23, 1943, 740.00115 PW/1498, SpEm to DS, August 3, 1943, 311.943/73, DJ to DS, September 8, 1943, 311.943/75, SpEm to DS, August 4, 1943, and August 12, 1943, and DS to SpEm, December 2, 1943, 740.00115 PW/ 1781, 1798, and 1949, RG59, NA.

61. This account of Fort Missoula is based on the following: DS (Gufler and Herrick) report of visit of August 3–6, 1942, 740.00115 EW1939/4022, RG59, NA; conversation with John Kunio Takeshita, August 28, 1976; conversations with Arthur Shinei Yakabi, October 1–2, 1977; *Perū Jihō*, December 1972; and Mangione, *An Ethnic at Large*, pp. 343–47.

62. *FRUS 1942*, 1:448–49, and *FRUS 1943*, vol. 3 (Washington: GPO, 1963), pp. 877, 898–99, 917, 922. After stops at Rio de Janeiro and Montevideo the *Gripsholm* carried 1,513 passengers and experienced two births at sea.

63. Hull to AmLeBern, September 3, 1943 (includes list of passengers), 701.-0090/2158b, RG59, NA; Emmerson, *The Japanese Thread*, p. 139; and Michi Weglyn, *Years of Infamy: The Untold Story of America's Concentration Camps* (New York: William Morrow and Company, 1976), p. 62. In an aside concerning the relationship of the Peruvian Japanese to the wartime exchanges between the United States and Japan, William Petersen, "Success Story, Japanese-American Style," *New York Times Magazine*, January 9, 1966, p. 43, grossly errs in saying, "Actually none was ever so used."

64. INS Files, nos. 1305, 1891, 1892, 1893, and 1449, RG60, WNRC, and *FRUS 1943*, 3:944, 946–52.

## 5. Grinding to a Halt

1. Ennis to Keeley, September 4, 1943, and Biddle to Hull, September 6, 1943, 740.00115 EW1939/7593 and 7290, RG59, NA.

2. SpEm to DS, August 10, 1943, WD to DS, September 4, 1943, DS to SpEm, September 25, 1943, and DS Circular, October 8, 1943, 740.00115 EW1939/1790, 1841, 1841, and 7442a, RG59, NA.

3. DJ to DS, September 25, 1943, DS to SpEm, October 22, 1943, SpEm to DS, October 18, 1943, and Ryuchi Fujii to Keeley, October 18, 1943, 740.00115 PW/ 1888, 1888, 1944, and 2001, RG59, NA.

4. Francis M. Sullivan (officer of the American Legion) to Hull, October 20, 1942, 740.00115 EW1939/7518, RG59, NA.

5. Butler to SS, October 9, 1943, and November 18, 1943, 740.00115 PW/1928 and 2018, RG59, NA.

6. Hoover to Berle, November 27, 1943, 894.20210/Yamamoto, Yoshitomo/2, RG59, NA.

7. SpEm to DS, November 20, 1943, December 4, 1943, and December 6, 1943, 740.00115 PW/2042, 2061, and 2063, and Muccio to SS, Panama, November 29, 1943, 740.00115 EW1939/7727, RG59, NA; and James D. Bell to CHG, April 15, 1977. One to assist writers inclined to worship him and his bureau, J. Edgar Hoover apparently thought little of the wartime operations of his Special Intelligence Service operations against the Japanese in Latin America, because they are almost totally ignored in such works as Don Whitehead, *The FBI Story: A Report to the People* (New York: Random House, 1956), and Frederick L. Collins, *The FBI in Peace and War* (New York: G. P. Putnam's Sons, 1962).

8. INS Files, nos. 2133–44, 2146, 2158, 2160, 2161, 2226, and 2274, RG60, WNRC; Patterson to SS, January 18, 1944, 740.00115 EW1939/8064, and SpEm to DS, September 1, 1944 (includes letter by Victor K. Tateishi, June 30, 1944), 740.00115 PW/9–144, RG59, NA.

9. Patterson to SS, March 3, 1944, 740.00115 EW 1939/8645, RG59, NA; INS Files, nos. 2280, 2156, 2224, and 2202, RG60, WNRC; Paul Shuhei Katsuro to CHG, Houston, Texas, September 27, 1976, and June 27, 1977; conversation with George Hisao Fujii, August 29, 1976; and conversations with Victor Kazuki Tateishi, Tokyo, December 6–8, 1978.

10. INS Files, nos. 2213, 2296, 2226, and 2218, RG60, WNRC.

11. Conversation with Masao Kishi, San Diego, May 13, 1977, and INS Files, nos. 2208, 2209, and 2211, RG60, WNRC.

12. INS Files, nos. 1393 and 2301, RG60, WNRC, and conversation with O. Kaneko, May 15, 1977.

13. INS Files, nos. 2265, 2269 and 2144, RG60, WNRC.

14. INS Files, nos. 2137 and 2152, RG60, WNRC, and SpEm to DS, September 1, 1944, 740.00115 PW/9–144, RF59, NA, "The Story and Diary of Kami Kamosato," in Takeo Kaneshiro, comp., *Internees: War Relocation Center Memoirs and Diaries* (New York: Vantage Press, 1976), p. 34.

15. DS (R. L. Bannerman) Report, March 28, 1944, 740.00115 PW/3–2844, RG59, NA, and conversation with G. H. Fujii, August 29, 1976.

16. Ryuchi Fujii to Consulate of Spain, May 26, 1944, and Lafoon to Clattenburg, July 8, 1944, 740.00115 PW/2473 and 7–844, RG59, NA.

17. SpEm to DS, September 1, 1944, 740.00115 PW/9–144, RG59, NA.

18. Patterson to SS, March 1, 1944 (includes Javier Correa to Patterson, March 1, 1944), 740.00115 EW1939/8740, RG59, NA.

19. Patterson to SS, March 9, 1944, 740.00115 EW1939/8790, Hoover to Berle, August 15, 1944, November 17, 1944, October 12, 1944, November 24, 1944, and

December 11, 1944, 894.20223/8–1544, 11–1744, 10–1244, 11–2444, and 12–1144, RG, NA.

20. For the table and the remainder of this section, see Patterson to SS, March 13, 1944 (includes Welch Memorandum, March 11, 1944), Clattenburg to Kelly, March 18, 1944, and Patterson to SS, April 1, 1944, 740.00115 EW1939/9032, 8790, and 9091, RG59, NA.

21. White to SS, June 17, 1944, 740.00115 EW1939/10076, RG59, NA; INS 56125/88E, INS 55125/88G, and INS Files, nos. 533, 1304, 1326, 1329, 1334, 1335, 1338, 1344, 1347, 1351, 1358, 1363, 1380, 1382, 1385, 1404, 1410, 1412, 1413, 1419, 1424, 1524, 1743–46, 1748, 1749, 1753, 1757–60, 1789, 1792, 1793, 1796, 1797, 1801–7, 1819, 1820, 1824–26, 1832–34, 1836, 1840, 1843, 1844, 1867, 1869, 1870, 1872, 1873, 1886, 2136, 2139, 2146, 2147, 2149, 2151, 2160, 2181, 2190, 2199, 2226, and 2232, RG60, WNRC.

22. INS Files, nos. 1380, 1820, 1793, 2147, and 2146, RG60, WNRC.

23. Avra M. Warren to SS, Panama, June 23, 1944, 740.00115 EW1939/10139, Patterson to DS, October 9, 1943, 894.20223/196, RG59, NA, and INS Files, nos. 2229 and 2354, RG60, WNRC.

24. INS Files, no. 2232, RG60, WNRC; U.S., DS, *The Proclaimed List*, Supplement 5, December 9, 1941, p. 12; and Hiroko Stevenson to CHG, March 25, 1978.

25. DS (E. J. Dorsz) Memorandum, May 31, 1944, 740.00115 PW/2482, RG59, NA, and Mangione, *An Ethnic at Large*, pp. 347–48.

26. Conversations with Arthur Shinei Yakabi, October 1–2, 1977; INS Files, nos. 1864 and 1859, RG59, NA; "Work Projects for Interned Alien Enemies," INS *Monthly Review*, 2, no. 12 (June 1945): 16; and "Kooskia Internment Camp Is Abandoned by Service," INS *Monthly Review*, 2, no. 11 (May 1945): 148.

27. INS Files, nos. 1332, 1339, 1341, 1388, 1394, 1396, 1402, 1409, 1422, 1442, 1453, 1459, and 1473, RG60, WNRC.

28. Conversations with A. S. Yakabi, October 1–2, 1977, and INS Files, nos. 1406, 1423, 1439, 1756, 2187, 2191, and 2206, RG60, WNRC.

29. INS, *Annual Report of the Immigration and Naturalization Service, for the Fiscal Year Ending June 30, 1945* (n.p., n.d.), p. 27.

30. Will Harrison, "The Santa Fe Internment Camp," INS *Monthly Review*, 3, no. 10 (April 1946): 298–300; conversations with John Kunio Takeshita, August 28, 1976, with Saburo Ushida, August 29, 1976, and with A. S. Yakabi, October 1–2, 1977; and Mangione, *An Ethnic at Large*, pp. 337–42.

31. Conversation with R. C. Tate, Crystal City Texas, May 20, 1977; *Zavala County Sentinel*, April 23, 1943; and Rucker, "United States–Peruvian Policy," p. 52.

32. Conversation with Tate, May 20, 1977, and Mangione, *An Ethnic at Large*, p. 327.

33. Conversation with Kiyoko Naganuma Matsuoka, San Francisco, May 6, 1977.

34. Conversation with Eugenia Yoshiko Kato, San Francisco, May 5, 1977.

35. Conversation with Mary Momoko Sato Sato (who as six-year-old Momoko Kaneko had come to Crystal City in 1944), May 15, 1977; conversation with Tate, May 20, 1977; and *Zavala County Sentinel*, August 18, 1944.

36. Conversations with Mitsutaro and Victor Tawara, Englewood, Colorado, and with Tosh (Toshiharu) Tawara, Aurora, Colorado, September 27, 1976; SpEm to DS, August 14, 1944, 740.00115 PW/8–1444, RG59, NA; "Civilian Alien Enemies in the Custody of the Service," INS *Monthly Review*, 2, no. 6 (December 1944): 75; and Rucker, "United States–Peruvian Policy," pp. 50–51.

37. SpEm to DS, August 31, 1944, September 1, 1944, September 4, 1944, and September 6, 1944, and Kelly to Keeley, September 27, 1944, 740.00115 PW/8–3144, 9–144, 9–444, 9–644, and 9–2744, RG59, NA.

38. Hoover to Berle, July 19, 1944, and August 18, 1944, 894.20223/7–1944 and 10–1844, RG59, NA; and Emmerson, "Japanese and Americans in Peru, 1942–1943," *Foreign Service Journal*, 54, no. 5 (May 1977): 47.

39. INS Files, nos. 2141 and 2300, RG60, WNRC; Hoover to Berle, July 19, 1944, August 11, 1944, August 25, 1944, October 12, 1944, and October 18, 1944, 894.20223/7–1944, 8–1144, 8–2544, 10–1244, and 10–1844, RG59, NA.

40. Hoover to Berle, November 10, 1944, 740.00115 EW1939/11–1044, RG59, NA.

41. Hoover to Berle, July 19, 1944, 894.20223/7–1944, RG59, NA.

42. Hoover to Berle, August 15, 1944, 894.20223/8–1544, RG59, NA.

43. Avoiding details, numerous past internees known by the writer merely smiled and nodded when the matter of buying influence and hiding was introduced.

44. Clattenburg to F. B. Lyon, August 12, 1944, 740.00115 EW1939/7–1944, RG59, NA.

45. DS (Norman Armour) Memorandum, August 17, 1944, and Armour to White, September 7, 1944, 740.00115 EW1939/7–1944 and 8–2344, and Clattenburg to Keeley, August 24, 1944, 894.20223/8–2444, RG59, NA.

46. SpEm to DS, August 21, 1944, 740.00115 PW/8–2144, and White to SS, September 9, 1944, September 22, 1944, and October 7, 1944, 740.0015 EW1939/9–944, 9–2244, and 10–744, RG59, NA.

47. Welch to SS, October 11, 1944, and Warren to SS, Panama, October 17, 1944, 740.00115 EW1939/10–1144 and 10–1744, RG59, NA; and INS Files, nos. 275, 1293, 2189, and 2463–68, RG60, WNRC.

48. T. F. Fitch to Clattenburg, October 30, 1944 (includes Bannerman to Fitch), 740.00115 EW1939/10–3044, RG59, NA.

49. INS Files, nos. 1348, 1378, 1383, 1386, 1390, 1414, 1754, 1835, 2232, 2260,

2261, 2272, 2284, and 2285, RG60, WNRC, and DS to AmEmLima, January 10, 1945, 740.00115 PW/1–1045, RG59, NA.

50. SpEm to DS, January 30, 1945, and Major L. E. Griffith (WD) to DS, April 24, 1945, 740.00115 PW/1–3045 and 4–2445, RG59, NA.

51. N. D. Collaer to Plitt, March 23, 1945, and Kelly to Gufler, March 2, 1945, 740.00115 PW/3–2344 and 3–245, RG59, NA.

52. INS Files, nos. 1373, 1393, 1747, 1759, 1760, 1840, 2079, and 2151, RG60, WNRC.

53. INS Files, no. 2474, RG60, WNRC, and Patterson to DS, October 9, 1943, 894.20223/196, RG59, NA.

### 6. Beyond War's End

1. *FRUS 1945*, 9:273; Welch to SS, June 20, 1945, 740.00115 PW/6–2045, RG59, NA; INS, *Annual Report...for the Fiscal Year Ending June 30, 1945*, pp. 26–27; and "Alien Internment Station at Seagoville Is Closed," INS *Monthly Review*, 2, no. 12 (June 1945): 163.

2. U.S., *Code of Federal Regulations: Title 3—The President, 1943–1946, Compilation* (Washington: GPO, 1957), pp. 57–58.

3. SwLeg (Weingartner) to Spokesman of the Japanese Internees at Crystal City, August 7, 1945, Kelly to Plitt, August 11, 1945, and Collaer to Plitt, August 13, 1945, and August 20, 1945, 740.00115 PW/8–1845, 8–1145, 8–1345, and 8–2045, RG59, NA.

4. Thomas C. Mann, "Elimination of Axis Influence in This Hemisphere: Measures Adopted at the Mexico City Conference," DS *Bulletin*, 12, no. 308 (May 20, 1945): 925, and *FRUS 1945*, 9:266–85 passim. The quoted material is on pp. 273–74.

5. Ibid., pp. 278–80.

6. U.S., *United States Statutes at Large*, 59, pt. 2 (Washington: GPO, 1946): 880–81, and "Alien Enemy Control Section," DS *Bulletin*, 13, no. 332 (November 4, 1945): 737–38.

7. DS (J. E. Doyle) Memorandum, September 29, 1945, 711.62115 AR/9–2945, RG59, NA, and *Washington Post*, October 5, 1945, p. 16. The numerical discrepancy between the INS and the Department of State concerning the number of Japanese internees from Latin America held as of June 30, 1945, defies reconciliation.

8. DS to American Missions in Latin America except Argentina, Brazil, Chile, Mexico, Uruguay, and Venezuela, November 8, 1945, 711.62115 AR/11–845, RG59, NA.

9. INS Files, nos. 1863, 1371, 2261, and 2150, RG60, WNRC.

10. Ibid., nos. 2144, 2366, 2276, 2223, 2269, 1381, 2079, and 2277.

11. Ibid., nos. 1455, 1832, 1387, 1353, 2280, 1860, and 2284.
12. Ibid., nos. 1844, 1765, 2220, and 1762.
13. Ibid., nos. 1420, 2474, 1424, 1864, 1865, 1845, and 2187.
14. Ibid., nos. 1821, 1849, and 2266.
15. Ibid., nos. 2468, 2148, 2226, and 2301.
16. Ibid., nos. 1830, 1847, 2295, and 2136.
17. Conversation with Kakuaki Kaneko, May 17, 1977.
18. Conversations with Tosh (Toshiharu) Tawara, September 27, 1976, and April 27, 1977.
19. "Proposed Exchange of Nationals Between United States and Japan," DS *Bulletin*, 12, no. 292 (January 28, 1945): 132, and numerous items in the file 711.94115 Exchange, RG59, NA.
20. Tosh (Toshiharu) Tawara, "Autographs," LL 28, 52, 58, 29, 60, and INS Files, no. 1825, RG60, WNRC. The unnumbered leaves of the Tawara autograph book have been numbered and the translations made by the writer.
21. Tawara, "Autographs," LL 33, 39.
22. Ibid., LL 36, 43, and INS Files, no. 2284, RG60, WNRC.
23. Tawara, "Autographs," LL 61, 61r.
24. DS to Peruvian Embassy, November 20, 1945, 711.94115 AR/11–2045, RG59, NA.
25. INS Files, nos. 1536, 1801, 1886, 2135, 1825, 1419, 1351, and 2284, RG60, WNRC.
26. Ibid., nos. 2223, 1862, 2194, 1874, 1275, and 1404.
27. For example, see ibid., nos. 1395, 1772, 1855, 1771, 1769, and 1854.
28. Ibid., nos. 1447 and 1761.
29. Ibid., no. 1455, and Patterson to SS, January 16, 1943, 740.00115 PW/1344, RG59, NA.
30. Ibid., no. 1422, and Patterson to SS, January 16, 1943, 740.00115 PW/1344, RG59, NA.
31. Ibid., nos. 1860, 1762, and 1853.
32. Ibid., nos. 2133, 2214, 2158, 2359, and 2201.
33. For example, see ibid., nos. 2189, 2359, 2366, 2376, and 2466.
34. "7,159 Japanese Depart from United States," INS *Monthly Review*, 3, no. 7 (January 1946): 253, and INS Files, nos. 1765, 1764, 2343, 2229, 2354, and 1331, RG60, WNRC.
35. "Disposition of Enemy Aliens from Other American Republics," DS *Bulletin*, 14, no. 340 (December 30, 1945): 1061, and *FRUS 1945*, 9:294–95.
36. *FRUS 1945*, 9:295–96.
37. DS (J. B. Binhgam) Memorandum, December 13, 1945, 711.62115 AR/12–1345, published in *FRUS 1945*, 9:298.
38. Ibid., p. 299.

39. "626 More Japanese Leave United States," INS *Monthly Review*, 3, no. 9 (March 1946): 285, and INS Files, nos. 1747 and 1391, RG60, WNRC.
40. DS, Policy on Alien Enemies from Latin America, December 15, 1945, 711.62115 AR/12-1245, RG59, NA.
41. Kiyoshi Fujiwara to Bingham, December 28, 1945 (includes letter by Victor K. Tateishi and list of names), 711.94115 AR/12-2845, RG59, NA.

## 7. Challenging Human Endurance

1. DS (Lafoon) Memorandum, January 4, 1946, 711.94115 AR/11-2045, William D. Pawley to SS, January 17, 1946 (includes copies of Javier Correa Elías to Edward G. Trueblood, January 8, 1946, and Javier Correa Elías to Pawley, January 14, 1946), 711.62115 AR/1-1746, Dean G. Acheson to AmEmLima, January 21, 1946, 711.92115 AR/1-1746, RG59, NA; and INS Files, nos. 517, 1344, and 2258, RG60, WNRC.
2. DS (Bingham) Memoranda, January 15, 1946, 711.62115 AR/1-1546, RG59, NA.
3. I. B. White to Lafoon, January 30, 1946, 711.62115 AR/1-3046, RG59, NA. The differing counts of the Latin American Japanese as of January 15 and 30 by the Department of State cannot be reconciled.
4. "Notice to the Internees from Latin America" (copy), January 4, 1946, 1946 File, WMC Papers.
5. Gongoro Nakamura to AmEmLima, February 4, 1946, Nakamura to DS, February 6, 1946, and DS to DJ, January 13, 1946, and March 23, 1946, 711.94115 AR/2-1246, 2-646, 1-1346, and 3-2346, RG59, NA; and Nakamura to Hugh Borton (copy), March 29, 1946, 1946 File, WMC Papers.
6. Pawley to SS, February 9, 1946, and February 14, 1946, and James F. Byrnes to AmEmLima, February 26, 1946, 711.62115 AR/2-946, 2-1446, and 2-1446, RG59, NA. Ambassador Pawley's interests in Peru, which were overwhelmingly economic, revolved around bonds, salt, and petroleum; see *New York Times*, December 6, 1945.
7. Acheson to Tom C. Clark, March 22, 1946, 711.94115 AR/3-2546, RG59, NA.
8. Peruvian Internees in Santa Fe to President Harry S Truman, March 27, 1946, and Ricardo Toshiaki Nakagawa to Truman, March 29, 1946, 711.94115 AR/3-2746 and 3-2946, RG59, NA.
9. Copies in 1946 File, WMC Papers.
10. Bingham to Officer in Charge, INS Camp Santa Fe, March 27, 1946, March 28, 1946, and April 1, 1946, 711.94115 AR/3-2646, 3-2746, and 3-2946, RG59, NA.
11. Kosuke Kitsutani, Koshiro Mukoyama, and Ginzo Murono to Spruille

Braden, March 29, 1946, and to DS (SWP), March 29, 1946, 711.94115 AR/3-2946, RG59, NA.

12. Warrant (Form I-200) for the Arrest of Alien Iwamori Sakasegawa (copy), March 21, 1946, Iwamori Sakasegawa File, WMC Papers.

13. Nakagawa to Byrnes (copy), April 1, 1946, and to Truman (copy), April 1, 1946, 711.94115 AR/4-146, RG59, NA; Nakagawa to Clark (copy), April 2, 1946, and to Embajada del Perú (copy), April 2, 1946, 1946 File, WMC Papers.

14. Kelly [?] to Bingham, April 2, 1946, 711.94115 AR/4-246, RG59, NA.

15. Contract (copy), April 4, 1946, 1946 File, WMC Papers.

16. "List of Peruvian Internees and Families" (copy), April 8, 1946, 1946 File, WMC Papers, and "Disposition of Enemy Aliens from Other American Republics," DS *Bulletin*, 14, no. 341 (January 6 and 13, 1946): 33.

17. Acheson to Clark, April 3, 1946, and Clark to Byrnes, April 12, 1946, 711.94115 AR/3-2546 and 4-1246, RG59, NA.

18. Pawley to SS, April 13, 1946, and April 15, 1946 (includes copy of Enrique García Sayán to Pawley, April 10, 1946), 711.94115 AR/4-3346, and 4-1546, RG59, NA. García Sayán's visit to Japan in 1938 had resulted in his *La economía japonesa, reseña sobre su evolución...* (Lima, 1939). See also *Revista conmemorativa del centenario de las relaciones diplomaticas entre el Perú y Japón* (Lima: Editorial Perū Shimpō, 1973), p. 17.

19. Walter J. Donnelly to SS, April 16, 1946 (includes copy of García Sayán to Pawley, April 12, 1946), 711.94115 AR/4-1646, RG59, NA.

20. Internees to J. B. Tietz (copy), April 13, 1946, 1946 File, WMC Papers.

21. Dillon S. Myer, *Uprooted Americans: The Japanese Americans and the War Relocation Authority During World War II* (Tucson: University of Arizona Press, 1971), pp. 261–70, and U.S., *United States Reports*, vol. 323 (Washington: GPO: 1945), pp. 214–48, 283–310.

22. Harry T. Takeuchi to Collins (copy), April 15, 1946, 1946 File, WMC Papers, and Ernest Besig to CHG, San Francisco, August 30, 1977.

23. Byrnes to AmEmLima, April 16, 1946, and April 19, 1946, Byrnes to Clark, April 19, 1946, and J. Howard McGrath to Byrnes, April 25, 1946, 711/94115 AR/4-1646, 4-1946, 4-1246, and 4-2546, RG59, NA.

24. Mukoyama to Nakamura (c/o Wayne M. Collins) (copy), April 23, 1946, and April 24, 1946, Nakamura to Besig (copy), April 24, 1946, 1946 File, WMC Papers; Nakamura to Bingham, April 23, 1946, 711.94115 AR/4-2346, RG59, NA; and INS Files, no. 2266, RG60, WNRC.

25. Besig to Roger N. Baldwin, April 22, 1946, ACLU Archives, 1946, vol. 25, p. 111, Princeton University, and Baldwin to Braden, April 26, 1946, 711.94115 AR/4-2646, RG59, NA.

26. J. P. Pradervand to Howard J. Carroll (copy), April 26, 1946, [Carroll] to Amleto G. Cicognani (copy), May 9, 1946, and Cicognani to Carroll, May 13,

1946, International Affairs; Immigration, Office of the General Secretary, NCWC, USCC.

27. Masao Yoda et al. to Collins, May 6, 1946, 1946 File, WMC Papers; Bruce M. Mohler to Cohill, May 28, 1946, International Affairs: Immigration, Office of the General Secretary, NCWC, USCC; and Mike Masaoka to Bingham, April 2, 1946, 711.94115 AR/4–246, RG59, NA.

28. "List of the Internees Brought from Peru Who Are Detained at Terminal Island Immigration Station" [May 1, 1946], and Yoshinaga Roberto Furuya and Seiho Inamine to Besig and Collins, May 15, 1946, 1946 File, WMC Papers.

29. Collins to Internees (copy), May 9, 1946, 1946 File, WMC Papers.

30. Usaburo Maoki to Besig (copy), May 16, 1946, and Collins to Hajime Kishi (copy), May 17, 1946, 1946 File, WMC Papers.

31. Iwamori Sakasegawa to Ennis, April 12, 1946, Sakasegawa to Bingham, March 26, 1946, G. C. Wilmoth to Chief, Expulsion Section, "Warrant for Arrest of Alien," March 31, 1946, Hearing in re Iwamori Sakasegawa, April 6, 1946, Application and petition for writ of habeas corpus, June 25, 1946, Stipulation and order continuing order to show cause, September 6, 1946, Iwamori Sakasegawa File, WMC Papers. See also Charles Gordon, "The Writ of Habeas Corpus in Deportation Proceedings," INS *Monthly Review*, 3, no. 5 (November 1945): 218–23, and Paul G. Werner, "Expulsion of Aliens from the United States," INS *Monthly Review*, 8, no. 9 (March 1951): 114–17.

32. Heishiki Hori to Collins, May 31, 1946, 1946 File, WMC Papers, and INS Files, nos. 1412, 1376, and 1871, RG60, WNRC.

33. "Two Japanese Deportation Parties Due to Leave in June," *American Civil Liberties Union—News* (San Francisco), 11, no. 5 (May 1946): 1–2.

34. *San Francisco Chronicle*, June 7, 1946; *San Francisco News*, June 25, 1946, p. 5; "Two Kidnapped Peruvian Japanese File Test Suits to Prevent Their Deportation to Japan," *American Civil Liberties Union—News*, 11, no. 7 (July 1946): p. 1, and ACLU Bulletin 1238, New York, July 7, 1946, ACLU Archives, 1946, vol. 25, p. 119, Princeton University.

35. Kishi to Besig and Collins, June 26, 1946, 1946 File, WMC Papers, and *FRUS 1946*, vol. 11 (Washington: GPO, 1969), pp. 76–85.

36. War Relocation Authority, *The Relocation Program* (Washington: GPO, 1946), pp. 90, 104.

37. Mukoyama to Collins, June 5, 1946, 1946 File, WMC Papers.

38. Mukoyama to Collins, August 14, 1946, 1946 File, WMC Papers.

39. INS Files, nos. 2136, 1393, 2266, 2300, and 1793, RG60, WNRC.

40. Tawara, "Autographs," LL 16, 50, 51r, 53r, 54, 55, 60r.

41. Isamu E. Kurotobi to Collins and Besig, August 20, 1946, 1946 File, WMC Papers.

42. Collins to Clark (copy), August 26, 1946, 1946 File, WMC Papers.

43. Donnelly to SS, May 8, 1946, 894.20223/5–846, RG59, NA; Gardiner, *The Japanese and Peru, 1873–1973*, p. 92; and Tigner, "The Okinawans in Latin America," pp. 617–19.

44. Hoover to Lyon, July 9, 1946, Prentice Cooper to SS, July 18, 1946, and Hoover to Jack Neal, August 1, 1946, 894.20223/7–946, 7–1846, and 8–146, RG59, NA.

45. Cooper to SS, August 16, 1946, Neal to Lt. Col. Charles B. Smith, August 20, 1946, and Cooper to SS, August 23, 1946, 894.20223/8–1846, 8–1646, and 8–2346, RG59, NA.

46. INS Files, nos. 2147, 2232, 2226, 2280, 2139, 2156, 2148, and 1409, RG60, WNRC; Cooper to SS, August 9, 1946 (includes García Sayán to Cooper, July 31, 1946), 711.94115 AR/8–946, RG59, NA; Taro Ohashi to Collins, September 6, 1946, 1946 File, WMC Papers; conversation with Victor K. Tateishi, December 6, 1978; and *FRUS 1946*, 11:1232–51.

47. Collins to Mukoyama (copy), August 21, 1946, and U.S. District Court for the Northern District of California, "Dismissal without Prejudice" (copy), February 24, 1947, Iwamori Sakasegawa File, WMC Papers.

48. INS Files, nos. 1442, 2134, 2185, 1868, 1848, 1458, 1402, 2239, 1794, and 1423, RG60, WNRC.

49. Ohashi to Collins, September 6, 1946, and Mukoyama to Collins, September 10, 1946, 1946 File, WMC Papers.

50. INS Files, nos. 2187, 1376, 2294, 2155, 1277, 1412, 1870, 1872, 1349, 2264, and 1367, RG60, WNRC, and Ohashi to Collins, September 6, 1946, 1946 File, WMC Papers.

51. Iwao Shimizu to Collins, October 9, 1946, 1946 File, WMC Papers.

52. Ohashi to Mohler, October 21, 1946, and Isamu Kurotobi to Besig, October 14, 1946 (copies), 1946 File, WMC Papers, and "Chartered Planes Effect Deportation of Aliens," INS *Monthly Review*, 4, no. 5 (November 1946): 66.

53. Isamu Kurotobi to Besig and Collins, October 14, 1946, 1946 File, WMC Papers; "Chartered Planes Effect Deportation of Aliens," p. 66; INS Files, nos. 2289, 1820, and 1378, RG60, WNRC; and Sakasegawa to Collins, October 20, 1946, Iwamori Sakasegawa File, WMC Papers. The withdrawal at midyear of the "American Blacklist" which had forced "the liquidation, forced sale, reorganization, or vesting of many Axis enterprises" had inspired no expression of Peruvian Japanese gratitude, see "The Proclaimed List of Certain Blocked Nationals: Announcement of Withdrawal of List," DS *Bulletin*, 15, no. 368 (July 21, 1946): 112, 114.

54. Otokichi Aida, Ricardo T. Nakagawa, Kosuke Kitsutani, and Takichi Kaneshige to Mohler, November 5, 1946, International Affairs: Immigration, Office of the Secretary General, NCWC, USCC.

55. Conversations with Kakuaki and Otari Kaneko, May 15, 1977, with John

Kunio Takeshita, August 28, 1976, with Saburo Ushida, August 29, 1976, with George Hisao Fujii, August 29, 1976, with Victor Tawara, and Tosh (Toshiharu) Tawara, September 27, 1976, and with Masao Kishi, May 13, 1977.

56. Mervin W. Logan to D. V. Aitken (copy), October 9, 1946, and Isamu Kurotobi to Collins, November 3, 1946, 1946 File, WMC Papers.

## 8. Drawn Out Finales

1. "List of the Peruvian Japanese in Crystal City Internment Camp," List of the Peruvian Japanese at Seabrook Farms, Bridgeton, New Jersey," and "List of Peruvian Japanese on Parole in the United States" (copies), 1947 File, WMC Papers, and Collins to Cardinal Stritch (copy), April 29, 1947, International Affairs: Immigration, Office of the Secretary General, NCWC, USCC.

2. Collins to Marshall (copy), February 7, 1947, 1947 File, WMC Papers.

3. Isamu E. Kurotobi to Collins, February 14, 1947, 1947 File, WMC Papers. Remembering Collins's labors on behalf of Japanese Americans, Michi Weglyn dedicated her volume, *Years of Infamy: The Untold Story of America's Concentration Camps*, to Collins, "Who Did More to Correct a Democracy's Mistake Than Any Other One Person."

4. Collins to Jorge Prado (copies), February 8 and 17, 1947, and H. Fernández-Dávila to Collins, February 18 and March 11, 1947, 1947 File, WMC Papers.

5. Clattenburg to Collins, February 26, 1947, and Collins to Clattenburg (copy), March 3, 1947, 1947 File, WMC Papers.

6. Collins to Marshall, March 3, 1947, 711.94115 AR/3–347, RG59, NA.

7. Collins to Clattenburg, April 29, 1947, 711.94115 AR/4–2947, RG59, NA.

8. Acheson to AmEmLima, March 19, 1947, 711.94115 AR/3–1947, RG59, NA.

9. I. E. Kurotobi to Collins, February 14, 1947, Kelly to Collins, February 17, 1947, Yoshisada Shiga to Collins, March 1, 1947, and Collins to Shiga (copies), March 6 and 7, 1947, 1947 File, WMC Papers.

10. Collins to J. J. Allen, F. H. Havenner, N. Poulson, S. Downey, W. F. Knowland, and R. F. Wagner (copies), May 9, 1947, 1947 File, WMC Papers.

11. Collins to Marshall, May 14, 1947, 711.94115 AR/5–1447, RG59, NA.

12. Ellis O. Briggs to Havenner and Allen, June 13, 1947, Briggs to Downey and Wagner, June 13, 1947, Briggs to Poulson, June 25, 1947, Briggs to Knowland, June 30, 1947, Briggs to Celler, June 13, 1947, Briggs to Farrington, July 7, 1947, and Briggs to Wiley, July 21, 1947, 711.94115 AR/5–1547, 5–2247, 6–1147, 6–1747, 5–2147, 6–2747, and 6–3047, RG59, NA.

13. DS (R. W. Flournoy) Memorandum, May 28, 1947, FW711.94115 AR/5–1547, RG59, NA, and *Paetau v. Watkins*, 164 *Federal Register*, 2d ser., p. 457.

14. INS Files, no. 2287, RG60, WNRC, Prado to SS, June 13, 1947, and Braden to Prado, June 27, 1947, 711.94115 AR/6–1347, RG59, NA.

15. "Peru's Minister of Foreign Affairs Visits Washington," *Bulletin PAU*, 81, no. 9 (September 1947): 486–89.

16. Armour to H. Fernández-Dávila, October 8, 1947, and DS (J. Espy) Memorandum, December 16, 1947, 711.94115 AR/6–1347 and 12–1647, RG59, NA.

17. Collins to Marshall, January 27, 1948, and R. M. de Lambert to SS, February 4, 1948 (includes Collins to Cooper, January 27, 1948), 711.94115 AR/1–2748 and 2–448, RG59, NA.

18. Armour to Cooper, January 30, 1948, and Kelly to Walter F. Chappell, January 5, 1948, FW711.94115 AR/1–548, RG59, NA.

19. De Lambert to SS, February 4, 1948 (includes copy of García Sayán to Ralph Ackerman, June 17, 1947), Chappell to AmEmLima, March 12, 1948, and De Lambert to SS, March 18, 1948, 711.94115 AR/2–448, 2–448, and 3–1848, RG59, NA.

20. Collins to Truman, February 16, 1948, 711.94115 AR/2–1648, RG59, NA.

21. Marshall to AmEmLima, March 16, 1948, 711.94115 AR/2–448 (the second point, present in a draft of this instruction, does not appear in the document transmitted to Lima), Celler to DS, August 9, 1948, and Theodore J. Hadraba to Celler, August 30, 1948, 711.94115 AR/8–948, RG59, NA.

22. Marshall to AmEmLima, August 16, 1948, A. O. Pierrot to SS, August 31, 1948, Peurifoy to Alfredo Ferreyros, October 14, 1948, Ferreyros to Robert A. Lovett, October 19, 1948, and Collins to Marshall, December 29, 1948, 711.94115 AR/8–1648, 8–2748, 10–1448, 10–1948, and 12–2948, RG59, NA.

23. Lovett to AmEmLima, January 6, 1949, and Harold H. Tittmann, Jr., to SS, March 24, 1949, 711.94115 AR/12–2948 and 3–2149, RG59, NA.

24. Ginzo Murono, Hajime Kishi, and Manuel E. Ykari to SS, April 13, 1949, 711.94115 AR/4–1349, and DS (B. C. Davis) Memorandum, April 15, 1949, FW711.94115 AR/4–1349, RG59, NA.

25. Taro Ohashi to Willard F. Kelly (copy), September 18, 1947, Taro Ohashi File, WMC Papers.

26. Order of Parole (Form I-220), signed by I. F. Wixon (copy), October 6, 1947, Collins to Commissioner of Immigration (copy), November 28, 1947, Submission to Deportation Process and Application for Suspension of Deportation (Form I-256) (copy), December 29, 1948, Board of Immigration Appeals, In Deportation Proceedings Motion (copy), November 4, 1949, Taro Ohashi File, WMC Papers.

27. Lloyd E. Cowen to Taro Ohashi (copy), July 25, 1952, Asst. Commissioner, In re Ohashi family (copy), September 3, 1952, Bruce G. Barber to Taro Ohashi (copy), September 18, 1953, Taro Ohashi file, WMC Papers, and conversation with Taro and Fusae Ohashi, May 5, 1977.

28. Conversations with Mitsutaro and Victor Tawara, September 27, 1976, with Masao Kishi, May 13, 1977, with Yoshisada Shiga, Los Angeles, May 12,

1977, with Yoshinari Honda, Los Angeles, May 12, 1977, with Yoshiko Eugenia Kato, May 5, 1977, and with Kiyoko Naganuma Matsuoka, May 6, 1977, and Mitsutaro Tawara File, WMC Papers.

29. Conversations with John Kunio Takeshita, August 28, 1976, with George Hisao Fujii, August 28, 1976, and with Saburo Ushida, August 29, 1976; INS Files, nos. 2136 and 2260, RG60, WNRC; and *Chicago Peru Kai Directory* (January 1971).

30. For example, see Alfred Steinberg, " 'Blunder' Maroons Peruvian Japanese in the U.S.," *Washington Post*, September 26, 1948, sec. 2, pp. 1, 4.

31. U.S. *United States Statutes at Large*, vol. 68, pt. 1 (Washington: GPO, 1955), pp. 1044–45.

### Epilogue

1. INS Files, no. 191, RG60, WNRC, and conversation with Shinzo Shimabukuro, Naha, Okinawa, December 10, 1978.

2. INS Files, no. 2266, RG60, WNRC; Hiroko Stevenson to CHG, March 25, 1978; conversations with Victor K. Tateishi, Yasuhiko Ohashi, Kishiro Hayashi, Shoichi Mishima, and Ricardo T. Nakagawa, Lima, Peru, January 16, 1979, and with Juan Iida, Chihito Saito, and Enrique Shimabukuro, Lima, Peru, January 19, 1979; *Inmigración japonesa al Perú 75 aniversario*, pp. 49–50; and "Ichitaro Morimoto,'" *Nikko* (Lima), 26, no. 241 (August–September 1979): 22–23.

3. Conversations with Arthur Shinei Yakabi, Lima, Peru, January 15, 1979, with Taro Ohashi, May 5, 1977, with Kakuaki Kaneko, May 15, 1977, with Victor Tawara, September 27, 1976, and with Saburo Ushida, August 29, 1976; Paul Shuhei Katsuro to CHG, Houston, Texas, June 27, 1977; and *Chicago Peru Kai Directory* (1971).

4. Ginzo Murono to CHG, Seabrook, N.J., September 29, 1976; Seiki Murono to CHG, New York, N.Y., November 20, 1978; Eisuke Murono to CHG, Amherst, N.Y., November 26, 1978; and Mary Jo Mather (Alumni Office, Franklin and Marshall College) to CHG, January 25, 1979.

5. Emmerson, *The Japanese Thread*, p. 149.

6. INS Files, no. 1420, RG60, WNRC, and conversation with Saburo Ushida, August 29, 1976.

# Directory

NOTE: This list is primarily composed of officials. Most, whose assignments and titles changed frequently, it simply identifies and locates. For a few topmost officials, terms of service are indicated.

| | |
|---|---|
| Acheson, Dean G. | Assistant SS, 1941–45; Under SS, 1945–47; SS, 1949–53 |
| Ackerman, Ralph | DS, Lima |
| Allen, J. J. | Congress |
| Armour, Norman | DS, Washington |
| Baldwin, Roger N. | ACLU, New York |
| Bannerman, R. L. | DS, Washington |
| Barber, Bruce G. | DJ–INS, San Francisco |
| Bell, James D. | DJ–AECU and DS, Washington |
| Bellido, Dr. Hernán C. | Peruvian official, Lima |
| Beltrán, Pedro | Peruvian Ambassador, Washington, 1944–46 |
| Berle, Adolf A., Jr. | DS, Washington |
| Besig, Ernest | ACLU, San Francisco |
| Biddle, Francis | Attorney General, 1941–45 |
| Bingham, Jonathan B. | DS, Washington |
| Bonsal, Philip W. | DS, Washington |
| Borton, Hugh | DS, Washington |
| Braden, Spruille | DS, Washington |
| Brandt, George L. | DS, Washington |
| Breese, Lt. Col. Howard F. | WD, Washington |
| Briggs, Ellis O. | DS, Washington |
| Bustamante Rivero, José Luis | President of Peru, 1945–48 |
| Butler, George H. | DS, Lima |
| Byrnes, James F. | SS, 1945–47 |

| | |
|---|---|
| Cárdenas García, César | Peruvian official, Lima |
| Carroll, Monsignor H. J. | Catholic clergy, Washington |
| Celler, Emanuel | Congress |
| Chapin, Seldin | DS, Washington |
| Chappell, Walter F. | DS, Washington |
| Cicognani, Amleto G. | Catholic clergy, Washington |
| Clark, C. | DS, Washington |
| Clark, Tom C. | Attorney General, 1945–49 |
| Clattenburg, Albert E., Jr. | DS, Washington |
| Collaer, N. D. | DJ–INS |
| Collins, Wayne M. | Attorney, ACLU, San Francisco |
| Cooley, Tom | DJ–AECU, Washington |
| Cooper, Prentice | U.S. Ambassador, Lima, 1946–48 |
| Correa Elías, Dr. Javier | Peruvian Foreign Minister, 1945–46 |
| Cowen, Lloyd E. | DJ–INS, San Francisco |
| Dasso, David | Peruvian official, Lima |
| Davis, B. C. | DS, Washington |
| Dawson, Allan | DS, La Paz |
| De la Puente, Ricardo | Peruvian official, Lima |
| De Lambert, R. M. | DS, Lima |
| Donnelly, Walter J. | DS, Panama and Lima |
| Dorsz, E. J. | DS, Washington |
| Downey, Sheridan | Congress |
| Doyle, J. E. | DS, Washington |
| Dreyfus, Louis G., Jr. | DS, Lima |
| Duggan, Laurence | DS, Washington |
| Emmerson, John K. | DS, Lima |
| Ennis, Edward J. | DJ–AECU, Washington |
| Eslinger, Ernest L. | DS, Washington |
| Espy, J. | DS, Washington |
| Fahy, Charles | DJ, Washington |
| Farrington, J. R. | Congress |
| Fernández-Dávila, H. | Peruvian Embassy, Washington |
| Ferreyros, Alfredo | Peruvian Ambassador, Washington, 1948 |
| Fitch, T. F. | DS, Washington |
| Flournoy, R. W. | DS, Washington |
| Gallagher, Manuel | Peruvian Foreign Minister, 1944–45 |
| Garay, José María | Spanish Consul, New Orleans |
| García Sayán, Dr. Enrique | Peruvian Foreign Minister, 1946–48 |
| Garrido Lecca, Dr. Guillermo | Peruvian official, Lima |
| Green, Joseph C. | DS, Washington |

# Directory

| | |
|---|---|
| Greenup, Julian C. | DS, Washington |
| Grew, Joseph | U.S. Ambassador, Tokyo, 1931–41 |
| Griffith, Major L. E. | WD, Washington |
| Groth, Edward M. | DS, Washington |
| Gufler, Bernard F. | DS, Washington |
| Hadraba, Theodore J. | DS, Washington |
| Hanley, J. Daniel | DS, Washington |
| Havenner, F. H. | Congress |
| Henkin, Louis | DS, Washington |
| Herrick, P. W. | DS, Washington |
| Hill, J. C. | DS, Washington |
| Hoover, J. Edgar | DJ–FBI, Washington |
| Hudson, Aubrey S. | DJ–INS, Texas |
| Hull, Cordell | SS, 1933–44 |
| Ickes, Raymond W. | DJ–AECU |
| Keeley, James H., Jr. | DS, Washington |
| Kelly, Willard F. | DJ–INS |
| Knowland, William F. | Congress |
| Lafoon, Sidney K. | DS, Washington |
| Larrañaga, Jorge | Peruvian in Washington |
| Long, Boaz | U.S. Ambassador, Quito, 1938–43 |
| Long, Breckinridge | DS, Washington |
| Lovett, Robert A. | DS, Washington |
| Lyon, Frederick B. | DS, Washington |
| Mangione, Jerre | DJ–INS |
| Marshall, George C. | SS, 1947–49 |
| Masaoka, Mike | Japanese American Citizens League |
| Mathewson, Col. L. M. | WD, Washington |
| McGrath, J. Howard | Attorney General, 1949–52 |
| McGurk, J. F. | DS, Lima |
| Mohler, Bruce M. | NCWC, Washington |
| Muccio, John J. | DS, Panama |
| Norweb, R. Henry | U.S. Ambassador, Lima, 1940–43 |
| Odría, Manuel A. | President of Peru, 1948–56 |
| O'Rourke, Joseph L. | DJ–INS, Crystal City |
| Patterson, Jefferson | DS, Lima |
| Pawley, William D. | U.S. Ambassador, Lima, 1945–46 |
| Peurifoy, John E. | DS, Washington |
| Pierrot, Albert Ogden | DS, Lima |
| Plitt, Edwin A. | DS, Washington |
| Poulson, N. | Congress |
| Pradervand, J. P. | International Red Cross, Geneva |

| | |
|---|---|
| Prado, Jorge | Peruvian Ambassador, Washington, 1946–47 |
| Prado, Manuel | President of Peru, 1939–45 |
| Rivera Schreiber, Ricardo | Peruvian Minister, Tokyo, 1936–41 |
| Rockefeller, Nelson | DS, Washington |
| Roosevelt, Franklin D. | President, 1933–45 |
| Rowe, Leo S. | Pan American Union, Washington |
| Sakamoto, Ryūki | Japanese Minister, Lima, 1941 |
| Seward, Lee H. | DS, Washington |
| Smith, Lt. Col. Charles B. | WD, Washington |
| Snow, William | DS, Lima |
| Solf y Muro, Alfredo | Peruvian Foreign Minister, 1939–44 |
| Stannard, Amy N. | DJ–INS, Texas |
| Stettinius, Edward R. | SS, 1944–45 |
| Stimson, Henry L. | Secretary of War, 1940–45 |
| Stritch, Cardinal | Catholic clergy |
| Tate, R. C. | DJ–INS, Crystal City |
| Tietz, J. B. | Attorney, Los Angeles |
| Tittmann, Harold H., Jr. | U.S. Ambassador, Lima, 1948–55 |
| Trueblood, Edward G. | DS, Lima |
| Truman, Harry S | President, 1945–53 |
| Wagner, Robert F. | Congress |
| Warren, Avra M. | DS, Panama and Washington |
| Warren, Fletcher | DS, Washington |
| Wechsler, Herbert | DJ, Washington |
| Welch, Rolland | DS, Lima |
| Welles, Sumner | DS, Washington |
| White, I. B. | DS, Washington |
| White, John Campbell | U.S. Ambassador, Lima, 1944–45 |
| Wiley, Alexander | Congress |
| Williams, Ivan | DJ–INS, Texas and New Mexico |
| Williams, Margaret Nan | DJ–INS, Crystal City |
| Wilmoth, G. C. | DJ–INS |
| Wilson, Edwin C. | U.S. Ambassador, Panama, 1941–43 |
| Wirin, A. L. | ACLU, Los Angeles |
| Wixon, I. F. | DJ–INS, San Francisco |
| Woo, George Tsung-yuan | Chinese Legation, Lima |
| Wright, J. H. | DS, Washington |
| Yodokawa, Masaki | Japanese Chargé, Lima, 1941–42 |
| Young, Whitney | DS, Washington |
| Zacharias, Captain E. | ND, Washington |

# Bibliographical Essay

The previously published materials related to this theme include the following: (1) several brief articles and editorials in San Francisco newspapers and the San Francisco-based ACLU publication (1946); (2) Alfred Steinberg's illustrated essay " 'Blunder' Maroons Peruvian Japanese in the U.S." in the *Washington Post* (September 26, 1948); (3) the terse and revealing accounts in Edward N. Barnhart's "Japanese Internees from Peru," *Pacific Historical Review* (May 1962) and his related "Citizenship and Political Tests in Latin American Republics in World War II," *Hispanic American Historical Review* (August 1962); (4) very brief references in the survey of the total Japanese experience in Peru by *Perú Shimpō*, the Lima-based newspaper, *Zai Peru hōjin 75 nen no ayumi (The 75th Anniversary of the Japanese Resident in Peru)*, and its accompanying Spanish summary *Inmigración japonesa al Perú 75 aniversario* (Lima, 1974); (5) an exceedingly brief reference to the deportation-internment program in the present writer's general survey, *The Japanese and Peru, 1873–1973* (Albuquerque, 1975); (6) those few pages of discussion and illustrative documents wherein Michi Weglyn's *Years of Infamy: The Untold Story of America's Concentration Camps* (New York, 1976) introduces the Latin American Japanese problem as a backdrop to her biting study of the Japanese American issue; (7) the tantalizingly brief 5-page item, "The Story and Diary of Kami Kamisato," in Takea Kaneshiro, comp., *Internees: War Relocation Center Memoirs and Diaries* (New York: Vantage Press, 1976), stands as the only published record of the wartime experience of a Japanese Peruvian; (8) John K. Emmerson's eyewitness-participant account, "Japanese and Americans in Peru, 1942–1943," *Foreign Service Journal* (1977), a slightly modified version of which is in Emmerson's *The Japanese Thread* (New York, 1978); and (9) Jerre Mangione's *An Ethnic at Large* (New York, 1978), which tells of author's personal identification with the INS internment program.

It is noteworthy that numerous high American officials—among them Hull, Byrnes, Acheson, Biddle, and J. E. Hoover—who were connected with the deportation-internment program saw fit to ignore it in articles and books about their public service.

## Manuscripts

More than 95 percent of this work derives from manuscript sources. For the formulation of the deportation program and its execution, the files of the Department of State in the National Archives are of basic importance. In RG59 extensive use was made of the following files: 311.9415, 311.943, 701.0010, 701.00112, 701.0090, 711.94115 AR, 711.94115 Exchange, 740.00115 EW1939, 740.00115 PW, 894.20200, 894.20210, 894.20211, 894.20214, and 894.20223. Herein are relevant instructions, dispatches, memoranda, and interdepartmental and general correspondence, including that of the protecting power, Spain.

For the operation of the internment camps the records of the Immigration and Naturalization Service at the Washington National Records Center are likewise indispensable. Especially significant are the Closed Legal Case Files (series 146–13–2 consisting of 2,488 entries), Alien Enemy World War II, Detention and Internment, RG60. Herein are forty-six large boxes of detailed data concerning the individual internees. The General Information Form (I-55), for example, is a twenty-page document that poses fifty-eight multipart questions. One can trace the movements of internees via the "Report of the Enemy Alien in Custody" and the "Application for Repatriation" (I-540) in these files. Also containing World War II Internment Files at the WNRC, RG85 offers valuable papers concerning the internment camps, their origins, physical nature, operations, and closings.

For the legal complexities and personal experiences concerning those internees who remained in the United States after 1946, the massive files of the late Attorney Wayne M. Collins are indispensable. Held by Attorney Wayne M. Collins, Jr., in Berkeley, California, these papers include the following kinds of materials relevant to the present study: (1) annual files, for 1946, 1947, and so on, which reflect basic issues and Collins's handling of them, including his efforts to solicit the support of politicians, clergy, and others; (2) some files that concern special groups of internees, such as those whose threatened deportation he blocked in 1946; and (3) many files for individual internees—for example, the file for Mitsutaro Tawara holds eleven items, that of Iwamori Sakasegawa contains twelve items, that of Ginzo Murono thirteen items, and that of Taro Ohashi twenty-one items. The Collins papers, in the aggregate, detail the legal, economic, and social problems faced by numerous Peruvian Japanese internees and the persistent effort of one man to help solve those problems.

Additional manuscript sources include correspondence between former officials or former internees and the writer, notes resulting from the writer's conversations with both groups of former participants, the autograph book of Tosh Tawara, correspondence in the ACLU Archives at Princeton University, correspondence in the archives of the United States Catholic Conference in Washington, D.C., James Lawrence Tigner's "The Okinawans in Latin America," a Ph.D. dissertation at Stanford University (1956), and Warren Page Rucker's "United States–Peruvian Policy Toward Peruvian-Japanese Persons During World War II," an M.A. thesis at the University of Virginia (1970).

### Printed Documents

Peruvian sources consulted include: Perú, Cámara de Diputados, *Compilación de la legislación peruana*, 5 vols. (Lima, 1950–56); Perú, Dirección Nacional de Estadística, *Censo nacional de población y ocupación 1940: Primer volúmen, Resumenes generales* (Lima, 1944); and Arturo Nieves Ayala, ed., *Los extranjeros ante la ley peruana* (Lima, 1961).

United States sources include: *United States Statutes at Large*; *United States Reports*; *Federal Reporter* (Second Series); *Code of Federal Regulations, Title 3*; Department of Commerce, Bureau of Marine Inspection and Navigation, *Merchant Vessels of the United States 1941* (1941); Department of State, *The Proclaimed List of Certain Blocked Nationals*; Department of State, *Foreign Relations of the United States*; Department of State, *Bulletin*; Department of State, *Diplomatic Register*; Department of Justice, *Annual Report of the Attorney General of the United States*; and Department of Justice, *Annual Report of the Immigration and Naturalization Service*. Titles for which no dates are listed were employed over considerable periods.

Other documents include: League of Nations, *Treaty Series* (1931–32); Emergency Advisory Committee for Political Defense, *Annual Report Submitted to the Governments of the American Republics* (Montevideo, 1943–44); and the *Chicago Peru Kai Directory* (1971).

### Books

Although no prior book-length study of the deportation and internment of the Peruvian Japanese existed, the voluminous literature regarding the Japanese Americans invited study, for background and comparative purposes.

Among the official accounts of the War Relocation Authority program the following were informative: WRA, *The Relocation Program* (1946); WRA, *Wartime Exile: The Exclusion of the Japanese Americans from the West Coast* (1946); WRA, *Community Government in War Relocation Centers* (1946); and Dillon S. Myer, *Uprooted Americans: The Japanese Americans and the War Relocation Authority During World War II* (1971). Illuminating accounts by Japanese American internees included Miné Okubo, *Citizen 13660* (1946); Daisuke Kitagawa, *Issei and Nisei: The Internment Years* (1967); Daniel I. Okimoto, *Americans in Disguise* (1971); Estelle Ishigo, *Lone Heart Mountain* (1972); Jeanne Wakatsuki Houston and James D. Houston, *Farewell to Manzanar* (1973); and the book by Michi Weglyn, which, more than any other, also recognized the Peruvian Japanese wartime problem. Detailed coverage and analysis of the Japanese American experience by nonparticipants is afforded by Jacobus ten Broek, Edward N. Barnhart, and Floyd W. Matson, *Prejudice, War and the Constitution* (1954); Allan P. Bosworth, *America's Concentration Camps* (1967); Audrie Girdner and Anne Loftis, *The Great Betrayal: The Evacuation of the Japanese-Americans During World War II* (1969); Maisie and Richard Conrat, *Executive Order 9066* (1972); and Roger Daniels, *Concentration Camps USA: Japanese Americans and World War II* (1972). A poignant statement of the Canadian experience is in the Japanese Canadian Centennial Project, *A Dream of Riches: The Japanese Canadians, 1877-1977* (Toronto, 1978).

Although a comparative approach to internment programs leads inevitably to the condemnation of all, the experience of the Peruvian Japanese was especially monstrous and deplorable.

### Periodicals

For many years tight government controls over the deportation-internment program limited the sources for related articles to the agencies concerned. The Department of State *Bulletin* offered such items as "Alien Enemy Control Section" (1945), "Disposition of Enemy Aliens from other American Republics" (1945 and 1946), Thomas C. Mann's "Elimination of Axis Influence in This Hemisphere: Measures Adopted at the Mexico City Conference" (1945), and "The Proclaimed List of Certain Blocked Nationals: Announcement of Withdrawal of Lists" (1946). All such items are somewhat oblique and distinctly limited considerations of the Peruvian Japanese issue. Another official periodical, the *Monthly Review* of the Immigration and Naturalization Service, offered such pieces as "Civilian Alien Enemies in the Custody of the Service" (1944), "Work Projects for Interned Alien Enemies" (1945), Charles Gordon's "The Writ of Habeas Corpus in Deportation Proceedings" (1945), "Chartered Planes Effect Deportation of Aliens" (1946), N. D. Collaer's "The Crystal City Internment Camp" (1947), Will Harrison's "The Santa Fe Internment Camp" (1946), and Paul G. Werner's "Expulsion of Aliens from the United States" (1951).

To the previously mentioned articles by Barnhart and Emmerson, the following are to be added: J. Irizarry y Puente's "Exclusion and Expulsion of Aliens in Latin America," *American Journal of International Law* (1942), and the present writer's "El desarrollo de sentimiento antijaponés en el Perú, 1899-1941," *Boletín de la Academia de Historia del Valle del Cauca* (Colombia) (1973).

### Newspapers

Here, too, there was little coverage of the deportation-internment program. Two Texas newspapers, located in towns housing internment camps, namely the *Kenedy Advance* (Kenedy, Texas) and the *Zavala County Sentinel* (Crystal City, Texas), did more than the rest of the American press. During the deportation fight of 1946, Attorney Collins inspired some coverage in the *San Francisco Chronicle*, the *San Francisco News*, and the *ACLU–News* of San Francisco. In 1948 the aforementioned article by Steinberg appeared in the *Washington Post*. In 1972 *Perū Shimpō* (Lima) carried the recollections of one veteran of the program.

\* \* \*

The foregoing statement of sources employed is selective, not exhaustive.

# Index

Abe, Kenzo (from Brazil), 152
Abe, Kimi (wife of deportee), 93
*Acadia*: transporting internees, 23, 34, 35, 37, 42, 48, 62
Acheson, Dean: quoted, 131, 136, 175
*Aconcagua*: transporting internees, 79, 80, 85, 109
Agreements: U.S.-Peru, 10
Aguirre, Carlos (Peruvian official), 104
Aikoku Doshi-kai (secret society), 151, 152, 153
Aita, Hisao: deported, 78
Aita, Tokio: deported, 78
Alien Enemy Act of 1798, viii, 176
Alien Enemy Control Section, 116, 117
Alien Enemy Control Unit, 70, 73, 86, 115, 130
Allen, J. J. (congressman), 164
Amemiya, Kenzi (Lima merchant): deported, 35
American Civil Liberties Union, 141, 143
American Friends Service Committee, 61
Ampudia, Eduardo V. (Mexican official), 105
Aprista: appraisal by, 10
Arakaki, Yosei (Lima restaurant worker): deported, 9, 29
Araki, Genichi (Peruvian Japanese), 104, 105
Aray, Nakataro (Lima bazaar owner–farmer): deported, 96–97; shake-down, 104, 105; death of, 127–28
Arequipa, Peru: trip to, 53; deported from, 68, 71, 77, 79, 89, 118, 153

Argentina: on committee, 17; at Rio Conference, 18–19
Arias Schreiber, Javier (Peruvian lawyer), 105
Asano Bussan: representative of, 27, 48
Asato, Kosuke (Lima barber): death of, 127
Ascope, Peru: deported from, 68, 79
Asiatic Exclusion League in Canada, 9

Baldwin, Roger L. (ACLU), 143
Bank accounts, 62
Barranco, Peru: deported from, 89
Barrios, Alejandro (Peruvian official), 104
Bazaar owners: deported, 6, 44, 96
Becerra, Gonzalo (Peruvian official), 104
Bell, James D. (U.S. official), 86, 133
Bellido, Hernán (Peruvian official), 52
Beltrán, Pedro (Peruvian official), 53, 106
Benavides, Alfredo (Peruvian official), 90, 91
Besig, Ernest (ACLU), 143, 150
Biddle, Francis (U.S. official): conclusion by, 22; actions by, 41, 74, 86; quoted, 56, 64, 70
Bingham, Jonathan (U.S. official): conclusions of, 129; quoted, 133; appeal to, 137
Blacklisted persons: 28, 35, 45, 61–62, 65, 68, 71, 72, 89, 91, 97, 107
Blacklisting: initiation of, 14; economic effects of, 15; closed out, 147
Bolivia: Japanese in, 23, 35, 42, 46, 84, 86, 107, 131
Brazil: Japanese in, 3, 4, 6, 7, 9, 56; on committee, 17

214

## Index

Briggs, Ellis O. (U.S. official): quoted, 164–65
Bustamente Rivero, José Luis (Peruvian president), 113, 137; toppled, 168
Byrnes, James (U.S. official): on compromise, 136; appeal to, 137, 139

Callao, Peru: settling in, 5; rioting in, 9; port of, 18; deported from, 44, 68, 71, 73, 79, 89, 90, 92, 107, 125
Camp administration, 30
Camp Livingston, Louisiana: internees at, 49, 58, 75
Canada: Japanese in, 3, 4, 6, 7, 9, 13
Canada Japanese Association, 7
Cañete, Peru: deported from, 44, 71, 72, 125, 126
Cárdenas García César: "protection" of, 88, 104
Carroll, Howard J. (American churchman), 143
Catacaos, Peru: trip to, 53; deported from, 68
Celler, Emanuel: in U.S. Congress, 164, 167
Census: Peruvian, 9
Central Japanese Association of Peru, 6, 96
Chacra, Peru: deported from, 68
Chancay, Peru: deported from, 44, 77
Chancay Valley: control of, 8, 42, 45
Chepén, Peru: deported from, 68
Chiba, Niichi (Lima farmer): quoted, 118
Chiclayo, Peru: deported from, 44, 66, 68, 79, 118, 119; trip to, 53
Chiclín, Peru: deported from, 68
Chile: on committee, 17; at Rio Conference, 18–19; agreement sought, 86
Chimbote, Peru: deported from, 44
Chincha Alta, Peru: trip to, 53
Chinese: in Peru, 7, 53
Chosica, Peru: Japanese officials in, 35
Chulacanas, Peru: deported from, 68
Cicognani, Amleto (church official), 143
Clark, Tom (U.S. official), 136, 140, 150
Clattenburg, A. E. (U.S. official): quoted, 162
Collins, Wayne M. (lawyer): quoted, 144, 150, 161, 162, 163, 164, 166, 167; mentioned, 141, 142, 143, 146, 147, 148, 150, 155, 164, 168

Colombia: Japanese in, 9, 23, 29, 35, 55, 86
Commercial associations, 6
Compañía Sud Americana de Vapores, 78
Contract system, 4
Cooper, Prentice: on report, 151; query to, 166
Correas Elias, Javier (Peruvian official): urges deportation, 64; quoted, 94
Costa Rica: Japanese in, 22, 48, 49, 58, 59, 75, 107, 113, 127
Council-spokesman system, 61
Count de Bureta (Spanish official), 87
Crystal City Internment Camp: facility at, 36, 75, 79, 80, 82, 87, 92, 96, 98, 102, 110, 112, 120, 122, 124, 127, 130, 134, 137, 139, 143, 147, 149, 150, 155, 156, 158, 160, 169; described, 59–61
Cuba: internment plans, 55; Japanese in, 90, 91, 92, 93, 95, 97, 103, 107, 109, 110, 126

Daigo, Matao (Huaral school official): deported, 85
Dasso, David (Peruvian official): visits Washington, 39
Deaths, 86, 109
De la Puente, Ricardo (Peruvian official), 52, 104
De la Riva Agüero, José (Peruvian lawyer), 105
Downey, Sheridan: in U.S. Congress, 164

Ecuador: Japanese in, 23, 29, 35, 48, 55, 107, 113, 130, 132
El Salvador: Japanese in, 113, 128, 130, 132
Emergency Advisory Committee for Political Defense: creation of, 17
Emigration companies: in Peru, 3–4
Emmerson, John K.: quoted, 22, 40, 42, 53, 81, 104, 175; conclusions by, 39–40; trip by, 53; report by, 81, 82; mentioned, 22, 64, 67, 68, 80–81, 95, 130
Endo, Fumio (Lima farmer): deported, 117; quoted, 117
Endo, Mitsuye (U.S. nisei): case of, 142
Endo, Noriyoshi (Lima merchant): deported, 44
Endo, Tae (wife of Lima merchant): deported, vii

Enemy aliens: internment of, 12
*Etolin*: transporting internees, 23, 24, 27, 28, 29, 30, 32, 34, 35, 42, 48, 50, 62, 84, 85; described, 25
Executive Order 9066: in U.S., 13, 176
Exclusion laws of U.S., 8
Export-Import Bank Credits, 21

Farrington, J. R.: in U.S. Congress, 164
Federal Bureau of Investigation: activity of, 10, 54, 87, 95, 151
Fifth Column: potential of, 10
*Florida*: transporting internees, 48, 49
Flournoy, R. W. (U.S. official): quoted, 165
Foreign ministers: conference of, 166
Fort Missoula, Montana: internees at, 82
Fort Sill, Oklahoma: internees at, 49, 86
*Frederick C. Johnson*: transporting internees, 65, 67, 69, 70, 71, 77, 107, 125
Frias, Peru: deported from, 68
Fujii, Jorge (George) Hisao (Lima merchant): deported, 4, 90; wages of, 158; settles in Chicago, 170
Fujimoto, Juan Ichisuke (Lima merchant): deported, 16
Fujishima, Kinsaku (Lima merchant): deported, 125; quoted, 126
Fukushima prefectural society, 66

Ganoza Chopitea, Ismaei: Peruvian blocks deportation of, 104
Garay, José Maria (Spanish diplomat): visits internees, 32, 38
García Sayán, Enrique (Peruvian official): appeal to, 137; visits Washington, 165; mentioned, 141, 167
Garrido Lecca, Guillermo (Peruvian official): inactivity of, 21, 41–42, 46, 52
*General Ernst*: transporting internees, 130
*General Gordon*: transporting internees, 127
*General Meigs*: transporting internees, 130
*General Randall*: transporting internees, 124
Geneva Convention (1929), 30, 33, 58, 84, 89, 94, 103
German internees, 29, 33, 38, 42, 46, 57, 60, 67, 79, 88, 130

Gibo, Takeo (Callao merchant): deported, 125
Grew, Joseph (U.S. official): report by, 55
*Gripsholm*: transporting internees, 28, 32, 35, 48, 49, 50, 55, 84, 85, 87, 121
Gushiken, Kohei (Lima tailor): deported, 63, 124
Gushiken, Koho (Lima laborer): deported, 107

Hachiya, Juan Hiroshi (Huancayo business agent): deported, 92
Hamamura, Hikoichi (Huancayo merchant): deported, 15–16, 90
Hara, Hikoichi: death of, 109
Haraguchi, Kunio (Piura merchant): deported, 118; quoted, 118
Hasegawa, Jiro (Lima glass manufacturer): deported, 15, 97, 109, 174; naturalized Peruvian, 153
Hashimoto, Pedro Minoru (Lima accountant): deported, 90, 118; quoted, 118; mentioned, 153
Havenner, F. H.: in U.S. Congress, 164
Hawaii: immigration to, 3
Haya de la Torre, Víctor Raúl: appraisal by, 10, 135
Higa family, 28–29
Higa, Kentoku: deported, 122; quoted, 122
Higa, Rensuke: deported, 124
Higa, Renyu (journalist): deported, 124
Higa, Yasuko: deported, 80
Higashide, Seiichi (Ica merchant): deported, 120, 149; quoted, 120, 170; settles in Chicago, 170; mentioned, 155
Hiramine, Nobu (wife of Lima bakeryman): deported, 110
Hiramine, Takeji (Lima bakeryman): deported, 110
Hoover, J. Edgar: posts agents, 10; report by, 151
Horiba, Katsutaro (Lima farmer): deported, 130
Hosokawa, Masakado (Callao ship chandler): deported, 92, 93
Hosokawa, Tomiko (wife of Callao ship chandler): deported, 92, 93
Huacho, Peru: deported from, 44, 67, 68, 71, 79, 89, 117, 155

# Index

Huancayo, Peru: deported from, 44, 71, 89, 90, 92, 104, 105
Huaral, Peru: deported from, 68, 71
Huaura, Peru: deported from, 68
Hudson, Aubrey S. (U.S. official): quoted, 31
Hull, Cordell: quoted, 56
Hurricane: at Kenedy, Texas, 60

Ica, Peru: deported from, 76, 89, 120, 126, 149
Ickes, Raymond W. (U.S. official), 70, 71, 73, 86; recommendations by, 74; quoted, 74
Ikari, Manuel Enrique (Piura merchant): deported, 68, 168; quoted, 119
Ikeda, Fukuichi (Lima factory owner): deported, 45
Ikeda, Kazaemon (Lima merchant): deported, 93
Ikeda, Kino (wife of Lima merchant): deported, 93
Ikeda, Shoichi (Lima merchant): deported, 156
Immigration quotas, 8
*Imperial*: transporting internees, 79, 80, 85, 108
Inaga, Nisaburo (Cañete barber): deported, 118, 126; quoted, 118
Inamine, Seiho (Lima merchant): deported, 97
Inayoshi, Junichi (Callao merchant): deported, 93
INS officials: questions by, 69–70
Intelligence, American: in Peru, 11
International Petroleum Company, 41, 164
International Red Cross: inspections by, 61, 78, 137
Ishikawa, Luis Sadaichi, 105
Ishikawa, Matsu (farmer): deported, 107
Ishu, Choki (Lima merchant): deported, 44
Italian internees, 29, 38, 40
Iwai Shoten: representative of, 27, 48
Izumi, Hikozo (Chiclayo importer): deported, 118; mentioned, 110
Izumi, Masako (wife of Chiclayo importer): deported, 110

Japanese American Citizens League: in U.S., 141
Jauja, Peru: deported from, 71
Jensen, L. H. (U.S. official), 98
Junín, Peru: deported from, 44
*Jus sanguinis*: principle applied, 8, 9

Kadena, Chitsu (Lima importer-merchant): deported, 44
Kage, Mantaro (Chulucanes restaurateur): deported, 155, 156
Kakutani, Sansuke (Tacna merchant): deported, 153
Kamada, Kay (Japanese-American interpreter), 145
Kamisato, Junken (Lima bakery owner): deported with family, 92
Kanashiro, Ricardo (nisei from Callo): deported, 119
Kaneko, Kakuaki (Lima merchant): reunion with family, 91; deported, 149; wages, 157; moves to California, 163; quoted, 70; mentioned, 155
Kaneko, Kakumi (Lima merchant): deported, 110
Kaneko, Otari (wife of Lima merchant): deported, 66, 91, 157
Kaneshige, Takichi (Lima merchant): deported, 90
Kato, Chuhei (Lima merchant): deported, 149; family of, 101, 149; mentioned, 101, 155
Kato, Eugenia Yoshiko: recalls Crystal City, 101
Katsuro, Shuhei (Lima clerk): deported, 90
Kawai, Koichi Manuel (Huancayo merchant): deported, 104
Kawai, Segoro (deported Lima businessman): death of, 128
Kawakami, Shigeru (Piura merchant): deported, 69; quoted, 69; injury to, 103
Kawamoto, Seigoro, 104, 105
Kawano, Kazuo (Panamanian Japanese): deported, 50
Kenedy Internment Camp: facility of, 3, 46, 49, 50, 58, 59, 70, 75, 79, 82, 88, 92, 96, 97, 98, 100, 126; described, 29–34
Kishi, Hajime (Lima farmer-executive):

deported, 90, 91, 104, 105, 158, 168; settled in California, 169
Kishi, Katsumi: deported, 91; settled in California, 169
Kishi, Masao: deported, 91; settled in California, 169
Kishimoto, Kensho (Lima laborer-chauffeur): deported, 92, 93; quoted, 118
Kitsutani, Fumiko (wife of Lima merchant): deported, 93
Kitsutani, Kosuke (Lima merchant): deported, 155, 156
Knowland, William: in U.S. Congress, 164
Kobashigawa, Kamei (Lima salesman): deported, 125–26; quoted, 118, 126
Kobashigawa, Yukihiko: death of deportee, 31–32
Koike, Ryohei (Lima merchant): deported, 125
Koizumi, Tomiji, 105
Kooskia, Idaho: activity at, 97, 98, 99, 126
Korematsu Case: in U.S., 142
Kudo, Nami: deported, 149
Kudo, Rokuichi (Lima importer): deported, 149
Kurotobi, Enrique Isamu (Lima merchant): deported, 71; quoted, 150
Kurotobi, Tatsujiro (Lima merchant): deported, 44

La Huaca, Peru: deported from, 68
La Oroya, Peru: deported from, 44
Larrañaga, Jorge (propagandist), 39
Lawrence, Audrey L., 145
Legislation: anti-Japanese, 8
Lend lease agreement, 21
Ley 9586: in Peru, 187n21
Ley 9592: in Peru, 187n21
Lima: settling in, 5; commercial associations in, 6; rioting in, 9; conference in, 9
*Lima Daily*, 9
*Lima Nippō*, 9, 45
Long, Breckinridge (U.S. official): quoted, 19; announcement of, 57
López Rubio, Humberto (Peruvian official), 104
Lourenço, Marques (now Maputo), 47
Lozano G., Enrique (Mexican official), 105
Lurín, Peru: deported from, 71

*Madison*: transporting internees, 88, 89, 92
Maeoko, Lucho Kenji (deported minor): quoted, 123–24
Maeoko, Sakutaro (Trujillo carpenter): deported, 124
Makimoto, José Kiyoto (Pisco restaurateur): deported, 110
Mangione, Jurre (U.S. official): quoted, 29
Maoki, Usaburo (Chiclayo merchant): deported, 155
Maputo (formerly Lourenço Marques), 47
Marshall, George C. (U.S. official): appeals to, 162, 166; mentioned, 164, 167
Masaki, Kengo (Callao dairyman): deported, 92, 117; quoted, 117–18
*Matsonia*: transporting internees, 124, 125
Matsubayashi, Michie: minor deported, 123
Matsubayashi, Natsuko (wife of Lima factory worker): deported, 124
Matsubayashi, Shigezo (Lima factory worker): deported, 124; quoted, 118
Matsuda, Carlos Ichitaro (Lima farmer-merchant): deported, 111; quoted, 119
Matsuda, Kunichi (Lima farmer): deported, 155
Mexico: Japanese in, 3–4, 6, 7, 17, 49, 55
Mier y Teran, Moises (Peruvian official): described, 104
Minamoto, Enzo (Huancayo merchant): deported, 155, 156
Miró Quesada, Luis (Peruvian publisher), 105
Mishima, Kikuno (wife of Lima merchant): deported, 165
Mishima, Shoichi (Lima merchant): deported, 67, 165
Missoula, Montana: facility at, 78, 88, 98, 126
Mitsui: representative of, 27, 48
Miyakawa, Heiji (Lima merchant): deported, 125
Miyashiro, Kenyu (barber): deported, 9
Mizuta, Noboru (Lima merchant), 118
Mochizaki, Luis Yoshitake (Chimbote merchant-barber): deported, 43
Mochizuki, Masao (Supe teacher): deported, 126
Mohler, Bruch M., 143

## Index

Monma, Eisaburo (Barranca farmer): deported, 96
Monma, Kumayo (wife of Barranca farmer): deported, 96
*Monterey*: transporting internees, 77
Moran, R., 104
Morimoto, Ichitaro (Lima farmer): deported, 153; inspiration by, 174; mentioned, 96
Morimoto, Ko (wife of Lima farmer): deported, 96
Morioka Emigration Company, 3
Moriyama, Kurata (Cañete merchant): deported, 119; quoted, 119
Muccio, John J. (U.S. official), 88
Mukoyama, Jorge Koshiro (Lima importer): deported, 120, 143; quoted, 120, 148, 149; spokesman, 148, 155; settles in Venezuela, 174
Murata, Yaichi (Lima tailor): deported, 63
Murono, Ginzo (Lima merchant): deported, 15, 65, 79, 168; family of, 79
Muroy, Luis Masaru (Lima laundry-owner): deported, 118; quoted, 118
Muto, Toshiaki (Arequipa merchant): deported, 119
Muto, Yoshihisa (Arequipa engineer): deported, 68, 118; quoted, 118

Naganuma, Isoka (wife of Callao laundry-owner): deported, 100
Naganuma, Iwaichi (Callao laundry-owner): deported, 100, 155
Naganuma, Kiyoko: recalls Crystal City, 100–101
*Naichijin*, 46
Nakachi, Mankichi (Lima restaurateur): deported, 130
Nakagawa, Ricardo Toshiaki (Lima merchant): deported, 120; quoted, 120
Nakamura, Gongoro (Japanese American), 143, 147
Nakamura, Hachiyoshi (Callao merchant): deported, 118
Nakamura, Katsue (Trujillo photographer): deported, 96
Nakamura, Victoria (wife of Trujillo photographer): deported, 96
Nakamura, Shogoro (Huacho farmer): deported, 119; quoted, 119

Nakao, Iwazo (Lima merchant): deported, 157
Nakashima, Shintaro (minor): deported, 123
Nakasone, Katsuo (Lima farmer): deported, 126; quoted, 127
Nasca, Peru: trip to, 53
National Catholic Welfare Conference, 61, 143, 157
Nimura, Genji: career, vii; naturalized Peruvian, 120, 153
Nisei, 6, 28, 43, 45, 68, 71, 72, 75, 78, 79, 80, 89, 90, 96, 110, 119
Nishino, Chieko (wife of Lima merchant): deported, 80
Nishio, Tomiji (Lima merchant): deported, 43
Nobuhira, Kiroku (Japanese Panamanian): interned, 50
Nonomiya, Motozo (Lima merchant): deported, 35
Noriego Calmet, Alberto, 104–5
Norweb, R. Henry (U.S. official): quoted, 13, 23, 54, 74, 76; conclusions of, 39; mentioned, 14, 40, 55

Occupations: of deportees, 6, 8, 9, 15, 26–31 passim, 35, 43–45, 63–68 passim, 71, 72, 75–77, 83, 84, 89–92, 98, 104, 105, 107, 109, 117–20, 124–27, 149, 155, 173
Oda, Zenkichi (hacienda administrator): quoted, 118
Odria, Manuel A. (Peruvian president), 168
Oguchi, Haruemon (Lima student): deported, 126
Ohara, Hidea (Barranco teacher): deported, 155, 156
Ohara, Shigeo (Japanese Panamanian): deported, 49
Ohashi, Fusae (wife of Lima manufacturer): deported, 79; case of, 169
Ohashi, José Shinichi (Jauja merchant): deported, 71
Ohashi, Taro (Lima manufacturer): family of, 79; case of, 169; in U.S. Postal Service, 175; mentioned, 65, 79, 155
Ohashi, Yasuhiko (Lima merchant): deported, 15, 65
Okada, Nikumatsu (Huaral farmer): deported, 15; mentioned, 43, 45, 75, 82

Okada, Ikiro, 104
Okada, Onishiki, 104
Okinaga, Yoshio (Huacho mechanic): deported, 117; quoted, 117
Onishi, Taiichi (Lima merchant): deported, 31
Orlando, Capt. Philip, 108
Oshio, Hideo, 29
Oshiro, Ryusuke (Lima commercial employee): deported, 120; quoted, 120
Otani, Tokumatsu (Lima importer): deported, 117; quoted, 117
Ouchi, Alejandro (Japanese Panamanian deportee): death of, 86
Oyakawa, Yoshihara (Lima merchant): deported, 120

Paijan, Peru: deported from, 68
Paita, Peru: trip to, 53; deported from, 68, 125
Panama: Japanese in, 4, 9, 22, 48, 57, 58, 59, 75
Panama Canal Zone: authorities in, 38
Paraguay: Japanese in, 86
Pawley, William D. (U.S. official): quoted, 135
Perú Chūo Nihonjin, 6
*Perú Jihō*, 45
Peru Menka, 90
*Perú Shimpo*, 174
Picado, Teodoro (Costa Rican president), 113
Pimentel, Peru: deported from, 68, 79
Pisco, Peru: trip to, 53; deported from, 71, 125, 127
Piura, Peru: trip to, 53; deported from, 66, 68, 118, 126
Poulson, N.: in U.S. Congress, 164
Prado, Jorge (Peruvian official): quoted, 162, 165
Prado, Manuel (Peruvian president): visits U.S., 41, 52; mentioned, 42, 46, 66, 73, 104, 107
Prefectural societies, 6, 29, 66
Press coverage, 8, 61
Protecting powers: inspection by, 61
*Puebla*: transporting internees, 69, 75, 85

*Randall*: transporting internees, 125, 126, 127

Rio de Janeiro, Brazil: conference at, 16–18, 47
Rioting: in Lima-Callao (1940), 9, 29, 91, 125
Rivera Schreiber, Ricardo (Peruvian official), 55, 66
Rockefeller, Nelson: report by, 55
Roosevelt, F. D., 41, 55, 68, 106

Saiki, Masao (Tacna merchant): deported, 110
Sakairi, Takeo (Lima farmer): deported, 92
Sakamoto, Kane (wife of Japanese minister), 35
Sakamoto, Ryūki (Japanese minister to Peru), 10–11, 35
Sakasegawa, Iwamori (Huacho mechanic): case of, 144–45, 147; quoted, 144–46, 156; case dismissed, 155; mentioned, 137–38
Sakata, Kotaro (Lima merchant): deported, 44
Sakoda, Eiichi (Piura barber): deported, 159
Sakurai, Susumu (Lima author): deported, 35
San Pedro INS facility, 142, 144
Santa Fe Internment Camp: facility at, 98, 99, 112, 124, 126, 127, 136, 137, 138, 141, 145
Seabrook Farms, New Jersey, 148, 150, 153, 155, 160, 163, 169, 170, 176
Seagoville Internment Camp: facility at, 36–38, 46, 50, 58, 59, 75, 98, 112
Senoh, Naonobu (Lima resident): deported, 85
Sharp Park, California, 77, 84
*Shawnee*: transporting internees, 42, 43, 45, 46, 50, 53, 54, 58, 62, 63, 80, 85, 173
Shibayama, Elisa Fusako (deported minor): quoted, 149
Shibayama, Isamu (minor): deported, 149
Shibayama, Yuzo (Lima importer): deported, 120
Shibukawa, Hisao (Lima merchant): deported, 119
Shiga, Yoshisada (Lima merchant): deported, 104, 149, 163–64
Shimabukuro, Koshio (Lima resident): deported, 68

Shimizu, Ichiro (Arequipa farmer): deported, 153
Shimura, Toshio (Lima baker): deported, 125
Shindo Remmei, 151, 152, 153
Shiroma, Zunsuke (Callao businessman): deported, 119
Sociedad Agricola Retes Ltd., 91, 96
Solf y Muro, Alfredo (Peruvian official), 10, 91
Spain: as protecting power, 25, 33, 61
Stannard, Amy (U.S. official), 38
Stimson, Henry L. (U.S. official): quoted, 74
Sugiyama, Hideko (wife of Lima merchant): deported, 124
Sugiyama, Ichitaro (Costa Rican resident): deported, 49
Sugiyama, Shigeko (minor): deported, 123
Sugiyama, Shiheru (Lima merchant): deported, 124
Sugiyama, Takeshi (minor): deported, 123
Sugiyama, Toyo (Costa Rican resident): deported, 49
Sullana, Peru: trip to, 53; deported from, 68
Sumitaka, Nishimuta (Huacho carpenter): deported, 67
Supe, Peru: deported from, 71, 126
Suwa, Tetsuo (Ica merchant): deported, 76, 126
Suzue, Aiko (Costa Rican resident): deported, 49
Suzuki, Atsumi (deported minor): quoted, 149
Suzuki, Eiichi: death of, 109
Suzuki, Kin (deported widow), 109, 155; settles in Chicago, 170
Suzuki, Suzuko (deported minor), 149

Tacna, Peru: deported from, 89
Taira, Carlos Shinkyu (Chiclaya farmer): deported, 68; naturalized Peruvian, 153
Taira, Mercedes (wife of Chiclayo farmer): deported, 68
Taira, Ryosho (Lima teacher): deported, 173
Takahashi, Banemon (Cañete merchant): deported, 119; quoted, 119
Takahashi, Kakichi (deported Pisco barber): death of, 127
Takahashi, Kaneichi (Lima printer): deported, 125
Takaki, Saju (Chiclayo merchant): deported, 118; quoted, 118
Takeshita, Kunio (Lima merchant): deported, 72, 99, 158; settles in Chicago, 169–70
Talara, Peru: port of, 18, 20–21, 53, 67, 68, 70, 71, 79, 125, 152, 156
Tamashiro, Kinsuke (Lima merchant): deported, 126, 127
Tameshiro, Jorge Kame (Callao deportee), 78
Tanaka, Shigeyuki (Trujillo barber): deported, 68
Taniguchi, Tadao (Lima merchant): deported, 65, 90
Tate, R. C., 99–100
Tateishi, Victor Kazuki (deported Lima nisei student), 90, 131, 153
Tateyama, Mitsue (wife of Panamanian deportee), 49
Taura, Shizuo (Cane bakeryman): deported, 119; quoted, 119
Tawara, Kiwa (wife of Cañete merchant): deported, 72, 96, 102; settles in Colorado, 169
Tawara, Mitsutaro (Cañete merchant): deported, 72, 96, 102, 122, 149, 158; settles in Colorado, 169
Tawara, Toshiharu (minor): deported, 102, 122, 149; wages of, 158
Tawara, Victor (minor): deported, 102, 158
Tenney, Daniel (U.S. official), 133
Tietz, J. B. (lawyer), 145
Tochio, Luisa Villanueva (wife of Arequipa merchant): deported, 96
Tochio, Octavio Taijiro (Arequipa merchant): deported, 72, 77, 96, 156–57; poetry of, 77; letter by, 84
Torigoe, Takeshi, 152
Tosa, Alberto Bunken (Huacho farmer): deported, 126
Trujillo, Peru: deported from, 44, 68, 79, 96, 109, 124, 125
Truman, Harry S: quoted, 115; mentioned, 136, 139, 165, 167

Tsuchiya, Harue (wife of Lima merchant): deported, 124
Tsuchiya, Yasuo (Lima merchant): deported, 124
Tuna Canyon Detention Center, California, 70

Uchiyama, Atsuko (minor): deported, 123
Uema, Samatsu (Piura cook): deported, 126
Uesugi, Akira Masamu (Lima shipping representative): deported, 63
Uno, Cecilia de Gracia (wife of deported Panamanian Japanese), 50
U. S. Bureau of Prisons, 37
United States Catholic Conference, 143
U. S. Immigration and Naturalization Service, 16, 29, 30
U. S. Public Health Service, 36, 76, 79, 83
Uruguay: on committee, 17, 86
Ushida, Saburo (Chiclayo merchant): deported, 66, 119; quoted, 119, 175–76; wages, 158; settles in Chicago, 170; mentioned, 69, 99, 176
Uozaki, Shozo (Lima merchant): deported, 124
Uozaki, Tomiko (minor): deported, 123

Venezuela: on committee, 17; mentioned, 55, 86
Virú, Peru: deported from, 68
Vitarte, Peru: deported from, 68

Wagner, Robert F.: in U.S. Congress, 164
War Prisoners Aid of the YMCA, 61
War Relocation Authority: in U.S., 13, 22, 148
War Shipping Administration: in U.S., 78
Watanabe, Isamu: death of deportee, 109
Watanabe, Kimiko (minor): deported, 123, 124
Watanabe, Masaji (Lima merchant): deported, 124
Watanabe, Shima (wife of Lima merchant): deported, 124
Waterson, W. J. (U.S. official), 145, 146
Wechsler, Herbert (U.S. official), 115
Welch, Rolland (U.S. official), 95, 130

Welles, Sumner (U.S. official), 22
White, John C. (U.S. official), 106
Wiley, Alexander: in U. S. Congress, 164
Williams, Ivan (U.S. official), 32, 98, 100, 183n12
Williams, Margaret Nan: quoted, 79
Woo, George Tsung-yuan, 42, 53, 61, 68
Wirin, A. L. (attorney), 146
Wirin, Maneo and Tietz (attorneys), 139, 141

Yakabi, Arturo (Arthur) Shinei: career, vii; quoted, 119; mentioned, 71, 72–73, 79, 83, 90, 96, 97, 98, 99
Yaki, Sentei (naturalized Lima office worker): deported, 90, 120, 153
Yamamoto, Masagi (Lima deportee), 78
Yamamoto, Yoshitomo (Lima barber): deported, 87–88
Yamasaki, Chika (deported tailor): case of, 144, 147
Yamashiro, Alfredo Minoru (deported minor), 96
Yamashiro, Bunsei (Lima teacher): deported, 117; quoted, 117
Yamashiro, Kotoku (Trujillo merchant): deported, 96, 149, 155
Yatoh, Nobuo (Lima resident): deported, 78
Yatomi, Aiko (deported Lima widow): 76, 91; quoted, 120
Yatomi, Ichiroku: death of deportee, 75, 82, 91
Yodokawa, Masaki (Japanese official), 19, 35
Yoshimoto, Pedro Kushinosuke: deportation of, blocked, 104
Yoshinaga, Fumiko (minor): deported, 123; quoted, 123
Yoshizumi, Ichijiro (Chincha merchant): deported, 155
Yumoto, Sadajiro (Lima merchant): deported, 4
YWCA: at Crystal City, 61

Zapata Veiez, Arturo (Peruvian official), 104
Zorritos, Peru: port of, 18